"*Maximize Performance* is a must-read for boards, superintendents, district leaders, and school leaders. The book describes the process our school district uses to transform our culture as we face constant changes in our profession. It contains a wealth of information that helps leaders think about how to face the challenges in front of us to achieve excellence. The process described promotes an open and transparent communication approach in which leaders are called to reflect on their own leadership skills and practices to be the best they can be."

—Tim Wyrosdick, Superintendent, Santa Rosa County
School District, Florida

"Several years ago, the Arlington Independent School Board and Superintendent Cavazos decided to partner with Studer Education to apply the Evidence-Based Leadership^{SM} framework described in *Maximize Performance*. The focus on measurable goals for the district that roll down to all leaders provides a tool for the board to analyze the progress that the school district is making toward achieving the goals. Our board has worked diligently to build collective thought around the continuous improvement process outlined in the book. Our board's dedication and commitment positioned us to receive the 2014 Outstanding School Board Award from the Texas Association of School Administrators. The focus and alignment of measurable goals provide direction for achieving excellence."

—Jamie Sullins, School Board Member, Arlington
Independent School District, Arlington, Texas

MAXIMIZE
PERFORMANCE

Creating a Culture for Educational Excellence

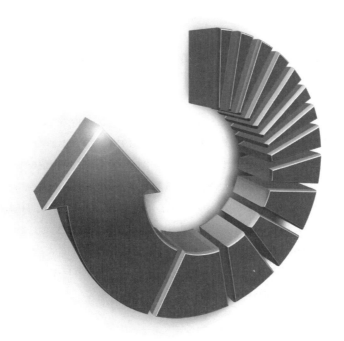

Quint Studer, MSE

Janet Pilcher, PhD

Published by:
Fire Starter Publishing
350 W. Cedar Street
Pensacola, FL 32502
Phone: 866-354-3473
Fax: 850-332-5117
www.firestarterpublishing.com

ISBN: 978-1-622-18014-1

Library of Congress Control Number: 2014959502

Printed in the United States of America

TABLE OF CONTENTS

Acknowledgments

We are grateful for the good fortune to make a difference to all the difference makers in our lives.

We also thank the many people who have traveled the fire-starting journey in healthcare and inspired us to do the same in education. We are grateful for the people in our professional fields who touch and heal lives.

We appreciate the work of others referenced in this book that continues to positively influence us.

Thanks to the leaders in this book who have become the first movers for creating high-performing school systems. We learn from you, and those who read this book will, too.

Special thanks to the Studer Education team members who have reviewed the book at each stage and supported the work to the end. Thank you for always encouraging and believing in the work we do.

Special thanks to our wonderful families, especially those at this time in our lives who are going through some painful illnesses and are continuing to fight the cancer battle. Our families are one of life's greatest blessings.

To Margaret Stanzell: Thank you for believing in this book and pushing us over the finish line. The added humor made the journey fun. We appreciate you.

To Joan Kocsis: Thank you for the thorough and timely editing of this book. You are the finest example of the descriptors associated with high performers. We got lucky when we found you.

Thank you to Fire Starter Publishing for publishing *Maximize Performance* to add to the list of many outstanding books.

Thank you to Lauren Westwood for creating all the wonderful graphics that add to the learning experience of this resource.

Thank you to Kira Freed for providing the final proofing to get us to completion.

Thank you to Dottie DeHart for your work early in this process to provide structure and guidance, which helped make this book everything we hoped it would be.

Introduction

A Reflection

It's the last day of school, and you have an exciting yet empty feeling in your stomach—this year even more so because you are retiring after many years of service as a teacher and leader. You take your last stroll down the halls as one of your students is walking out with his teacher. The student thanks you for being a great principal and for the many times you've been helpful to him and his parents. The teacher smiles and says, "We are sure going to miss you."

You make your way to a favorite area of the school—the courtyard, where students have planted gardens and displayed "yard art" designed with their creative minds. You chuckle as you think about the countless interactions with them and the teachers that made school such a fun and engaging place. You pause and wonder about the type of legacy you will leave for others to follow.

Over time, you think about changes that have occurred in education and, in particular, how they've affected your school system. There have been tremendous external pressures and changes. You take a deep breath as you reflect on the times you had to unsettle yourself. You had to work through your own discomfort before you could work with others to do the same. The voice of Ralph Waldo Emerson creeps into your thoughts: "People wish to be settled; but only as far as they are unsettled is there any hope for them." You've learned from some hard knocks along the way that we can only take others as far as we can take ourselves. Again, you chuckle, thinking, "I wish I had learned that sooner." You learned that one way to help people with change is to explain why the change is needed, what impact the change will have on their work environment, and how change will personally affect them.

Now your mind turns to daydreaming about your retirement celebration. The teachers get up to speak on your behalf. They say one of the reasons they loved working for you is because you often came into their classrooms. You always made sure they understood exactly what was expected of them, and they really liked having clear expectations. They felt that when they did a good job, you recognized them. The teachers acknowledged that sometimes the messages were difficult to hear. They appreciated that you engaged with them in a constructive and coaching manner. They specifically mentioned that you gave them explicit feedback rather than relying on hearsay. They also applauded you for being consistent and timely with classroom walkthroughs and observations. Your way of using data to guide a conversation helped them trust that you were there to help them achieve their best. The teachers also recognized that you addressed performance issues with subpar performers. They acknowledged that you had difficult conversations with people when needed. It was clear that you did not tolerate negative attitudes or unskilled teachers and staff. In fact, one teacher joked about how she thought she could outlast you at the school. It was the day when the two of you had a very difficult conversation that made her realize she wanted to reignite the passion she once had as a teacher. You loved this story. It made you feel proud because she had become known as one of the best teachers in the district.

Finally, the teachers talked about how much they appreciated the opportunity to complete employee engagement surveys. Initially, they were skeptical about taking the survey. They wondered what would be done with the results and whether the process would be completed in a fair way. The teachers mentioned that when you rolled out the survey results and presented them as your report card, they felt their voices and opinions were heard. They recognized you for supporting a best-place-to-work environment and listening to their input when you made decisions that affected their jobs. They helped you be the best leader you could be. The school had a "we are all in it together" attitude. They saw you making changes and realized that if you could change, so could they. As you listened, you felt so proud of them and grateful to be their leader.

The parents spoke next. They acknowledged that you called them quite often and said that when you called, you were very specific in telling them the good things about their children. One parent who moved to your town this past year said that she cried after the first phone call. Every year up to this point, she had only received negative comments about her child. You called her to welcome the family to town and told her your school was glad to have her son there, and you mentioned that you appreciated the humor her child brought to the school. No one before you had ever seen her son's humor in a positive light.

In unison, a group of parents repeated the questions you would ask them on those phone calls. "What's going well for you at our school?" "Is there anything that we could do better?" "Has anyone been especially helpful to you?"

It made you recall the same type of conversations you had with teachers. The teachers were very appreciative of you asking if the systems were working. They knew that if not, you would try to solve the problem, and if you could not do so, you would explain why. Also, you were always asking if they had the resources in the classroom so that students had the very best opportunity to learn.

The parents also applauded the teachers at your school. In particular, they appreciated that the teachers called every child's parent at the beginning of the school year. The teachers introduced themselves and their skill sets, provided a brief overview of the first few weeks of school, provided a process for parents to contact them, and thanked the parent for sending their child to the school.

As you thought about what the parents and teachers were saying, you realized this was not taught to you in college, but you were so glad your school district provided the training that gave you the skills to take these actions. You thought back to the Leadership Development

Institutes your school district offered about every 90 days. You had fun learning with your colleagues about the best ways to hire people, coach them to improve their performance, reward and recognize employees, and apply processes to become efficient and effective.

You appreciated the fact that your school district invested in you. What a privilege it was to work for this district. Every school had consistent and reliable leadership. The superintendent modeled excellent leadership and expected the senior leaders to do the same. You felt lucky to work in a place where parents were not asking for one school over another. In fact, the whole school district had a great reputation because of the consistency of practices among all schools. Another thing you liked was how this practice transferred to your school. Parents were not saying to you, "I want this teacher but not that one." As you transition your leadership post to the next leader, you can say with confidence that all teachers are highly effective and eager to learn.

As the superintendent spoke, you thought about what a difficult job that is. You remembered years ago when the school board met for hours, trying to figure out how to evaluate the superintendent. The process was very subjective and was influenced by the last crisis or the loudest complaints. Now the school board applies an evaluation tool that is objective and weighted. The superintendent no longer worries about playing politics with the school board. In fact, that's not why the school board members joined the school board. They ran for this office to contribute to providing the best learning environment for students, and that seems to be what everybody is focused on. You appreciate the superintendent and the board for creating priorities and holding themselves accountable. You appreciate how they rolled the accountability process to all leaders. You always knew what was expected of you as a leader. You also knew how your school's success influenced the success of the district. It helped you motivate your school team to victory year after year. As the results came in at the end of the year, your team felt great pride in their accomplishments.

You were amazed that when the president of the school board got up to talk at your retirement, she mentioned some of these very things—how the school district made the decisions to invest in leader development and recognize and repeat best practices. The actions of the board members demonstrated that they were committed to helping each individual become successful. They made decisions to support compensation plans that retained high performers.

You were touched when several of the district department leaders spoke on your behalf. Every 45 days, you completed a survey evaluating the services you received from the district. You had an opportunity to give feedback to human resources, maintenance, food service, curriculum and instruction, and other departments. They mentioned that you always reinforced how important the departments were to your school's success and that they valued your feedback. It made their departments better. You knew that if these services were not provided in an effective and efficient way, you would not have had the time you needed to work with the students, teachers, and parents. Then you looked out into courtyard and through the windows into the hall. You were grateful for the staff who supported such a beautiful place to work and educate students.

The retirement celebration was coming to a close. For a short moment, you remembered the time when you had an offer to go to another school district but didn't take it. You didn't want to leave this excellent culture. You knew then that you would only leave the district when you decided to retire. That time had come. And now, you were nearing the last presentation—from the students.

It was so gratifying to hear some of the students talk. They said school was fun. They were learning a lot. They loved being in their classrooms with their teachers and classmates. The students expressed how confident they were that the teachers were preparing them to achieve success. That was really exciting for you to hear.

You are eager to enter the next phase of your life. You want to travel to places you've always wanted to go, spend more time with your family, and have time to engage in long-awaited projects around the house.

Most of all, you are very grateful. You've worked in a school district that provided you with clear expectations and defined priorities, invested in your development, recognized you for high performance, and expected consistency of leadership starting at the top. Tomorrow you will be a member of a community that takes great pride in its schools. The professionalism of the school board and the superintendent serves as a model for other districts and allows leaders, teachers, and staff to excel in their jobs.

At the end of the retirement celebration, the students presented a tribute to you. More than ever, you knew you had been blessed to work in one of the best professions in the world. You are going to miss the students. You're going to miss the teachers. You're going to miss the parents. You're going to miss working for the superintendent and school board.

The best part about being in education is that you have a legacy in your community. That legacy is defined by the generations of people you've touched. On behalf of the entire school district, the students presented you with a plaque with the words, "Thank you for touching our lives. Never underestimate the difference you have made."

What This Book Is About

This book is about consistent and reliable leadership. Education leaders deserve to feel that they've made a difference in the lives of those they touch—just like the leader in the opening story. Similar to teaching, we believe leadership is a calling. We also know it's hard work, especially in today's world of continuous change. In education, even the way we *change* has changed. To survive and thrive, we need to perform at an even higher level—continuously.

Our professional field has always dealt with change, but the environment we're navigating now requires change at a new level. We've moved from occasional change to continuous change—and as leadership expert John Kotter has famously noted, that requires a whole different set of skills and a new level of urgency.

In *Maximize Performance: Creating a Culture for Educational Excellence*, we explain how to leverage the powerful values that have always defined educators—passion, fortitude, and a willingness to learn—to meet the challenges of our disruptive external environment.

Together, we lay out the framework, principles, processes, and tactics that maximize performance in educational systems. We present the tools for setting up a culture of consistent and reliable execution that drives quality higher—and sustains that excellence. The book will help you:

- Apply organizational and leadership assessments to diagnose your system's strengths and its areas needing improvement

- Manage data to create key drivers of performance that align with board and executive team priorities

- Align key performance drivers in all schools and all departments

- Determine the best metrics to monitor progress aligned to the key performance drivers

- Choose core system-wide strategies aligned with key drivers to roll down to schools and departments

- Coach executive teams to work with leaders in choosing strategies for schools and departments that align to the key drivers

- Implement district, department, and school performance reviews to validate the execution of strategies at the system, school, and department levels

- Determine which processes need improvement to achieve results

- Integrate key performance driver metrics into leader evaluations

- Apply leadership behaviors that create service and operational excellence

- Train leaders in core leadership skills: performance management, key communication skills, and teamwork

- Expand leadership by identifying and training future leaders

Packed with targeted research and fresh insights—all brought to life with thought-provoking and inspiring stories—this book was written to serve as a go-to resource for superintendents and executive teams, school board members, school leaders, and district department leaders. It was written for leaders who support and inspire people to maximize performance and maintain excellent outcomes in an environment of continuous change. It's about building highly consistent and reliable systems that promote effective communication, trust, and credibility as key priorities for maximizing performance.

Maximize Performance is divided into three sections and one closing chapter. The goal of the first two sections is to set the stage for presenting ways leaders apply what we call the Evidence-Based Leadership[SM] (EBL) framework. In education, we're accustomed to using student data and evidence to make good decisions about student learning. The Evidence-Based Leadership framework guides leaders to gather and analyze information to make good system-wide decisions that improve organizational performance. The framework includes components associated with aligned goals, behaviors, and processes that will be described in the third section.

Since we are in the thrust of continuous change and disruption, the first section focuses on change. It provides us with *why* leadership is so important in creating high-performing school systems. The second section provides the foundational concepts we used years ago to create the framework. Think of these concepts as the foundation of the house that holds the framework together. The third section details the parts of the framework and provides a road map for leaders to follow to improve performance. The closing chapter circles back to why we lead and how the Evidence-Based Leadership framework presents us with a tool to succeed.

To gain insight into how leaders maximize system-wide performance, we suggest reading from the beginning to the end of the book. If you want to focus on key leadership behaviors that create a best-place-to-work environment, start with Chapters 11 and 12 (the aligned behavior part of Evidence-Based Leadership) prior to starting at the beginning.

Education leaders want to do their best. They choose to lead so they can make a difference in the lives of teachers, staff, students, and their families. We hope this book provides you with a resource to do just that.

SECTION ONE:

CHANGE

We've met quite a few strong leaders. Strong leaders know how to navigate change in a way that creates new opportunities. Today, organizational results depend on how well leaders guide their teams to achieve. Equally important, leaders and teams must be good problem solvers and thinkers. The best leaders

- create a system-wide vision,
- clearly set and communicate a direction for people to go,
- align behaviors to priorities,
- create best-place-to-work environments that motivate people to action, and
- reinforce critical and strategic thinking on how to achieve well-defined outcomes.

The first four chapters of *Maximize Performance* set the stage for how we think about change and why relying on the Evidence-Based Leadership℠ framework described in this book is essential to good leadership. The first chapter highlights changing times but mainly focuses on the qualities that have stayed the same. The eternal qualities of passion, fortitude, and willingness to learn have drawn some great people into our professions. People who work in education want to have purpose, do worthwhile work, and make a difference in the lives of those they touch.

In Chapter 2, we use two sources of evidence to show leaders' readiness for change. We summarize the results of a 2004 Studer Group study that set the stage for introducing the Evidence-Based Leadership framework. The Straight A Leadership Assessment tests organizations and serves as a means of gathering evidence in the field. We share some of the results gathered through this assessment tool on organizational alignment, readiness for change, leadership fundamentals, self-awareness, consistency, and accountability.

Chapter 3 focuses on some critical behaviors that accountable leaders use to manage change and maximize system-wide performance. We discuss the importance of validating how well people consistently execute required actions. People might not do what is required without knowing why it is important. For any change to succeed, leaders first explain why it is important and only then explain what needs to be done and how to do it.

The final chapter of Section 1 describes what individual and organizational change looks like and what we can expect when change is introduced. This chapter first introduces the four phases of individual change: unconsciously unskilled, consciously unskilled, consciously skilled, and unconsciously skilled. When change is introduced, the organization goes through a sequence of natural phases: the honeymoon, reality setting in, the uncomfortable gap, and consistency.

The trend is for K–12 system results to be transparent to our communities. The daily tasks of running departments and schools remain demanding, but leaders need to do more than that or they risk failure. Our goal is for leaders to apply the Evidence-Based Leadership framework to do what's advocated by a leading thinker about managing change, John Kotter. Kotter suggests that leaders identify obstacles and opportunities early on, quickly formulate strategic initiatives, and implement change quickly. These actions, coupled with gathering and reviewing evidence, create consistent and reliable systems that maximize leadership performance.

CHAPTER ONE:

CHANGING TIMES, CONSTANT VALUES

We live and work in interesting times. More than ever, educators face continuous pressure to reform established practices in order to improve outcomes throughout the school system. Many executive leaders and boards of education are doing all this with declining budgets. As educators, we've faced decades of reform initiatives, but some current mandates are opening up uncharted territory.

Yes, many things *have* changed, and the changes are dramatic. Yet many other things—which may ultimately be the most important things—have stayed the same.

The premise of this book is that, in order to survive and thrive, leaders need to focus on improving systems by creating and maintaining a culture that reinforces high performance. Essentially, the task involves disrupting some parts of our educational systems and building up other parts. In K–12 systems, for example, we're being asked to consider student achievement as we evaluate teachers and leaders. In postsecondary institutions, funding depends on the number of students retained over various time periods while they are completing their degrees. Increased pressures in educational systems demand that leaders enhance their skill sets to better manage human performance.

The skills leaders need today build on those needed in the past, with some key differences. But before we can discuss how to develop these needed skills and transform our cultures, let's take stock of exactly what has changed in education and what has held constant.

What Has Changed in Education?

The biggest and most profound challenge we've had to deal with— and the one that's requiring the greatest adjustments inside organizations—is **the education sector's move from *episodic* change to *continuous* change**. In John Kotter's book on managing change and motivating employees, *A Sense of Urgency*, he talks about the challenges and intense pressures that arise when business cultures go from one kind of change to the other. Certainly this is true in educational institutions. Moving from episodic change to continuous change is like a sprinter becoming a marathon runner.

Different Muscles, Different Endurance

Justin Gatlin, who lives in Pensacola, Florida, is an Olympic gold medalist in the 100-meter dash and a two-time world indoor champion in the 60-meter dash. He is truly a world-class sprinter. It is safe to say that no one in Pensacola can beat Justin in the 100-meter dash. Another Pensacola resident, Andrew Rothfeder, runs triathlons and marathons. It is probably safe to say that in a marathon race, Andrew would beat Justin every single time because running marathons requires different types of muscles and a different endurance level—different skills.

This is why today's **external environment** is so hard on frontline supervisors, leaders, directors, and employees: everything they do is based on episodic change. Now they need a whole different muscle set, mind-set, and range of emotional skills to operate in a field of continuous change. In this book, we show how to create those muscles because today we're no longer sprinters; we're high-performing marathon runners.

Now let's talk about some specific changes that are shaking up our external environment. We can think of them as disruption. Although it's uncomfortable, disruption is an effective way to force change. One can disrupt an environment—via a new invention, a new technique, or a new tool—in a way that challenges the status quo and causes us to rethink and adjust.

Many imposed changes in education are creating an ever-shifting landscape. In K–12 systems, changes include directives such as the inclusion of student achievement measures in teacher evaluations, the growth of charter schools, the creation of national standards and testing, and the rendering of school and school district report cards transparent to the public. In higher education, many states are moving toward a performance-based funding model that involves receiving financial rewards only when defined outcomes are achieved.

Efforts such as these indicate the government's goal at times of disrupting the current educational environment in such a way that leaders become responsible for improving systems. In this book, our purpose is not to judge what is driving this movement but rather to manage the upheaval that government-driven accountability pressures are causing in our profession.

Although it's uncomfortable, disruption is an effective way to force change. One can disrupt an environment—via a new invention, a new technique, or a new tool—in a way that challenges the status quo and causes us to rethink and adjust.

Some of the K–12 reform efforts at the top of mind for educational leaders are Common Core State Standards, standardized testing, state report cards, and personnel evaluation systems, to name just a few.

To date almost all states have adopted the **Common Core State Standards** and are moving toward adopting common assessments so that student achievement across states can be compared. The initiative, sponsored by the National Governors Association and the Council of Chief State School Officers, seeks to establish consistent educational standards across the states and to ensure that students graduating from high school are prepared to enter either two- or four-year college programs or the workforce.

As we've been writing this book, leaders of states adopting the Common Core State Standards are deciding how they will implement standardized assessments to evaluate student achievement levels for each standard. Two major challenges exist. Each state must ensure that all its school districts consistently apply the same practices. States will also assume increased costs for the development and administration of a new state assessment process.

Also in the forefront are **standardized testing** and comparing U.S. math and science scores to those of students elsewhere in the world. The continued decline of U.S. science and mathematics test results relative to global competitors is driving this movement.

The United States ranks below the Organisation for Economic Co-operation and Development average in every category. What's more, our country has slipped in all the major categories in recent years. The results from the 2012 Program for International Student Assessment (PISA) show that U.S. teenagers slipped from 25th to 31st in math since 2009; from 20th to 24th in science; and from 11th to 21st in reading, according to the National Center for Education Statistics, which gathers and analyzes the data domestically. A U.S. comparison of results on the National Assessment of Educational Progress (NAEP) has shown little gain in reading and mathematics student achievement over the last decade. NAEP is the largest nationally representative and continuing assessment of what America's students know in various content areas.

It allows states to compare results and provides a clear picture of academic trends over time.

State report cards are another significant change in education. In the past, few states held school districts accountable in highly transparent ways (though our home state, Florida, does). Today, more states are enacting a transparent accountability system by creating state report cards. They include multiple measures of student achievement as well as other indicators, such as graduation rates, school attendance, and discipline measures. The results become public, and therefore superintendents and boards of education feel heightened pressure to perform at high levels to remain in their positions and achieve reelection, respectively.

As they are doing with report cards, states are cascading accountability to school districts and schools by requiring that student achievement scores be part of school leaders' and teachers' **individual personnel evaluations**. In many instances, student achievement counts for 30 to 50 percent of the total score. We find that more and more boards of education are promoting some type of performance pay attached to personnel evaluations. Like most of the changes identified, performance pay aligns with the directives outlined in the current federal educational reform legislation.

Change is difficult, especially change that affects people personally. As leaders, we tend to think of significant changes as negative. However, most change is positive—a new baby, a new house, a new job. We need to learn to view change as a source of opportunity—the opportunity to take our mission to a higher level. This book provides the tools to do that.

Most change is positive—a new baby, a new house, a new job. We need to learn to view change as a source of opportunity.

Education leaders can view poor results on the Program for International Student Assessment (PISA), for example, in one of two ways. We can say it is unfair to compare our students to those in some of the highest-achieving countries—after all, we educate *all* children, whereas other countries have more selective processes for the type of education students receive. Alternatively, we can be grateful for the opportunity to make a difference in every American child's life as we set challenging goals and focus on making gradual, continuous progress.

When we choose the second approach, everyone wins: the students, the leaders and teachers who have the privilege of shaping them into productive adults, and the communities of which we are all a part.

To make the educational systems the best, it is vital to set and cascade the right goals for meeting these changes and be relentless in going after them. And we have to ensure that we're doing this inside a framework that allows the improvements we make to stick. That's what Evidence-Based Leadership℠, which is reviewed fully in Section 3 of this book, is all about.

What Is Constant in Education?

Let's look at a few examples of what has not changed in education. The first and most obvious value is **passion**. The primary concern of education professionals and parents is that students be well educated, and businesses and communities demonstrate their share in that concern by supporting those efforts. All these groups are passionate about effective education.

There is no better way to write about passion than to show examples with stories. Both of us connect back to purpose by relating stories from our days in the classroom. Here are some of Quint's childhood stories, which demonstrate so well the *why* behind our passion for what we do each day. Let us share them with you.

Quint's Beginning:
The Value of Believing in People

As a child, I had a rough time academically through all of grade school and high school. With a GPA under 2.0, I was not considered "college material." But after taking the ACT and scoring higher than anticipated, I and others realized that perhaps there was untapped potential, so I went to college. I majored in education because of three remarkable teachers who believed in me: Mrs. James, Mr. Fry, and Mr. King. I believe I would not have survived without them. Here are their stories, reprinted from my book *Hardwiring Excellence*.

Quint and Mrs. James:
Setting the Stage for Success

I was not a good student. I couldn't speak very well because I had a speech impediment. By the end of second grade, I still couldn't read. In fact, I'm pretty sure the only reason they agreed to promote me to third grade at all was because my mother was the vice president of the PTA.

By the time I was nine years old, I already knew I was a reject. I couldn't stay in my own classroom all day like the other kids: I was pulled out for speech therapy. But Mrs. James, my third-grade teacher, made a difference in my life. I can't tell you exactly what she did, but I would take risks for her that I would never take for any other teacher. She even invited me to stand up at the front of the room and perform in a skit once. It was the first time in my life a teacher had done that because people couldn't understand me. Performing just didn't come naturally. But Mrs. James set me up to succeed. She found a few words I could say: "I'm as poor as ever." She even had me visualize pouring milk so that I could say the word *poor*. I felt like I was important.

Today, I call it feeling worthwhile. I never would have believed then that eventually I would have the confidence to spend many of my days speaking in front of large groups, as I do now.

Mrs. James is one reason I am passionate about the importance of worthwhile work and making a difference.

Quint and Mr. Fry: Looking for the Positive

My sixth-grade teacher was Mr. Fry. What I liked about him was that he always looked for the positive. While other teachers told my mother that I couldn't sit still, Mr. Fry said, "Quint really has energy!" Other teachers complained that I couldn't focus. Mr. Fry said he was impressed by my ability to multitask. He made a point of noticing what was right, not what was wrong. It is because of Mr. Fry that I urge leaders to ingrain (or hardwire) systems and tools that recognize what's right and what's working well.

Quint and Coach King:
A Focus on *Can*, Not *Can't*

When I went to high school, I decided to play soccer because it was the only sport where they didn't cut anybody. My soccer coach, Mr. King, had a way of correcting me without destroying me. He would come up to me and say, "Quint, way to hustle! Way to get to that ball!" Then, almost as an afterthought, he'd add, "Next time, let's put the foot out. But hey, you got there! Way to go!"

You know how I felt? Pretty good. I had hustled. I had gotten there. And the next time, you better believe that I remembered to put my foot out. Suppose he had said, "Quint! What's the matter with you? What good does it do for you to run all that way if you don't kick the ball? Sit down now so I can put somebody else in." I might have run a little slower the next time to make sure I didn't get yelled at for missing the ball. Coach King taught me to go for the ball.

If we only hear about what we can't do, it seems easier to give up. Many of us do. In fact, of the people who leave their jobs, a great many leave within the first 90 days. About 27 percent of all employees who leave do so during this early period of employment. They don't leave to go work in some other industry. They just give up on their current employer and try another one. I believe this is because they hear too much about what they can't do instead of what they can do.

In fact, of the people who leave their jobs, a great many leave within the first 90 days. About 27 percent of all employees who leave do so during this early period of employment.

When we can pause in today's busy world, we see passion everywhere. Passion, or relentlessness in the pursuit of goals, is the same as ever, and it continues every day in education. As professionals and as members of giving and caring communities, we are blessed with an abundance of great people filled with passion.

Passion, or relentlessness in the pursuit of goals, is the same as ever, and it continues every day in education.

Another constant in education is **fortitude**. Working in education has always come with challenges, but with all the change happening today, it's become even more complex. It takes great fortitude and stamina to thrive in the midst of disruption. Change is difficult. It is hard for the people managing the change as well as for those on the receiving end.

We serve on university and college committees created to recommend a 21st-century curriculum for future leaders. One subject that comes up consistently is managing change. Yes, future leaders need skills in selection, the ability to understand a profit/loss statement, process improvement, and so forth. Being able to manage and navigate change is an absolute must for leaders. Without a doubt, this is as true in education.

Being able to manage and navigate change is an absolute must for leaders.

Leaders carry tough messages. Leaders are the ones who inform staff members that they will not be getting more resources, so they'll have to use current resources more efficiently and effectively. They are also the ones whom people point to when results are not as expected, even if these results are unrealistic at times. Although all organizations and institutions learn from failure, the experience is painful. Sometimes things get worse before they get better. Leading in today's changing environment takes tremendous fortitude.

Another element that remains constant in education is a **willingness to learn**. Every day, education professionals help people and are responsible for students' well-being. In the middle of all the intense emotions that come with their jobs, however, these leaders continue to learn. Whether it is mastering a new technology, learning a new strategy, or studying best practices, education professionals consistently show that a desire to learn is in their DNA.

In any given week, we help lead professional development sessions with district and school leaders. It is always encouraging to attend a training and watch attendees walk out feeling better and more hopeful. The feedback and comments we receive consistently show how grateful individuals are to acquire skills to be better leaders.

In addition to professional development, many individuals have entered teaching as a second career through professional teacher certification programs. It is rewarding to watch professionals devote time to learn, grow, and invest in not only themselves, but education as well.

Commitment to Learning:
Newsroom to the Classroom

Meet Sara Rabb, fourth-grade teacher at Oakcrest Elementary School in Escambia County, Florida. Prior to teaching, Ms. Rabb was an editor and reporter at the *Pensacola News Journal* in Pensacola, Florida.

Because of an incredibly strong desire to continue her learning and to use her time and talents to teach others, Ms. Rabb made a career decision to move from the newsroom to the classroom. With that goal in mind, she pursued an enhanced set of skills and learning, earning a professional teaching certification through completion of the TeacherReady® program. When asked about her new teaching role, Ms. Rabb reflects, "Watching my students' success gives me the greatest joy."

Four years later, not only does Ms. Rabb feel personal success regarding her decision, but her school does as well. The percentage of students meeting the state's writing standard at Oakcrest during her first year was one of the highest in the district. She continued to maintain and increase that in the second year.

Ms. Rabb provides an example of the multitude of educators who are eager to learn and improve their skills, refresh their motivation, and help others learn. Thank you, Ms. Rabb, for the difference you have made in the lives of your students.

We also continue to see a hunger to learn in today's educational systems; the key is the systems giving people the opportunity. We refer to a common theme in the book *Hardwiring Excellence*, which is that we can determine an organization's values by the investment it makes in leadership development (training). As the external environment in education gets increasingly tough, the need for skill building becomes greater and greater.

People have a tremendous **desire to do work that has purpose, is worthwhile, and makes a difference**. This attribute has stayed constant in education. People might initially feel that their work meets these criteria, but the feeling can be fragile. Traumas and problems over the course of a career make withdrawals from a person's emotional, mental, and physical "bank accounts." These withdrawals can cause people to lose sight of the fact that they have great purpose, do worthwhile work, and make a difference. It's up to organizational leaders to help connect people back to the positive difference they make each day in the lives of others.

It's true that many things have changed in education, but the values that drive people to do their best work—to throw their heart and soul into caring for those they serve—remain steadfast. It's those values that will pull us through the tough changes with our passion and dedication intact. In the pages ahead, we explain how to leverage those values to create the high-performance culture that will enable people working in educational systems to keep living the mission and values of doing their best for students every day.

Summary

At one time, education operated in a state of episodic change. Today, we've moved to a state of continuous change (Figure 1.1). As John Kotter explains, organizations must be able to increase and sustain their level of urgency in order to deal with the flow of continuous change that is coming our way.

To survive and thrive, today's leaders want to lead highly reliable organizations to create and maintain a culture of high performance. The skill sets needed in the next years build on the skill sets we needed in the past, but there are key differences. The good news is that the timeless values we possess—passion, fortitude, willingness to learn, and the desire to do worthwhile work and make a difference in the lives of others—will drive us to master the skills we need (Figure 1.2).

FIGURE 1.1 CHANGES IN EDUCATION	
· Episodic change to continuous change	· Competition with global assessments
· External environment	· Higher-stakes personnel evaluation systems and performance pay
· Common Core State Standards	· Performance-based funding model in higher education
· State report cards	

FIGURE 1.2 CONSTANTS IN EDUCATION	
· Passion	· Willingness to learn
· Fortitude	· Desire to do purposeful, worthwhile work that makes a difference

CHAPTER TWO:

USING EVIDENCE TO DRIVE CHANGE

Educators are highly familiar with research. Research helps us become better teachers and leaders, and expands the boundaries of our knowledge. Also, research can drive change.

It is impressive how quickly people—particularly educators—adapt to change they believe in. Given that, why might educators resist change? First, they might not understand the reason for the change, meaning they're not familiar with the research that determines the *why*. Second, intuitively they could feel there aren't enough data to back it up. Third, the change has not been explained well. Fourth, they don't think the new approach will last because they've heard for years that the organization is going to make a change, and it either never gets off the ground or quickly fizzles out.

The last point is interesting. Why are certain employees, leaders, and educators lacking in confidence that a new initiative will continue? Well, past initiatives have not succeeded in delivering the promised results. Initiatives often stop when they hit a barrier, and then the educational system moves on to the latest buzzword, book, or speaker.

When someone asks what's being done to improve leadership skills in an educational system, we often hear about a new book or an idea picked up at a conference. Now, we love books and conferences or we wouldn't be doing these two things ourselves, but books and conferences are not stand-alone items. As change is introduced, it is best when backed by solid evidence in order to achieve results. If performance gaps exist, leaders can acquire better skills. In other words, research makes the ideas stick and determines how to invest in leadership development.

Of course, research to validate educational work and practices has been available for years, with research priorities shifting from management of schools to instructional leadership. This is a positive trend. We want to see more educational research focused on leadership. Organizational research has focused on two things we are passionate about: (1) a senior leadership model of high-performing leadership, and (2) a leader focus on creating a best-place-to-work environment to help employees achieve their highest potential. The research highlighted in this chapter focuses on these two areas.

Relating versus Comparing

Sometimes we get pushback from education leaders when we refer to leadership studies from other fields, such as business, industry, and healthcare. Leaders in education can fall into the trap of feeling "terminally unique"—that is, if the data don't fit exactly, they don't apply to where I work. When someone or something is terminally unique, it's easy to come up with reasons that a proposed change might not work.

The solution is to relate, not compare. There is great benefit in pushing ourselves to transfer learning from other industries into the educational environment.

When someone or something is terminally unique, it's easy to come up with reasons that a proposed change might not work.

The solution is to relate, not compare.

The book *Results That Last* (written by Quint) was created for organizations other than healthcare providers. Around the time it was published, Microsoft sponsored a book tour for non-healthcare companies. The subject of the tour was various practices from the book that improve service, improve employee retention, improve quality, and reduce cost. Using healthcare examples, the best practices included the importance of pre- and post-visit phone calls to customers, key words to use when introducing oneself to a customer, how to hire talent using behavioral-based interviewing, and adding 30- and 90-day meetings for new employees to increase engagement and retention. At the end of these presentations, people would immediately share how they could transfer the learning to their own environment. Whether they worked for a hotel, a restaurant, a trucking company, or another service industry, they understood right away. It would be great if more education professionals learned to think this way as well.

The same thing happens when we administer employee engagement and parent satisfaction surveys for our partner school districts. As the results are rolled out, comments about the uniqueness of the district, school, or department surface. In fact, it is not unusual for leaders to spend more time and energy on excusing the results than on accepting them for what they are and engaging in an improvement-oriented conversation with their teams. We all can fall into this trap.

The good news is that most people in educational systems are open to learning from others who are not exactly like them. For example, each year Menomonee Falls School District in Wisconsin schedules two to three on-site visits for other district leaders to tour classrooms in which teachers are applying the Plan-Do-Study-Act approach. It isn't unusual for the district to have 75 to 100 visitors touring their schools during each visit.

When the supporting evidence is there, one can trust it enough to at least give the tool or tactic a solid try. The evidence gathered might not be perfect, and people may challenge the validity of the numbers. However, we have found time and time again that when somebody wants to believe the results, they will. When they don't want to believe the results, they won't. Isn't it ironic that although it takes only about six people to constitute an acceptable sample size, someone who does not want to believe the results could question the validity of a study with a sample size of two billion.

Another barrier to change can be expressed as "best" getting in the way of "better." Healthcare executive Mark Clement cautions his teams that perfection, or "best," can stall or stop action. Mark will ask, "Will this make it better?" If the answer is yes, he will say, "Then let's make it better." When put in those terms, the team can hardly argue or disagree.

"Best" can get in the way of "better."

A Look at Some Powerful Research

The remainder of this chapter highlights two studies focusing on leadership that were conducted by Studer Group. Both the high-performing organization study and the Straight A Leadership Assessment provide direct evidence of hardwiring excellence through leadership to build a culture of accountability and high performance.

The High-Performing Organization Study

Before digging into an initial organizational diagnostic tool we use called the Straight A Leadership Assessment, we'll look at a Studer Group study conducted in 2004. This important study set the stage for the Evidence-Based Leadership[SM] framework that our team applies with leaders to drive positive outcomes and continuous improvement processes.

The 2004 Studer Group study of high-performing organizations (*Organizational Change Process in High-Performing Organizations: In-Depth Case Studies with Health Care Facilities.* Gulf Breeze, FL: Alliance for Health Care Research, 2005) found that some key elements drove high performance. In this study, an organization was classified as "high performing" when it made and sustained statistically significant progress over a minimum of three years on measurable criteria, including:

(1) Increases in patient experience ratings

(2) Increases in employee engagement ratings

(3) Reductions in employee turnover

(4) Increases in market share, financial returns, or other growth indicators

(5) Improvements on quality indicators

These criteria boil down to the five pillars we always talk about at Studer Group (adapted from the concept identified by author Clay Sherman in his book *Creating the New American Hospital*): service, quality, finance, people, and growth.

To explore characteristics of high-performing organizations, our team of researchers completed in-depth personal interviews with all senior-level managers at each facility. Five factors consistently emerged as the most influential in their success (Figure 2.1). We summarize the findings and then provide an example of how the study results transfer to high-performing superintendent behaviors.

FIGURE 2.1	THE MOST INFLUENTIAL FACTORS IN SENIOR MANAGERS' SUCCESS, FROM HIGH-PERFORMING ORGANIZATION STUDY FINDINGS
· Executive and senior leadership commitment (relentlessness) · Leadership evaluation (accountability) · Leadership institutes and training (development)	· Employee forums (communication) · Knowing this was the right thing to do (connect to purpose and *why*)

High-Performing Organization Factor 1: Executive and Senior Leadership Commitment (Relentlessness)

The first success factor was the executive and senior leadership team's relentless commitment. These leaders didn't rationalize why they didn't get a particular result. They didn't make excuses. They were relentless in pursuing their goals. This is similar to what Jim Collins, in his book *Good to Great*, describes as a Level 5 leader. Collins describes these types of leaders as those who focus their drive on the success of the organization they're leading rather than on themselves.

Respondents agreed that without the passion, vision, and commitment of top leadership, their organizations would not be successful. They talked about the management team's unified vision, clear outlining of expectations, determination to stay focused, and discipline in following the process and vision. This team also "walked the talk" and modeled all the behaviors they expected others to perform.

Example: A Relentless Leader

Dr. Pat Greco is the superintendent of Menomonee Falls School District in Menomonee Falls, Wisconsin. She has been a superintendent of school districts for several decades and is a great example of leadership that is relentless about achieving results. Here's what makes her a relentless leader:

Dr. Greco and her entire leadership team show unified discipline in their pursuit of continuous-improvement processes, including Evidence-Based Leadership and Plan-Do-Study-Act in classrooms and school buildings as well as Lean and Six Sigma process-improvement tools. Dr. Greco models these behaviors herself, seeking opportunities to showcase the school district and continuing her lifelong work of making public education systems better for students and families. At meetings, she turns over the stage to the leaders and teachers who carry out the work every day. As Jim Collins says, it's not that Level 5 leaders do not have egos; rather, they channel their ego away from themselves and toward the larger good of the organization.

Dr. Greco is defined by her passion, vision, and commitment. She claims that for years she's been looking for the right formula to make a difference in school reform and improvement, and finally she sees success as a result of finding the right combination and not wavering from achieving the district's goals.

High-Performing Organization Factor 2: Leadership Evaluation (Accountability)

The second success factor was a leadership evaluation tool that created accountability. All the organizations studied had an objective, weighted evaluation tool that helped the leaders know exactly what they were going to accomplish and what their priorities were. This moved leaders away from making excuses such as "My plate is full" or "I have too many priorities." They might still have had a full schedule, but they understood their priorities.

Respondents also talked about getting those who were not willing to buy into the organization's emphasis on accountability "off the bus." Some employees (including leaders) at these high-performing organizations were asked to leave. Others left voluntarily when they determined it was not the best employment match for them.

Example: A Shift in Accountability

Our partner school districts apply a measurable leader evaluation system that integrates alignment of superintendents, executive team leaders, principals, and department leaders.

The Santa Rosa County School District in Milton, Florida, is a high-performing school district. In fact, every year it ranks in the state's top three districts for student achievement scores. The superintendent of schools, Tim Wyrosdick, partnered with us to apply the Evidence-Based Leadership framework as a way to sustain its success. In some Florida school districts, superintendents are elected, and Santa Rosa County is one of those.

Superintendent Wyrosdick acted bravely when he shifted his evaluation to a transparent, open, measurable evaluation that included growth measures on student achievement, employee engagement scores, parent satisfaction, satisfaction of principals with district services, and financial effectiveness. By bravely, we mean that Superintendent Wyrosdick is not evaluated by the board; in essence, he is evaluated by the citizens of the community. Therefore, he made a conscious choice to use "hard" measures and to make the results transparent to the board and the public. Superintendent Wyrosdick serves as a model for other leaders, who made at least 75 percent of their evaluation dependent on measurable goals.

Superintendent Wyrosdick said it took maturity for him and other leaders to face the brutal fact that they would not hit the highest rating in all categories every year. When 98 or 99 percent of leaders got the highest evaluations and the district did not, the Santa Rosa County School District leaders acknowledged the fact and embraced a culture of accountability to achieve high performance. Today, Santa Rosa County remains one of the highest-performing districts in Florida. The leaders made a conscious decision to be held accountable when being complacent may have been easier.

High-Performing Organization Factor 3: Leadership Institutes and Training (Development)

The third influential success factor was leader development. Each organization invested heavily in training. Every one of these organizations provided more than 60 hours a year in leadership and management development training. It was mandatory for everyone in a supervisory role, without exception.

Example: Leadership Development Is Priority One

As part of the Evidence-Based Leadership framework, we recommend that superintendents hold Leadership Development Institutes (LDIs) to develop all leaders and to engage teams of leaders to plan the curriculum. The Janesville School District in Janesville, Wisconsin, under the leadership of Superintendent Karen Schulte, committed to holding four LDIs each year.

The LDIs are planned by leadership teams that may include a curriculum team (during the event), linkage team (continuous learning from one event to the next), logistics team (event planning and setup), and social team (integrating relationship-building learning events into the day). The superintendent provides direction and begins each institute by presenting a current state address.

School districts tend to resist by claiming to be unable to put all their leaders in one room. Superintendent Schulte has created a "win-win" situation to counteract this objection. She schedules teams of teacher leaders (who could be the next generation of principals) to provide fill-in leadership to schools so that principals and assistant principals can attend LDIs.

High-Performing Organization Factor 4: Employee Forums (Communication)

High-performing organizations made a real commitment to employee communication, not only at the department level but also at the administrative level. Every organization conducted employee forums or town hall meetings led by senior leaders, thus allowing employees to hear key messages, be informed on key issues, and focus on what they can do to improve.

At Studer Group, we have found that when leaders have good communication skills, they also apply effective strategies to reward and recognize employees. High-performing organizations realize that people are more engaged and willing to go the extra mile when leaders frequently express their appreciation—in person, in thank-you notes, or both.

Example: Are There Any Questions?

Dr. Marcelo Cavazos, Arlington Independent School District superintendent in Arlington, Texas, exemplifies commitment to fostering transparent and open communication with leaders, teachers, and staff. During their monthly and quarterly meetings, Dr. Cavazos communicates key information to staff in an uncommon way. In each session, he presents key information and data, and connects strongly back to the district's goals by continuously repeating, "Failing to improve is not an option." But Dr. Cavazos doesn't just deliver his message; he also fosters interaction and feedback among his staff. He always ends his presentations by asking for questions. To ensure that his inquiry is sincere, he remains silent until people ask questions or make comments. He does not adjourn the meeting until all questions have been asked and answered.

High-Performing Organization Factor 5: Knowing This Was the Right Thing to Do (Connect to Purpose and *Why*)

The fifth influential success factor in the high-performing organization study was knowing when an action was the right thing to do. In these organizations, leaders didn't take for granted that people automatically knew *why* a change was being made. They spent time explaining why decisions were made, and they frequently and deliberately connected employees back to purpose, worthwhile work, and making a difference.

Example: Explaining Why

School districts often implement an employee engagement survey that can be benchmarked to other partner districts. The most important feature of the survey is that leaders use the results to provide teachers and staff with a work environment that supports them in reaching their highest potential. To reinforce this message, it is highly recommended that the superintendent explain why it is important for teachers and staff to complete the survey. Here's an example:

Dear ____,

Our school district is working each day to provide a great place for students to learn, a great place for teachers to teach, a great place for all employees to work, and a great place for parents to send their children for an excellent education. As a district, we are continuing to gather data that will allow us to set realistic goals for our district as part of our strategic plan for improvement. It is important that we get your input on how well your immediate supervisor (the person who completes your evaluation) provides a work environment that allows you to perform at the highest levels.

The survey will open on April 15 and will close on April 26. The data from this survey will be reviewed by all stakeholders and used to create action plans at school, departmental, and district levels. These action plans will focus on an area for improvement that will continue to move our school district to higher levels of excellence. Your input in this process is valuable, so please take a few minutes to complete the survey.

Thank you for your commitment to students, employees, and parents.

It's easy to see from the superintendent examples how the findings translate to education. The superintendents live out the five factors of relentlessness, accountability, development, communication, and connecting to purpose. Superintendents like the ones highlighted here want to engage in a partnership with us. We find that they have a great desire to move from good to great. They see value in continuous systems improvement, and thus they echo the value of the Evidence-Based Leadership framework.

We strongly believe that we can contribute to our professions by doing research with our partner organizations. One way we've been able to do so is through the Straight A Leadership Assessment tool. The remainder of this chapter describes the tool and our findings.

The Straight A Leadership Assessment

The second study we present is the Straight A Leadership Assessment, the largest data-collection process Studer Group has ever done. In fact, it might be one of the largest ever done in healthcare. It is now being applied to educational systems, so this chapter outlines the survey questions we use in K–12 systems. As this book is being written, more than 37,000 people have taken the survey (Studer Group, *Straight A Leadership Assessment*, 2013). The results represent what we've learned from healthcare systems that we are now testing in education.

The Straight A Leadership Assessment diagnoses a given organization in the key areas of: (1) alignment, (2) readiness for change, (3) fundamentals, (4) self-awareness, (5) consistency, and (6) accountability. Studer Group created this assessment tool to align with the five success factors identified in the 2004 study on high-performing organizations and with John Kotter's concept of urgency. In Kotter's book *A Sense of Urgency*, he identifies two types of urgency: episodic (false sense of urgency) and continuous (true urgency). When leaders experience episodic urgency, the organization experiences chaos. Continuous urgency requires leaders to understand that change is inevitably part of life in a system. To allow the data to be analyzed in detail, the first question of the survey asks, "What is your role?" Typically, the choices for K–12 educators are "School Board," "Superintendent/Executive Team," "Directors/Department Leaders," "Managers," and "Principals/Assistant Principals." Being able to analyze the data by role allows us to evaluate the degree of alignment among the leadership groups.

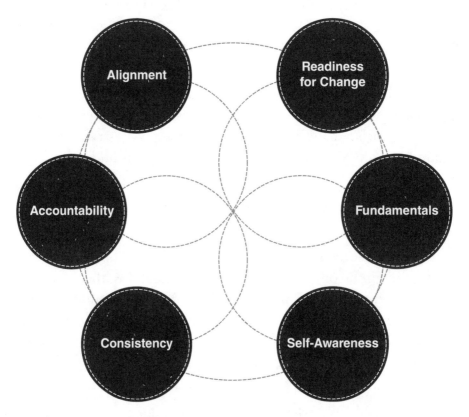

FIGURE 2.2 | KEY FACTORS TO ACHIEVE HIGH PERFORMANCE

As highlighted early on in the book *Straight A Leadership* (written by Quint), one skill CEOs need is the ability to take a hard look at themselves. Many organizations say they're high quality, but the survey results do not support their view. Leaders also say, "We're a great place to work," but sometimes the data show that employees don't agree. So the willingness to self-assess really matters.

Now let's look at the key factors for achieving high performance, one at a time.

Alignment

In our Straight A Leadership Assessment, we ask questions aimed at seeing how aligned the organization is in viewing the past and the future. The questions presented are those adapted for educational institutions. Figure 2.3 shows one example.

FIGURE 2.3 | ALIGNMENT

· Over the past 5 years, the external environment in your school district has been (1 = very easy to 5 = very difficult).

· Over the next 5 years, the external environment in your school district will be (1 = very easy to 5 = very difficult).

The cumulative assessment results show that senior leaders tend to see a more difficult environment than unit-level leaders see. The results show a difference between these groups when looking back but an even greater difference when looking forward. This is not unusual, since the executive team is closer to issues raised by the external environment than the rest of the organization is. They have a front-row seat for the huge changes occurring. However, if senior leadership does not get the rest of the organization to view the external environment as they do, others will not share their urgency. After all, leaders have performed well in tough circumstances before, so the rest of the organization may be lulled into a false sense of security. Senior leaders may be frustrated by not seeing quicker movement, and managers and directors may think senior leaders are overreacting.

> If senior leadership does not get the rest of the organization to view the external environment as they do, others will not share their urgency.

Readiness for Change

Another key component measured in the Straight A tool is an organization's readiness for change (Figure 2.4).

FIGURE 2.4 | READINESS FOR CHANGE

· If the district continues to perform exactly as it does today, your results over the next 5 years will be (1 = much worse to 5 = much better).

We find that leaders at the executive level tend to say, "If we don't change, our results are going to get worse or (most likely) much worse." Leaders at the school and departmental levels might not feel the same sense of urgency. In fact, about 37 percent of them say, "I think we can stay the same."

In *A Sense of Urgency,* John Kotter writes that probably the biggest reason organizations don't achieve high performance is that the executive team doesn't understand that other leaders might not be on the same page. We've found that executives live the urgency felt from change, but other leaders do not. The managers and directors believe that continuing down the same path will lead to better results. Executives believe that results will get much worse. The results show a variation in the degree of urgency felt in the leadership ranks.

We've found that executives live the urgency felt from change, but other leaders do not. The managers and directors believe that continuing down the same path will lead to better results. Executives believe that results will get much worse.

That's why we include the "readiness for change" quotient on the Straight A Assessment tool. It helps an organization measure the degree of urgency they have in the leadership ranks—which is the first step in making sure everyone understands the external environment.

Fundamentals

Two questions on the survey measure two critical fundamentals: leader accountability and leader training (Figure 2.5).

FIGURE 2.5 | FUNDAMENTALS

- How well does your current leader evaluation system hold people accountable? (1 = very poorly to 5 = excellent)

- How well does your current leadership training prepare you for your leadership role? (1 = very poorly to 5 = excellent)

First, let's look at what the study tells us about leader accountability. On a 1–5 scale, with 5 being excellent and 1 being very poor, the average score is about 3, or "fair." We find that one of the biggest impediments to organizations achieving high performance is that while many leader evaluation systems are good for collecting data for a number of human resource issues, the tools just do not work to drive high performance. Without an evaluation tool that drives performance, an organization will struggle to attain high performance.

> Without an evaluation tool that drives performance, an organization will struggle to attain high performance.

Next, let's dissect the responses to the question of how well the organization prepares leaders with the skills necessary to be successful. Once again, the average response is 3, or "fair."

Often leaders may not be getting the most effective training, or else increased challenges mean they need more development. Over the years, we've learned that it's important to start with a thorough assessment of leaders' skills to determine what's needed. Then, leaders need not only didactic and large-group training but also small-group training, online training, and, most important of all, mentorship.

Self-Awareness

The tool asks how well respondents think the organization is currently doing with their three stakeholders: (1) faculty and staff, (2) students, and (3) parents/community (Figure 2.6).

FIGURE 2.6 | SELF-AWARENESS

- From a teacher/staff perspective and point of view, how would a teacher/staff member rate your district? (1 = worst to 10 = best in class)

- From a parent/family perspective and point of view, how would a parent/family member rate your district? (1 = worst to 10 = best in class)

In other words, can the organization objectively look in the mirror? The good news is that, yes, organizations have good self-awareness and do have the ability to see themselves as they are. We have repeatedly found that organizations understand their level of performance.

That doesn't mean they understand how to make it better—if they did, they probably already would have—but they certainly understand where they sit in the areas of student achievement, employee engagement, stakeholder engagement, and financial stability.

Organizations understand their level of performance.

Consistency

The Straight A Leadership tool also measures another attribute for achieving and sustaining high performance: consistency, or reliability (Figure 2.7).

FIGURE 2.7 | CONSISTENCY

- Rate the skill set of your district in implementing and standardizing best practices throughout the district (1 = worst to 10 = best in class).

- Rate your perception of the consistency in leadership behavior/practices throughout the district (1 = worst to 10 = best in class).

One of the biggest frustrations for organizations of almost any type is inconsistency. This is always one of those "aha" moments, even for the executive team. What the executive team discovers is that if there are seven people on their team, on a scale of 1 to 10 they might actually have seven different leadership ratings. In fact, it's not unusual to go from a 3 to a 9, or a 4 to an 8—anywhere from a 4- to 6-point differential. Also, when senior leaders rate their own team's consistency as poor, there tends to be less consistency throughout the entire organization.

We don't believe anyone tries to be inconsistent. What we've learned is that leaders may not know how inconsistent they are until they decide to be consistent. It's comparable to not knowing how out of shape we are until we decide to start working out to get in shape.

So this tool creates conversation at the senior table about the areas in which they want to be more consistent. That's important because the next question asks how well the organization implements best practices. And guess what? The score on best practices implementation is almost exactly the same as the consistency score.

The score on best practices implementation is almost exactly the same as the consistency score.

One thing we've learned in coaching is to not say, "Okay, let's get consistent!" Again, we'll compare it to the workout example. No one has to say to those of us who are out of shape, "You're out of shape. You need to work out." We know that already. What we need is for someone to identify best practices for us, such as how long to walk when we're starting out, how much to stretch, what exercises have the most beneficial impact, and what sequence to do them in.

It's the same with education leaders. Educational systems need to decide what best practices to be absolutely consistent in. It might go this way: When we have our executive team meeting, exactly what message points do we want to communicate to the rest of the organization? When do we meet with the direct reports so we can have consistent timing for this communication? This is some of the low-hanging fruit that we find can improve communication very quickly.

Alternatively, somebody might choose an employee engagement strategy, such as leadership rounding or intentional touch points by leaders with their direct reports. This rounding would be for the purposes of recognizing areas that are working well, improving processes, and recognizing individual performance of those recognized by others. Standardization occurs by defining how often leaders will round (i.e., check in with in a meaningful way) with employees. How will the process occur? How will it be validated?

Most of our K–12 education partners administer some common questions we use to benchmark employee engagement. The superintendent first shares overall results with district employees. Then, all leaders are taught a results rollout process they use to present their unit results to their direct reports. The steps for rolling out the results and the process used to do so are standard and consistent practices that become part of the culture of the school system.

By choosing the right best practice, enacting it, and making it consistent, we get much better results. We won't be implementing actions just for the sake of doing something. As John Kotter says, we should not confuse activity with urgency. By creating less activity, we actually create more urgency. The key is choosing the right activity and making sure it's implemented to the fullest degree.

By creating less activity, we actually create more urgency. The key is choosing the right activity and making sure it's implemented to the fullest degree.

Accountability

The last component from the Straight A tool we'll discuss is accountability. Several questions address this issue (Figure 2.8).

FIGURE 2.8 | ACCOUNTABILITY

- How many employees do you directly supervise?
- How many of the employees you directly supervise are not meeting performance expectations?
- How many employees do you currently have working directly for you who are in formal corrective/disciplinary action?

As we discussed earlier, accountability is vital to an effective leader evaluation. But that's not the only place we address it. The tool asks respondents several questions related to performance management—in other words, how well are employees held accountable?

Responses to the first question have shown us that the average leader supervises a manageable number of employees. In fact, it's not the span of control that has the biggest impact on performance—it's the skill of the leader managing the employees. We also ask how many employees are not meeting performance expectations, and then we ask how many of them are being documented and dealt with.

The data in our study show that the great majority of employees met performance expectations. We've surveyed more than 34,000 leaders, and the average leader supervises 20 people. That means our study accounts for 600,000+ employees under supervision. Of those, 92 percent were meeting performance expectations.

So that means the first thing an organization has to do is focus on what's right. What can be done with the 92 percent who are meeting expectations to re-recruit and develop these individuals? They cannot be taken for granted. If we don't re-recruit and develop them, some will leave. Never take a person for granted. We need to be in the process of re-recruiting every single day.

This, of course, leaves the 8 percent who are not meeting performance expectations. First, we need to look at the leadership. If the leaders are not meeting performance expectations, how can they evaluate others? They obviously don't have the right skill set to make that judgment. Change starts at the top.

The study has shown that of the 8 percent not meeting performance expectations, 48 percent (or almost half of those not meeting performance expectations) did not know they were not performing well. That means almost half of them (a) had not heard from their supervisors that they're not meeting performance expectations, or (b) they may have had a conversation, but no documentation of it exists.

It really isn't fair to employees to be left unaware of their job performance. Chapter 12 details some specific techniques to help people in supervisory roles develop their performance management skills. The key is to connect performance management with values. Our values call for people to receive feedback so they can be developed to their fullest degree. If they're not successful after leaders attempt to help them develop the skill, either find a place in the organization where they can succeed or help them leave the organization so they can find an opportunity elsewhere.

The key is to connect performance management with values.

Straight A Leadership Summary

The Straight A Leadership Assessment tool provides a first step that leaders can take to gain insight about perceptions focused on the factors influencing high-performing educational systems. We have found that the tool leads to many "ahas" inside systems. Repeatedly, CEOs and superintendents say, "This has given me so much more than I thought it would!" Yet the survey takes only 10 to 15 minutes to complete.

This tool provides data that leaders can use to create a road map for maximizing performance (Figure 2.9). Once leaders know their scores, they have opportunities to tighten up the evaluation system, become more effective at providing skill development, adapt best practices for better leadership consistency, and use the clear accountability data for continuous improvement.

FIGURE 2.9	STRAIGHT A LEADERSHIP— DATA SUMMARY AND SUGGESTED TREATMENT		
AREA	**FINDING**	**SOLUTION**
ALIGNMENT	Senior executives have more urgency than the rest of the organization. When comparing executive team responses to those of managers and directors, the cumulative data show a gap looking backward, but an even bigger gap looking forward.	All levels of leaders need to feel the same sense of urgency to improve that the executive team does.
READINESS FOR CHANGE	More leaders than expected, or about 37% of respondents, feel that if the organization stays the same, the results will be the same, better, or much better.	Leaders communicate and educate all stakeholders on the external environment and the changes that are necessary for success.
FUNDAMENTALS	How well the leadership evaluation system builds leadership accountability and how well leader training prepares for success are both rated as fair.	Implement a measurable and weighted evaluation tool for leaders and develop leadership skills.
SELF-AWARENESS	Organizations are generally self-aware and understand where they sit in the areas of quality and engagement.	Use the data to identify performance gaps and create a continuous improvement plan.
CONSISTENCY	Data show a large degree of inconsistency in leadership practices, and there is a direct correlation between the ability to implement best practices and consistency of leadership practices.	Determine mandatory senior leadership practices and identify and implement those best practices.
ACCOUNTABILITY	The average leader supervises a manageable number of employees. About 8% of employees are not meeting expectations. Of those 8%, about one-third will be terminated. The other two-thirds will leave or improve.	Re-recruit high performers, re-recruit and develop middle/solid performers, and document and develop performance plans for all low/subpar performers.

For a Straight A Leadership Assessment for your organization, please visit studereducation.com.

Summary

This chapter provides only a sample of the evidence Studer Group has collected over the years, but it does offer a glimpse into why evidence is so important. The 2004 Studer Group study on high-performing organizations paved the way for hardwiring the pillars and reinforced the work of Clay Sherman. The pillars (see Chapter 8) guide leaders to create the key performance drivers of any organization. The study also found the most influential factors to be: (1) relentlessness in the executive team leadership, (2) accountability, using a measurable leadership evaluation process, (3) leadership development aligned to identify gaps in work performance, (4) communication by leaders using employee forums, and (5) connection to purpose and *why*, so that people know the right thing is being done.

Most of the chapter describes a diagnostic tool that Studer Group uses with healthcare and educational systems. The diagnostic tool focuses on gathering initial data to test the leadership alignment along several factors: alignment, readiness for change, fundamentals, self-awareness, consistency, and accountability.

The key, of course, is to learn from the evidence and execute on the behaviors we know are effective. We still have a lot of work to do. Despite the availability of evidence on best practices in our fields, tremendous inconsistency remains in leadership today. Studer Education's role as a leader in education is to hardwire excellence for better consistency, better reliability, better efficiency, and better effectiveness. That's what this book is all about.

CHAPTER THREE:

A STARTING POINT FOR CHANGE: ACCOUNTABLE LEADERSHIP

For decades, accountability and student test scores have been used to judge how well schools are doing. We are very familiar with this type of accountability. What we could perhaps focus on more is accountable leadership—leaders creating ways to let people know they can count on us to be committed to a culture of high performance.

As leaders, teachers, and staff, our profession allows us the wonderful opportunity to be engaged in extremely purposeful, worthwhile work every day. Think about it. All school district employees directly or indirectly influence classroom environments, whether they are teachers, facilities and grounds operators, bus drivers, custodians, food servers, or human resource officers. These employees deserve to work in a high-performing culture. Without accountable leadership, high-performing cultures are hard to find.

Leaders of school systems, working with all stakeholders, define the culture that best achieves the schools' desired outcomes. The most successful school systems have accountable leaders who focus on maximizing their own performance, which influences results throughout the system. Accountable leadership means leaders consistently perform certain behaviors using targeted tools and techniques that create the excellence needed to provide the highest-quality educational experiences for students and their families.

Accountable leadership means leaders consistently perform certain behaviors using targeted tools and techniques that create the excellence needed to provide the highest-quality educational experiences for students and their families.

So when accountable leadership is mentioned in this chapter, please think of it as a starting point for creating a high-performing educational system. A high-performing educational system is one with leaders who have the skills to create workplace environments in which people perform so as to create organizational excellence. Their performance must be consistent, reliable, effective, and efficient, and it must result in high-quality learning environments with the most effective use of resources.

This chapter focuses on what accountable leadership looks like in school systems. If you are a leader reading this chapter, think about how your actions serve as a model for those you lead. Before we can expect our teams to perform at high levels, we choose to show "what right looks like." Our behaviors and actions show others how to be held accountable for clearly defined outcomes and measures, and we want to work collectively with our teams to achieve these outcomes. We become the premier role models for applying the behaviors we expect of them.

To set the structure for best-practice leadership behaviors, let's focus on two graphics that help define the concept of accountability, or high performance.

The Results Triangle

The Results Triangle has three components: strategy, structure, and execution (Figure 3.1).

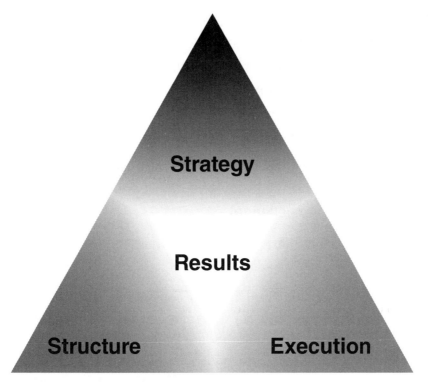

FIGURE 3.1 | RESULTS TRIANGLE

When things are not going well, it can be normal to discuss changing the organizational structure as a possible solution to the problem. Leaders might say something like, "If we reorganize and assign certain people to report to different leaders or align varying groups that have better working relationships, we may get better outcomes." Sometimes leaders change approaches or programs. When a certain program does not work after a year or two of implementation, senior leaders sometimes choose another without providing an exit strategy for the existing one. Employees are likely to think, "Another program, another approach—wait two or three years and it will go away." Change for the sake of change is unlikely to work; it's important to get the right structure and strategy.

We've read the works of many strategic thinkers in our profession who have contributed significantly to the field. But even with the best structure and strategy, if we fail to execute with consistency and quality, we face a difficult path to excellence.

Even with the best structure and strategy, if we fail to execute with consistency and quality, we face a difficult path to excellence.

The challenge in getting results lies in consistency and reliability of execution. For example, a school district might purchase a reading program for all schools to implement. Some leaders apply the program with fidelity, some apply it with little effort, and others don't apply it at all. The problem is not necessarily the program but rather its execution. In other words, we are great sometimes, good most of the time, and on occasion we have real issues. Obviously, we need to be great always.

The Execution Triangle

Since execution is so critical to maximizing organizational and individual performance, leaders have to know what quality execution looks like. The Execution Triangle components are accountability, consistency, and reliability (Figure 3.2).

FIGURE 3.2 | EXECUTION TRIANGLE

With execution, the key driver is accountability. It is important to realize that if we achieve accountability, the organization will also be consistent and reliable.

All organizations strive to become highly reliable. A highly reliable organization needs a highly consistent leadership team with a high level of accountability. So yes, strategy and structure are vital—but it is execution that creates that consistency and reliability. Therefore, consistency must be measured at the leadership level.

In order to execute well, we need the right strategy and structure; however, it is execution that creates that consistency and reliability.

What Gets in the Way of Execution?

Execution is the must-have to achieve an organization's desired goals. One of the most important responsibilities of a leader is to work collectively with professionals to create a best-place-to-work environment. As leaders, we know that we and our direct reports—and certainly anyone taking the time to read this book—want to execute well. People don't walk into work hoping to frustrate their supervisor by missing a deadline. They don't keep key information from their colleagues just to make them anxious, and they certainly don't insult their colleagues or stakeholders just to have some fun. Most people go to work with the intention of doing a good job.

As leaders, we model behaviors we expect those we lead to apply, but certain potential barriers keep us from maximizing performance. These barriers originate at a subconscious level, perhaps stemming from emotions that sit just below the surface. Our colleagues might not even notice that they are doing these things, and if they do, they may not know how to change them.

Let's examine some barriers to change that can get in the way of execution (Figure 3.3).

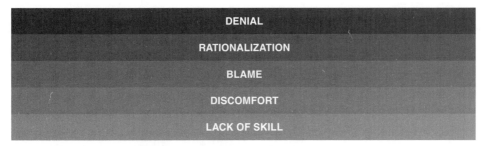

FIGURE 3.3 | BARRIERS TO CHANGE

Barrier 1: Denial

In our research, we find that organizations without good measurement tools may be unaware that certain things are happening. For example, we've found that when we present results using data and input from the workforce and stakeholders, senior executive teams are often so surprised that they say the data can't be right. Teams that deny the data impede progress toward creating a culture of excellence and improving organizational performance.

When sharing data and results in order to move to solutions, many organizations see a predictable pattern of denial (Figure 3.4). At first, many inside the organization will deny the data if they are not positive. If they do accept the data, they will think the problem is not theirs but someone else's. If they accept the data and the problem, they may think a solution can't be found. The goal is to move to the fourth step, in which the data are accepted, along with the problem and the need for a solution. When we know there is a problem, it's up to us to come up with the solution.

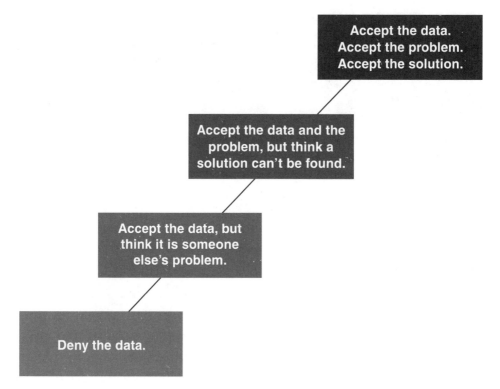

FIGURE 3.4 | **FOUR STEPS TO MOVING FROM DATA TO SOLUTIONS**

When educational systems are having issues, those issues usually begin at the top—sometimes the *very* top. The story "Change Starts with Me" illustrates what it means to become aware that sometimes the problem is us.

Quint's Story: Change Starts with Me

Back when I was president of a hospital, a department was experiencing some real challenges in productivity and the patient experience. I rounded on the staff in that area and quickly noticed some serious performance issues that we had accepted and tolerated. It wasn't just in their results; you could hear it when you listened to their attitudes.

Next I met with the vice president and department manager in that area to discuss the situation. Both mentioned that some employees weren't performing well. We discussed how to deal with the low performers and how to help the middle and high performers become more successful.

Three months later, nothing had changed. I started thinking perhaps the issue wasn't the hourly employees at all, but the manager. The vice president and I talked again, and I found out they had first placed the manager in the position as an interim and eventually gave him the job. In hindsight, perhaps he wasn't a good fit. So the vice president agreed to either provide the manager with the needed skill set or move him out of the organization. We both left the meeting feeling good about our solution.

Another three months went by and still no change. The employees and manager were still there, and the issues were continuing. I came to a new conclusion: if the problem wasn't the manager, perhaps it was his leader, the vice president of operations. I felt certain my conclusion was right, but decided I'd better end this little exercise because the next line of investigation might lead to me!

So I was really the one who needed to hold myself, and others, more accountable. As Gandhi said, "If I want change, I have to start with me."

Yes, the more we discuss the issues our systems face, the higher the progression leads, until we really have to hold up the mirror and look at ourselves. And the mirror doesn't belong only to leaders: no matter what position we're in, chances are we're all part of the problem. Denying that this is true keeps us from improving—and from realizing that if we're part of an organization, we have to be part of the solution.

If we're part of an organization, we have to be part of the solution.

Barrier 2: Rationalization

Another barrier to execution is rationalization. When we rationalize, we come up with reasons that something won't work, can't work, or will never work. Sometimes we can rationalize so much that not only will our excuses make sense to us, but they'll make sense to other people as well. We may even rationalize them so much that they become our reality and part of our nomenclature.

We've all heard rationalizations like those to explain why so few leaders hardwire reward and recognition. They manifest in statements like "Don't compliment them; they'll get complacent" or "If they get too many compliments, they'll get big heads." With all the time we have spent working in hospitals, we have never seen anyone in the emergency department with a swelled head and a diagnosis of being over-complimented! If such people exist, it is guaranteed they don't work in education.

We also hear rationalizations about geography. It's common to hear, "People in this area have high expectations and are hard to please" or "The best teachers don't apply for jobs at this educational institution, so we can't expect to achieve as much as other institutions."

We're having a little fun with these stories and not criticizing people for having certain perceptions. We don't mean that what people say is not valid—we are just saying that when issues come up, we need to research and dig a little deeper, beyond our initial thoughts. In fact, we have used all of these at times in our careers, and it is very easy to fall into the rationalization trap.

One of the most common rationalizations we hear is the lack of resources. We find that one of the best ways a leader can address this one is to find another organization with similar numbers and study it to see why it has better performance.

It's extremely helpful when leaders of an organization with better results share the issues they've experienced. They can share what they did to improve, and they can say, "I don't know if this will work for you, but here is what worked for us." It is important to always relate, not compare. If others can do it, we can, too, by learning and harvesting best practices from them.

It is important to always relate, not compare. If others can do it, we can, too, by learning and harvesting best practices from them.

In your leadership role, particularly when working with a peer, we have found that instead of saying, "Here's what you need to do," say, "I don't know if this will work for you, but here is what worked for me." Connect with an understanding of where the other person is coming from, show empathy, and share some struggles.

Leaders attract followers and imitators, and that's good. There's only so much innovation to go around. Plus, as Oded Shenkar pointed out in his April 2010 *Harvard Business Review* article "Defend Your Research: Imitation Is More Valuable Than Innovation," "Nearly 98 percent of the value generated by innovations is captured not by the innovators but by the often overlooked, despised copycats."

Why don't we have more imitators? It could be because we recognize the innovators more than we do the imitators. For instance, Bobby gets all this recognition because he was the first to invent or do something. Some people see this recognition and don't want to copy him; instead, they want to come up with their own solution, even if his is clearly working. This attitude, when it manifests inside an organization, leads to inconsistency.

By identifying others who've successfully overcome a problem we're experiencing, and by encouraging people to adopt their solution (and modify it if needed), we remove the basis for rationalizations. Our job as leaders is to do it in a way that doesn't point out that the person is wrong—and that subtly attracts him or her to the right solution.

Barrier 3: Blame

Blame is another common barrier to execution. Of course, it's tempting to blame easy targets like the government, difficult students or families, inadequate compensation and benefits, and so on. We like to point the finger at these "culprits" for the poor results or inconsistencies we are facing. A good way to reduce blame is to find those in your organization who are succeeding and then point out what they are doing well. Stephen Covey teaches us that the solutions to our problems usually lie with the people in our own organizations. Reaching out to those who are achieving their goals is an easy way to reduce the blame.

The Blame Game

We worked with a school district whose leaders said that their compensation and benefits were the reason for their poor employee engagement results. Yet, in reviewing the district's overall engagement results, we saw that the head of transportation had the highest percentile rating of all. Paradoxically, he had some of the lowest-paid employees. How was it that his employees felt more engaged and motivated than others in the same school district who were earning far more? The answer had to be that what people were blaming wasn't the real problem after all.

Another common entity to blame is that all-too-common scapegoat: the school board.

Blame Game Stopper

In one school district, the senior leadership team often insisted that the school board placed too many demands on their time by calling meetings too often, interfering in their everyday business, doing too much of this or too much of that, not caring about the problems of certain departments, and so on and so forth. The board did not know how to determine the value of district activities and did not know if the decisions they made about resourcing initiatives were good ones. Rather than remain silent, they asked for information that seemed threatening to district leaders.

To solve this problem, we engaged the board members and the district leadership in creating key goals and measures to define overall district priorities. From that point on, the board became interested in seeing the progress being made toward goals. They also asked for information on how the dollars invested in district-wide initiatives were paying off. The solution reduced the time district leaders were spending on preparing for board meetings. The board requests for information decreased and became more specific to the district goals. Focusing on goals with an accountable process saved time for both the district leaders and the board members.

Barrier 4: Discomfort

We have never seen a definition of leadership that includes "to be comfortable" or "to create comfort throughout the organization." And there is a good reason for that: it is uncomfortable to execute a plan that has transparent results. Transparency is not fun when your results aren't so great. (When they are great, of course, it's a different story.)

Quint's Story: The Cafeteria Thermometer

When I worked at Holy Cross Hospital in Chicago, the patient satisfaction scores were in the 14th percentile. The Measurement Team (a mix of internal experts who tracked the organization's numbers) wanted to put a big thermometer in the cafeteria, like the one a United Way fundraising campaign uses. They wanted a visible and central location so employees could see the hospital's current results, be reminded of the goal, and track the improvement.

I didn't think it was a good idea. All I could picture were family members and community leaders sitting in the cafeteria staring at that big thermometer and knowing exactly how low satisfaction was. I explained to the Measurement Team that it was better not to do this right now. I just didn't feel comfortable with going public in such a visible way.

This was the point at which I was challenged. An employee said to me, "They already know. Who do you think is filling out these surveys?" I had to admit she was right. So, the thermometer was placed in the cafeteria for all to see, and, yes, it was enormously uncomfortable. But that discomfort created results. The employees saw where they were every day, and they wanted to improve. In one year, the results moved from the bottom of the thermometer to near the top.

Many people are uncomfortable going to the doctor because they might hear something they don't want to hear. Like them, leaders often don't want to hear what they're doing wrong or badly. But if leaders aren't willing to be diagnosed, how do they know what to improve—and when they do improve, how will they know how far they've come?

One tool that has proven very effective in communicating results with the education team of Studer Group is the use of the green, yellow, and red measurement scorecard. At the beginning of each year, the senior team of Studer Group determines the key metrics for the year, and the final company scorecard is set by the company president. From there, each division aligns its metrics to the company's metrics. The education division has its scorecard, which is used as a tool to show progress and to gain input on areas that need improving. Progress on measures is shown by colors, with green meaning on target, yellow meaning making progress, and red meaning trending behind and in trouble. It is important to show the reds so that input can be gathered and support can be provided to move the troubled areas into yellow and then green.

Barrier 5: Lack of Skill

Another barrier to execution is lack of skill. Leaders are responsible for engaging in continued skill development, coaching, and supporting their direct reports to enhance their skills. We stress that the values of an organization are shown by the organization's commitment to developing its leaders. Research shows that the most important person in an employee's work life is his or her leader. The number one reason people leave an organization is their leader. It makes sense to do everything we can to invest in and develop the best leaders, who then apply the same principle to develop those they lead.

> The number one reason people leave an organization is their leader. It makes sense to do everything we can to invest in and develop the best leaders.

Many leaders have a rough time sleeping at night because they bring problems home from work. There's often something they wish they could do better or some change they wish they could make to be more effective.

In education, we administer an engagement survey to employees that measures the extent to which leaders provide an environment that gives employees the opportunity to reach their highest potential. We find that leaders generally have the most difficulty working through this type of feedback from their direct reports. At times, it's downright emotional for some. Our job as leadership coaches is to help leaders celebrate the wins and to carefully review the results to determine areas for improvement. We provide leadership development to train leaders to roll out the results with their staff as a way to gather additional input and identify particular needs that, when met, can enhance the work environment. The rollout process includes more than presenting results—leaders also gain input from their direct reports on ways they can improve their leadership skills.

Leadership training and skill development will build the skills leaders need, but there's also another dimension to consider: consistency in executing those skills. Even if someone becomes highly skilled, if those skills are inconsistently practiced, the organization doesn't get the full advantage of them, and other people can't learn from them. Furthermore, unless they are practiced frequently, skills erode.

Just because people are receiving leadership skill development training does *not* mean they don't need an on-the-job teacher. On the contrary, they need someone (either their leader or a successful, experienced leader designated by their leader) to guide and coach them even more. Why? Because when new leaders come out of training, they need to be held accountable at a high level in order to consistently implement and validate their skills. People have to continue practicing their new skills until they become comfortable with them. It's this comfort level that will generate the consistency needed to create a high-performance organization.

Before moving on from this discussion of barriers to change, here is a relevant example. We wanted to manage up a principal who was modeling new behaviors—that is, we wanted to publicly acknowledge her work. This principal did not push back on results. Rather, she worked hard with her team to gather data and then used the results to improve.

Pepperhill Elementary School, Charleston, South Carolina

Ms. Underwood is the principal of Pepperhill Elementary School in Charleston, South Carolina. At Studer Education, we administer employee engagement and parent satisfaction surveys in the school district. From day one, Ms. Underwood's school had the highest number of responses for both surveys, with almost 100 percent returned from parents. She also leads the district with some of the best results on those surveys.

What makes these such notable accomplishments is that her school is located in North Charleston, an area that struggles with poverty and changing demographics, including higher populations of students who are learning English as a second language. Yet despite these challenges, at no time has Ms. Underwood been out of compliance with the principles we teach—and never have we witnessed or heard of her making excuses. She sees her job as serving teachers, staff, students, and parents—and she does it all cheerfully and well. At a principal training session, we recognized Ms. Underwood's accomplishments to her peers and the senior leadership of the district.

Communicating Change: Start with *Why*

The way leaders communicate change influences how people work through the barriers to change. We have found that some of the best leaders communicate change to others. Accountable leadership relies on executing strategic actions consistently and effectively. To do so, leaders cannot act alone; teams need to be brought along as well. The essence of leadership is creating a work environment in which people are inspired to work together to achieve a common goal. So a primary responsibility of all education leaders is to build and guide teams to achieve defined goals that lead to high levels of student achievement and success.

The first skill that leaders need to have to create highly productive and reliable organizations is effective communication on why change is needed. Teams want to know why a particular goal is important and why particular tactics and process-improvement strategies are needed to help them achieve the goal. The better the *why* is explained, the better the compliance and execution.

As we strive to create high-performing educational systems, we do more than lay out a new process and set of behaviors and expect people to implement them. We, as leaders, present change in a way that makes people *want* to do it. Specifically, when the *why* behind the changes we're asking people to make is well communicated, they are more willing to do so—and that leads to far more success than if they were just following orders.

Even though understood, many communicate following the usual sequence: *what*, *how*, and *why* (Figure 3.5). Think about an occasion when a new process, technique, or practice was introduced. Most likely a training session was held to officially announce the new process, technique, or practice and to explain *what* it was and *how* to do it. After going into the details in depth, the training session might have concluded with *why* this change was so important. Or—and this is not uncommon—maybe the reason for changing was forgotten altogether. While there is nothing wrong with explaining the *what* and the *how* in great detail, if leaders want to achieve buy-in and build excitement right away, the sequence needs to be flipped around (Figure 3.6).

When communicating difficult information or a new process, technique, or practice to an organization, it's important to start by connecting to *why* it's so critical to make the change. This sequence is far more powerful than the one just described.

Yes, explaining *why* can be exhausting and even aggravating at times. If you have ever had a child ask you, "Why? Why? But why?" you'll understand what we mean. However, making the effort is worth it. Quite simply, when the reasons for change are explained, compliance is better. People want to be successful and fulfilled; they want their jobs to take care of their head and heart needs. Sometimes explaining *why* connects the two needs.

> People want to be successful and fulfilled; they want their jobs to take care of their head and heart needs. Sometimes explaining *why* connects the two needs.

Furthermore, when a message is connected to the *why*, we can actually gain time. People are much more eager to learn the behavior and carry it out when they know why it's needed, which means less time can be spent on the *what* and the *how*. And, by following the sequence of *why*, *what*, and then *how*, we reduce people's anxiety when they carry out the change.

WHAT
HOW
WHY

FIGURE 3.5 | USUAL SEQUENCE

WHY
WHAT
HOW

FIGURE 3.6 | SUGGESTED SEQUENCE

Superintendent Dan Evans of Jackson Public Schools in Michigan found that connecting back to *why* was extremely powerful when communicating a difficult message.

Jackson Public Schools, Jackson, Michigan

Along with many other leaders over the past several years, Superintendent Dan Evans had been through several years of major budget cuts. Each year an annual meeting was held with the school board that opened the floor for community members and employees to bring up their concerns about the budget cuts. These meetings had high attendance, and some comments about the board and the district leadership were negative.

Superintendent Evans was preparing for how to message the budget cuts this coming year. At a Leadership Development Institute, we talked about how to start tough messages by explaining what we call the *why*. By starting with why decisions are made, people tend to understand the reason behind them. Superintendent Evans did a great job of crafting a message explaining why certain budget cuts were made. He held several community forums throughout the district prior to the board session. As a result, at the board meeting only three members of the community spoke, and all three expressed appreciation for the message the superintendent had given them. Another plus: the press reported the meeting in a summary of events rather than relaying the usual noisy drama of the annual budget approval board meeting.

This story does not mean that community members or employees liked or necessarily agreed with the board's decisions, but explaining why cuts were needed focused people's input on factual rather than emotional appeals.

This may sound simple, but simple does not mean easy. If we can just adjust our mind-set and start with *why*, we'll find it's much easier to get others to comply with *what* and *how*. When we get compliance, we get the desired outcome. And when we get the desired outcome, we get closer and closer to fulfilling our mission of becoming a high-performing educational system.

Summary

Let's review. First, accountable leadership means that leaders consistently and effectively apply agreed-upon behaviors inside the organization that are aimed at meeting the desired outcomes. Accountable leaders also create a supportive environment to collectively engage teachers and staff to apply behaviors that lead to good results. Next are the strategy and execution triangles. Structure and strategy cannot provide answers to continuous systems improvement without quality execution. And execution is really about consistency and reliability, which are what the rest of this book is about.

To set the stage, we identify the barriers to change that leaders typically encounter: denial, rationalization, blame, discomfort, and lack of skill. Now that we've gotten barriers out of the way, we want to focus mostly on positives as we move forward. Peter Senge, author of the best-selling book *The Fifth Discipline*, says that if we focus on the goal, we'll hit the goal. If we focus on the barrier, we'll hit the barrier. Finally, we discuss the best way for leaders to communicate change to bring people in the school system along with them to achieve goals. We recommend that leaders connect people to the *why*—to the reasons change is being undertaken. Once they understand *why* they're being asked to make a change, most people are ready, and they're more eager to learn the *what* and the *how*.

Let's reiterate the *why* that's driving us: we want to hardwire excellence for consistency and reliability, which creates efficiency and effectiveness, which create a higher-quality learning environment with the most efficient use of resources, all of which is absolutely necessary not only for today's students, staff, and teachers but for all students, staff, and teachers in the future.

CHAPTER FOUR:

MANAGING INDIVIDUAL AND ORGANIZATIONAL CHANGE

One thing is certain in leadership: wherever we are or whatever we are doing, we will always be leading and managing some sort of change. Ralph Waldo Emerson famously wrote, "People wish to be settled; only as far as they are unsettled is there any hope for them." As leaders, a big part of what we do is to "unsettle."

"People wish to be settled; only as far as they are unsettled is there any hope for them."

—Ralph Waldo Emerson

As noted in Chapter 2, our Straight A Leadership Assessment asks, "If your organization continues to act/perform exactly as it does today (with the same processes, same cost structure, same efficiencies, same productivity, same techniques), do you think your results over the next five years will be (1 = much worse to 5 = much better)?" We have found that 37 percent of respondents feel that if they stay the same, their results in the future will be the same, better, or much better, despite the fact that the rapidly changing external environment makes it impossible to stay the same.

Thirty-seven percent of respondents feel that if they stay the same, their results in the future will be the same, better, or much better.

People don't always welcome change with open arms. In fact, it is natural to resist change—even positive change. However, leaders can be prepared to help people become more comfortable and move them through the "unsettled" feeling of change. From our diagnosis and research, we have found that even though members of an organization may think they are ready for change, they might not be.

As we seek to hardwire excellence by improving the levels of consistency, reliability, efficiency, and effectiveness, we see that individuals and organizations go through certain *predictable* phases of change.

Managing Individual Change

The first part of this chapter focuses on understanding the phases of competency and change through which an individual moves. We use this model to illustrate the various stages people will find themselves in at some point in their lives and careers. The four phases of individual change are: (1) unconsciously unskilled, (2) consciously unskilled, (3) consciously skilled, and (4) unconsciously skilled (Figure 4.1).

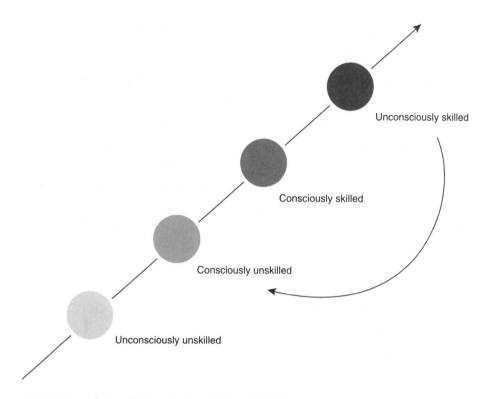

Unconsciously skilled

Consciously skilled

Consciously unskilled

Unconsciously unskilled

FIGURE 4.1 | PHASES OF CHANGE—INDIVIDUAL

Source: Abraham Maslow, 1940, "Four Stages for Learning Any New Skill." Gordon Training International by Noel Burch, 1970

Phase 1: Unconsciously Unskilled. During this initial phase, we are very new to a role, process, or skill. We don't know what we don't know because it is still too new. One could even say we are a bit incompetent. We're not saying we didn't bring competency to the job or that we're going to stay incompetent. It's just that in the current position, we are not nearly as competent as we need or want to be.

Sarah may be highly skilled, but if she is new to a job and is working with all new equipment, people, procedures, and software, she is not going to be at the same competency and skill level she was in her last job. We can usually recognize such people because they look happy. These are teachers prior to and on their first day of school or people in new-employee orientations before they realize what the job is really like. Ask leaders who have been on the job fewer than 60 days how they like their job and they'll say, "I love it!" They love their job because they haven't yet entirely figured out what the job is.

Recently we received a photo of a brand-new baby from an employee. The baby was fewer than 24 days old. It was a perfect child. The parents had so far experienced no terrible twos, no potty training, no homework struggles, no adolescent issues—only wonderful times together. New parenthood certainly is an exciting time, but it's also a time when we don't yet realize all the twists and turns of child rearing. We just have that rosy new-parent outlook. This is called unconsciously unskilled or inexperienced—we just don't know what we don't know.

When we're unconsciously unskilled, we just don't know what we don't know.

Phase 2: Consciously Unskilled. During the second phase, we are aware of what we don't know. We've identified a gap between our current skill set and where we need to be to become successful. This phase accounts for the large dropout rate in college early on. It's also why 27 percent of employees who quit leave within the first 90 days.

We become consciously unskilled when we start hitting bumps. Maybe that new supervisor realizes he has an employee who is rather difficult. Or he finds himself in a situation that he doesn't know how to solve. Or he is over budget and doesn't know what to do. He is learning policies and procedures he thought he understood but now realizes he doesn't—at least not to the extent needed.

At this point, a good values-based organization will have been proactive and put a mentor in place, some type of skill-building orientation program will be implemented, and an experienced supervisor will help the new supervisor navigate this phase.

This is why 30- and 90-day meetings are part of the selection process and are vital to success. The idea is to schedule a formal time to sit down one-on-one with an employee and do a temperature check. Asking key questions at these times can help identify what's needed to alleviate anxiety and to help an employee embrace change and work through the difficulties.

Phase 3: Consciously Skilled. In this phase, the skill set is there, but reminders or checklists are still needed to fully execute responsibilities. We are likely still unsettled, but we understand the need for change and have embraced it or at least have accepted it.

So the goal is for organizations to get people to the point where they know the needed skill and have the opportunity to take advantage of development and mentoring. This allows them to know "what right looks like" and to perform the skill frequently enough to become consciously competent in it.

An executive recently shared how bad he felt for letting a leader go. This woman had become a leader because the person before her had not done a good job. The executive realized this employee had never seen "what right looked like." Without a system in place for helping her become consciously skilled, she didn't have a chance. (Also, if a better system for selecting leaders had been in place, she would not have become one to begin with, which would have saved everyone a lot of time and energy.)

When a leader is going through this phase of change, the skill must be practiced and studied. It's important to provide opportunities for practice. Yes, it might take a little longer and it is not easy, but it gives the person confidence that the skill can be mastered.

Sometimes it helps to go outside the organization for help. It can be very powerful to connect leaders with leaders from other organizations who have achieved high performance.

Phase 4: Unconsciously Skilled. In this fourth phase, a task can be completed without reminders. It has become second nature, and we can't imagine doing it any other way. By executing the skill over and over, we become *unconsciously skilled*, or unconsciously competent. At this point, we can do more than one thing at a time, without even thinking about it.

Quint's Story: Bow Ties and Change

A while back, I went to a formal event. I put on my tuxedo and my clip-on bow tie. A friend, Jack Williams, gave me a hard time for wearing a clip-on at my age and later gave me a real bow tie. I really liked the tie and was happy to have it, but because I had no occasion to wear it, I put it away and forgot about it (Phase 1).

A year passed. I realized I was going to another tuxedo event and my friend was going to be there. I knew I needed to wear the bow tie, which meant that I had to learn how to tie a bow tie myself. Even though I had read about tying a bow tie and had pictures of the steps, I couldn't do it. I immediately realized I didn't have the skill. I was consciously incompetent (Phase 2).

So I went home and studied a YouTube video clip on how to tie a bow tie. I needed to see "what right looked like." I followed the video and after many tries was finally able to tie it on my own. Now, every time I wear a bow tie, I have to pull up that same video clip, watch it, and practice. I just don't wear a bow tie often enough to master the technique. So I understand I am unskilled, but I also understand how I can be skilled and follow a certain procedure to do it (Phase 3).

Now let's imagine that I wore a bow tie every day. After putting it on numerous times, I would be able to tie it without the video clip because I would have experienced the frequency to do it skillfully. In fact, I would get so comfortable with the process that not only could I tie my own bow tie, but I could probably also tie one for someone else. I might even be able to tie a bow tie while having a conversation or without a mirror as I walked to get my car keys. Eventually I would be able to perform the task without thinking about it at all (Phase 4).

In order to manage change, we have to understand the phases and know which phase we and others are experiencing. Each phase requires different conversations and actions.

In order to manage change, we have to understand the phases and know which phase we and others are experiencing. Each phase requires different conversations and actions.

Now let's look at the phases of organizational change.

Managing Organizational Change

There are also four phases of organizational change that occur as leaders apply the Evidence-Based Leadership[SM] framework in their organizations: (1) the honeymoon, (2) reality setting in, (3) the uncomfortable gap, and (4) consistency. We also look at how leaders can be sensitive to the changes the organization goes through.

Education professionals live in an environment of continuous change. We've experienced K–12 educational reform initiatives over the last three decades that seemed to be what Kotter would describe as episodic in nature. Today, change occurs constantly, and the types of changes occurring leverage higher levels of accountability. In the past, some states promoted higher-stakes accountability systems more than other states. State accountability for certain types of changes is gradually becoming the norm. These changes include: (1) school report cards, which make student achievement results transparent to the public, (2) leader and teacher evaluation systems that include student achievement results, (3) common standards and assessments for the purpose of comparing states, (4) single sign-on systems that consolidate operational and academic areas into one system, (5) performance pay for leaders and teachers, and (6) more pressure to improve student achievement in math and science on international tests so that the United States can compete globally.

As of this writing, about 25 percent of states have begun funding public colleges based at least partially on student outcomes such as degree production and completion rates. Soon the number is expected to grow to about 50 percent of states. The significance of this trend is that college ratings, tuition distribution, and federal financial aid could depend on how well public colleges perform on defined student performance indicators. Poor performance could hit colleges in the wallet.

The pressure is on to ensure that students gain the best opportunity to become successful and productive members of society. The challenge for K–12 systems is to create seamless systems of excellence that prepare students for the workforce in a highly competitive global economy. When something seems challenging, the best leaders do everything in their power to meet the challenge. This is what Evidence-Based Leadership in a culture of high performance is all about. Our constant goal as education professionals is to achieve a level of high performance and sustain it over time.

Of course, because we understand human nature, we know we might have some times of setback. As we explore the four phases of organizational change, it becomes clear that we can predict when these setbacks will occur.

Because we understand human nature, we know we might have some times of setback. As we explore the four phases of organizational change, it becomes clear that we can predict when these setbacks will occur.

Phase 1: The Honeymoon

When introducing any change, organizations go through what's called the honeymoon phase (Figure 4.2). Not surprisingly, this happens at the beginning. A sense of excitement, anticipation, and energy pervades the organization.

When introducing any change, organizations go through what's called the honeymoon phase. Not surprisingly, this happens at the beginning. A sense of excitement, anticipation, and energy pervades the organization.

FIGURE 4.2 | PHASE ONE—THE HONEYMOON

· Sense of excitement.	· Quick fixes are implemented.
· People feel they're working on the right to-do list.	· Skeptics and cynics emerge.
· "Things will get better" (hope).	

During the honeymoon phase, people feel as though they are working on the right to-do list. Maintaining high-quality learning environments is the mission of the educational organization in the first place, and most employees in a school district are committed to helping students succeed. Our work with school districts has shown that employees benefit when leaders commit to creating best-place-to-work environments for employees. That's why it is now common for the to-do list to include items focused on employee engagement, student engagement, parent satisfaction, and quality instruction. These focuses allow an organization to execute tactics that influence student learning outcomes.

In Phase 1, leaders and staff members have high hopes that things will get better. This doesn't mean there won't be setbacks. Today's organizations are dealing with budget reductions during a time when the stakes are higher than ever to produce key outcomes, yet people still like that these changes are happening because they feel they know what they have to do.

The honeymoon phase is generally the most evident after an organization's first leadership development session. As leaders leave this session, the room is typically buzzing with excitement because participants have connected with the superintendent and other leaders, they have had fun, and they are energized by their learning. Above all, they have hope that things are going to get better.

Phase 1 also brings some quick fixes. By addressing some problems quickly and early on, we show our workforce that the change they're undergoing will work. This, of course, adds to the excitement.

The next story shows how quick fixes can let people know that we trust them.

Quint's Story: It's a Matter of Trust

When I was president of Baptist Hospital, I was trying to get into my office late one night but didn't have my key. I ran into the housekeeper who cleans my office and asked her to let me in. She said she didn't have a key to the administrative suites and would call her boss to let us in.

When I asked her to explain, she said that every time she came to clean the administrative suites, she had to call her boss to let her in. What's more, when she left, she had to call again to get everything locked up for the night. I asked, "So you have to wait until they let you in or out to do your job?" She said yes. I asked, "Wouldn't it be easier if you could let yourself in?" She agreed it would.

The next day, I made sure we had keys made so the housekeepers could get into the administrative suites. We need to be careful not to make rules because of what might happen—and perhaps because we haven't dealt with performance issues—and instead make it easier for people to work. (Plus, if we can't trust people with keys, we have bigger problems.)

Quick fixes aren't meant to change the world, but they let people know they are being listened to and that leaders want things to get better.

Even in the excitement of the first phase, skeptics and cynics emerge. They may say things like, "The time is not right for this." However, the skeptics and cynics are a little quieter because of the excitement around them. They think, "If everybody is all excited, how can I go against them?"

By the way, the honeymoon phase, like the other phases, can last a few months or it can last longer. Typically a phase lasts anywhere from six to nine months and perhaps up to a year. However, things will gradually get a little more difficult as they go on, which leads us to Phase 2.

Phase 2: Reality Setting In

In Phase 2, the excitement has worn off a bit, and the reality of the change begins to sink in. Everyone realizes that this change is not going to be all fun and games—in fact, it's going to take quite a bit of work. People start realizing it is a little harder than they had anticipated (Figure 4.3).

FIGURE 4.3 PHASE TWO—REALITY SETTING IN	
· We/they phenomenon occurs.	· "This will have an impact on me."
· Inconsistencies become evident.	· Some people are getting it, and others are not.
· Transparency creates discomfort.	
· "This change is bigger than I thought."	

Phase 2 is when the **we/they** phenomenon can begin. We/they behavior is actually pretty easy to spot. It occurs when employees love their supervisor but don't care for their supervisor's boss. We/they is also happening when people look for someone to blame for the change that is occurring.

Phase 2 is when the we/they phenomenon can begin. We/they behavior is actually pretty easy to spot. It occurs when employees love their supervisor but don't care for their supervisor's boss.

For example, a supervisor who works really hard and achieves great success should be complimented, right? Believe it or not, some leaders may actually get a little jealous and start fixating on the notion that the successful manager has an easier job or has it better than we do. This is where the we/they mentality can start, and it's important to be on guard against it during this phase.

Inconsistency can become noticeable during this phase. After all, creating consistency, reliability, efficiency, and effectiveness is a hard thing to accomplish, and not everyone is likely to get it right all the time.

We were at a school board meeting this past year, and on the agenda was a discussion of the results of the employee engagement survey. This included the overall district results as well as results for every school and department. The board members realized which leaders showed improving results and which showed declines. The reality had set in: addressing leader skill sets and attitudes had become essential in order for the school district to improve. The school board meeting revealed the discomfort with transparency that becomes evident during this phase. In education, people tend to move in a herd. They are team oriented and like being part of one group. During the reality phase in a transparent organization, however, it becomes clear that some people perform better than others.

Interestingly, it's common for people who are performing better than others to actually back off or disown their progress. They may think, "Well, I have it easier," "My staff is more experienced," or "My location is better." They may downplay their own performance because they don't want others to feel that they think they're "better than them."

The book *Straight A Leadership* has a chapter on the challenges of implementing best practices. One challenge is that people who are achieving best practices often minimize what they're doing because they don't want the other people to feel bad—and they don't want to move out of the "club of acceptance." It's kind of like the smart kid in class playing dumb because she wants to fit in with her less academically inclined friends.

Over the years, we've even had to pull people aside and explain to them that their job is to raise the overall level of performance, not lower their performance to be on par with everybody else. Part of leadership is accepting that at times you're not the most popular person in the organization. The good news is that you could end up becoming the most valuable and respected person in the organization.

Consistency Is a Solution

An organization that was committed to reducing turnover and implementing a standardized way to hire became highly transparent with its data and began to measure and report turnover by department. It quickly became obvious that some departments and leaders were reducing turnover and implementing the new hiring best practices better than others. In fact, there was far more inconsistency than they had realized. The good news is that, rather than letting the inconsistency be a barrier, the organization identified opportunities for improvement, coached effective ways of change, and further standardized the best practices to help achieve the turnover goal.

During the reality phase, an organization may become aware that the change is bigger than originally thought, and people may begin to struggle. Some people might feel overwhelmed and think they don't have time to do their other tasks. At this point, leaders need to help them integrate and implement what is new into their normal job. The end of this chapter explains further.

Doing the Old Stuff Better

While we were working with one organization, one senior leader felt the "Studer Group stuff" was taking up too much time and he couldn't get to his "real work." So the CEO met the leader for dinner and listened to him talk about the problem.

The CEO broke it down this way: "Let's look at what we're asking you to do. We're asking you to meet with the employees. Haven't you been meeting with the employees?" The leader immediately said he had.

Next the CEO said, "We're asking you to develop leaders. Haven't you always developed leaders?"

Again the leader immediately answered yes.

The CEO then said, "We're asking you to make sure people understand their goals. Haven't you in the past talked about goals and people knowing their goals?"

The leader said yes.

They chatted some more, and by the time they were done, the leader got it. This was not "new stuff" at all; rather, it was doing the "old stuff" better, more efficiently, and more effectively. The change may be bigger than the leaders originally thought, but it's also a lot more rewarding than they thought.

In the reality phase, people realize, "These changes will affect me personally." Early on, they may think of our partnership as a "come in and go quickly" event, until we keep coming back and working alongside the leadership. We hear educators from most of our partners say to us, "You are like the Energizer bunny—you keep coming back and coming back." We do not call Evidence-Based Leadership (EBL) a program; we call it running a great organization. EBL partners are on a journey of creating excellent systems. Our point with the reality phase is that it soon becomes obvious that everyone is involved in setting measurable goals and that the standards and practices apply to everyone. If a best practice is being implemented, everyone does it. It's not a program—it's a way of life and work that will have an impact on everyone.

Finally, during Phase 2 it becomes apparent that some leaders are getting it and others are not. If people aren't getting it, their supervisors must zero in and start thinking in terms of high, middle, and low performance. If everyone isn't performing consistently, there will be a gap in the leadership team. This is where Phase 3 comes in.

Phase 3: The Uncomfortable Gap

Here's where things start to get really uncomfortable. Phase 3 cannot be avoided—and it's not "bad," because it really does spark tremendous change—but it can be made shorter and less painful.

Keeping the Throttle Down

To put into perspective what Phase 3 can be like, let's consider the 1983 film *The Right Stuff*. Set in 1947, this movie tells the story of a group of determined men gathered together in a remote California desert with the goal of breaking what is now known as the sound barrier. One of these men was a wartime pilot named Chuck Yeager. What made Chuck different from the others who had tried to achieve the same task is simply that at the moment of truth, he did not back off. As others approached the sound barrier, they would get uncomfortable when the plane began to shake and would pull back the throttle. Chuck Yeager did not. He kept the throttle down.

The film shows that Yeager ignites the rocket engine and zooms up into the sky, gaining more and more speed to close in on the barrier. The plane begins to vibrate and shake violently. All of a sudden we hear a loud boom, and the plane flies almost effortlessly past the sound barrier.

This same phenomenon happens inside organizations. In Phase 3, the performance gap has become so big that the organization "shakes." Some people are successful with the change, and others are not. The transparency of results makes this feel uncomfortable. The initial reaction is to slow down and back off because leaders tend to be uncomfortable with discomfort. Actually, this is the time to keep the throttle down.

> **The initial reaction is to slow down and back off because leaders tend to be uncomfortable with discomfort. Actually, this is the time to keep the throttle down.**

We have also seen organizations go back and forth as they approach Phase 4, throttling down and pulling back over and over. This will exhaust an organization. This "teeter-tottering" about making tough decisions actually gets an organization off balance, and employees' performance starts eroding.

When the going gets rough, remember Chuck Yeager. When we keep the throttle down and move through Phase 3, we will end up in Phase 4, which is where we want to be.

Let's take a deeper look at the good things and the challenging things that happen in the uncomfortable gap (Figure 4.4).

FIGURE 4.4	PHASE THREE—THE UNCOMFORTABLE GAP
· Performance gap is evident.	· Process improvement increases.
· Tougher decisions must be made.	· Inconsistencies are even more obvious than before.

No longer is it surprising that a performance gap exists between some departments and others, and between some people and others. Some are hitting the goals or at least coming close, and others are not. Now the need to use the tools for high, middle/solid, and low/subpar performance truly becomes apparent.

It's obvious that tougher decisions must be made. In Phase 2 we might have had to deal with people who had bad attitudes, but in Phase 3 we have to deal with people who have great attitudes but just don't have the skill. This is much harder.

On more than one occasion, we have been in educational organizations in which transparency of defined measures sheds a different light on historically popular leaders. Because of personalities, some underperforming leaders have been showcased as high performing. Here's the reverse of that scenario.

The Performance Gap Is Evident

High School Principal 1 was well known by his vibrant personality and was voted best leader of the year. However, as the measurable results started appearing on his scorecard, the superintendent saw something new. He saw low student achievement and marginal employee engagement and parent satisfaction results.

High School Principal 2, who was not as well known, quietly went about his job every day. As the measurable results started appearing on his scorecard, the superintendent again saw something new. This principal's student achievement, employee engagement, and parent satisfaction results were some of the highest in the district.

With this realization, the superintendent now had to recognize the work of the high-performing principal and put a performance plan in place for the lower-performing principal.

That's what we mean by the uncomfortable gap.

Sometimes these "skill" conversations turn out well for everyone involved, but not always. As leaders, we have to be prepared for some tough moments. We must do the right thing even when it's uncomfortable.

Quint's Story: It Isn't Always Comfortable

I currently own a minor league baseball team called the Pensacola Blue Wahoos, which is affiliated with the Cincinnati Reds. At the double-A level, most of the players have great attitudes. In fact, my wife and I have to be careful not to get too emotionally attached to the players because we take it personally when players have to be cut.

These players have spent their entire lives, since they were little boys, playing baseball. They were probably the stars of their Little League teams and the MVPs of their high school teams. They might have been drafted out of high school or college. They've now moved through the minor league organization from rookie ball to short-season rookie baseball to low-A, to advanced-A, and now they've hit double-A. In other words, they haven't experienced much failure.

Double-A is the defining level in minor league baseball—it determines whether a player is going to move up or move out. At this point, many players experience failure for the first time. Minor league baseball organizations know this. They feel it's healthy for players to work through failure, so they create situations in which the players are allowed to experience it.

For instance, a pitcher might be out on the mound and not be having a good inning when he looks over at the bullpen (where relief pitchers warm up during the game) and doesn't see anyone there. In the major leagues, a relief pitcher would already be warming up. But minor league coaches want that person to know he's got to get out of the situation himself. They want to see what he's got.

During this time, it also becomes clear how coachable a player is. Chances are he hasn't needed much coaching so far because up until now he's been a natural. Yet even with the best coaching and the greatest passion, sometimes players just don't have the ability to take their skills to the next level. They have to be released—and that is an extremely tough decision.

Obviously it's hard for the player, but it's also hard for the people who run baseball, especially the heads of minor league operations, because they drafted the players. They scouted them. They usually have a close relationship with the players and their families, so letting them go can be quite painful.

These decisions are as difficult in education as they are in baseball. When the inconsistency becomes glaring, however, the uncomfortable performance gap in the organization must be dealt with.

Finally, a positive: because there is a higher skill level in Phase 3, there's better training and performance, and because leaders have already lived through a year of the new evaluation system, process improvement is exploding.

In fact, Studer Group received a letter from a COO talking about how he sees process improvement everywhere because: (1) people are motivated, know they do worthwhile work, have a sense of purpose, and know they make a difference; (2) people are being held accountable; (3) leaders who have the skill now lead process improvement; and (4) due to reward and recognition, employees feel a sense of ownership and are committed to helping the organization fulfill its mission of providing higher-quality care at a lower cost. Because of the process improvement, inconsistencies become obvious.

Phase 4: Consistency

Organizations have completed their high, middle/solid, and low/subpar assessments, and change is well under way. Things are really rolling along. And then one day (at least sometimes it feels as though it happens in one day)—boom! You break through the barrier. And when you come out the other side, you are in Phase 4 (Figure 4.5).

FIGURE 4.5 | PHASE FOUR—CONSISTENCY

· High-performing results.	· Disciplined people and disciplined processes.
· Everyone understands the keys to success.	· Proactive leadership.

Jim Collins, author of *Good to Great*, would call Phase 4 the break-through. While the organization has steadily been improving the whole time, now the flywheel is really spinning. The organization is getting high-performance results. It has disciplined people and disciplined processes, and instead of a reactive senior leadership team, it now has proactive leadership. Everyone understands the key to success.

While the organization has steadily been improving the whole time, now the flywheel is really spinning. The organization is getting high-performance results. It has disciplined people and disciplined processes, and instead of a reactive senior leadership team, it now has proactive leadership. Everyone understands the key to success.

People have created a culture of high performance by hardwiring excellence for consistency, reliability, efficiency, effectiveness, high quality, and low cost, but what's even greater is that they feel really good about what they do. In fact, they probably feel better about working in an educational system than they have for a long, long time. And isn't that what this is all about?

It's sort of like watching children go through all the phases as they are growing up. Eventually a point is reached when even though some of the phases weren't that pleasant, we are awfully glad they were experienced. We feel really good about where our children are and where we are. That's what this phase is like. Getting here was tough, but it is really worth the effort.

Sustaining results at this stage is no cakewalk. Relentless leadership, always thinking the organization can improve, and maintaining the passion for the work we do each day are necessary to create the year-to-year consistency that promises continued success.

At this stage, our Studer Education coaches work alongside leaders to support the ongoing movement of the flywheel. In the prior stages, we coach leaders to align goals, select aligned behaviors, manage performance, and shift inefficient processes to productive ones. Now the attention shifts to validating the consistency and quality of execution.

We find that the Level 5 leaders Jim Collins refers to are relentless in their pursuit of success, and they value qualified people from outside the organization to coach leaders through these four phases and beyond. We've been lucky in our professional lives to work alongside many Level 5 leaders, and the field of education is better for their commitment.

Summary

Individuals and organizations go through certain predictable phases of change. Figure 4.6 shows the four phases of competency and change an individual moves through.

FIGURE 4.6 | FOUR PHASES OF INDIVIDUAL CHANGE

PHASE ONE: UNCONSCIOUSLY UNSKILLED	During this phase, we are new to a role, process, or skill. We don't know what we don't know because it is still too new. Ask leaders who have been at a job for fewer than 60 days how they like their job and they'll say, "I love it!" They love the job because they really haven't figured out what the job is.
PHASE TWO: CONSCIOUSLY UNSKILLED	During the second phase, we consciously know what we don't know. We've identified a gap between our current skill set and where we need to be to become successful. At this point a good values-based organization will intervene with assigned mentors, skill building, or other training identified by the supervisor to move through this phase. Also, 30- and 90-day meetings can help identify a person's needs.
PHASE THREE: CONSCIOUSLY SKILLED	In this phase, the skill set is there, but reminders or checklists are still needed to execute the plan fully. We are likely still unsettled, but we understand the need for change and have accepted it. The goal is for organizations to get people to the point at which they know the needed skill and have the opportunity to take advantage of development, mentoring, and using the skill frequently enough to become consciously competent in it.
PHASE FOUR: UNCONSCIOUSLY SKILLED	In this phase, a task can be completed without reminders. It has become second nature, and we can't imagine doing it any other way. By executing the skill over and over, we become unconsciously skilled or competent. At this point, we can do more than one thing at a time without even thinking about it.

Figure 4.7 shows the four phases of organizational change.

FIGURE 4.7	FOUR PHASES OF ORGANIZATIONAL CHANGE		
PHASE ONE: THE HONEYMOON	PHASE TWO: REALITY SETTING IN	PHASE THREE: THE UNCOMFORTABLE GAP	PHASE FOUR: CONSISTENCY
· Sense of excitement. · People feeling they're working on right "to-do" list. · "Things will get better" (hope). · Quick fixes are implemented. · Skeptics and cynics emerge.	· We/they phenomenon occurs. · Inconsistencies become evident. · Transparency creates discomfort. · "This change is bigger than I thought." · "This will have an impact on me." · Some people are getting it, and others are not.	· Performance gap is evident. · Tougher decisions must be made. · Process improvement increases. · Inconsistencies are even more obvious than before.	· High-performing results. · Everyone understands the keys to success. · Disciplined people and disciplined processes. · Proactive leadership.

The good news is that we don't need to start from scratch to help people move through these phases of individual and organizational change. Leaders can help position change to achieve maximum buy-in and compliance as we strive to become better, more reliable, more consistent, more cost-effective organizations.

SECTION TWO:

FOUNDATIONS

In Section 1, we focused on the evidence we've used to create Evidence-Based Leadership℠—the *why* of the framework. Section 3 shows *how* to apply the three parts of the framework. What comes between them—Section 2—outlines the concepts we rely on to help leaders achieve results in changing times. It lays out the *what*, or the details of the framework. These three chapters focus on the foundations of high-performing leadership: the Organizational Flywheel, the Nine Principles®, and the Execution Flywheel℠.

The Organizational Flywheel, presented in Chapter 5, is the same as the Healthcare Flywheel®, but positioned to align to K–12 settings. It includes passion, principles, and results. It demonstrates that school districts must have people with the right will (passion) and skill (principles) to achieve results.

The Nine Principles originate with the book *Hardwiring Excellence*, and they continue to be the cornerstone for defining high-performing leadership behaviors. They are part of the flywheel and are so important that we have devoted Chapter 6 to them. Studer Group applies the Nine Principles to achieve its own success. In this chapter, we show how the Nine Principles position school districts to do the same.

Over the years, we've found that the flywheel breaks down and loses momentum if leaders fail to fully execute a tactic, strategy, or process. For this reason, we created a process, defined by the Execution Flywheel

(Chapter 7), to hardwire compliance and ensure that the organization's plan is carried out with high fidelity. The Execution Flywheel surrounds the Organizational Flywheel. It shows how to apply the conceptual foundation to maximize leadership performance. The Execution Flywheel is applied to all actions and behaviors to achieve consistency and reliability of results.

CHAPTER FIVE:

THE ORGANIZATIONAL FLYWHEEL: BUILDING MOMENTUM

T his chapter and the next one present a number of Evidence-Based Leadership℠ teachings that lay the foundation for leaders who are creating high-performing educational systems. In school districts, we consider school board members integral partners in the leadership process. In this chapter, we transfer the components of the Healthcare Flywheel® to education. Influenced by Jim Collins's flywheel in his book *Good to Great*, we developed the Healthcare Flywheel, which is easily translated to education. Throughout the book, we will refer to this as the Organizational Flywheel.

A flywheel is a heavy wheel that regulates the speed of machinery. It takes awhile to get started, but once it starts, it turns smoothly and efficiently. Momentum takes over, and the wheel turns almost effortlessly. It's the same with the symbolic flywheels that power our organizations: once the flywheel is moving, it spins easily, and the momentum we build keeps working for us.

The flywheel illustrates the power that purpose, passion, and results have to create momentum in an organization. Studer Education applies the flywheel to help leaders embark on a results-driven journey. While doing so, they create an engaged workplace for employees, students, and communities.

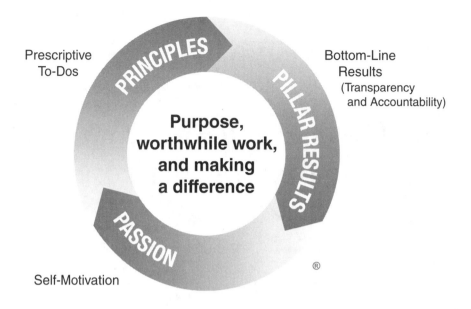

FIGURE 5.1 | ORGANIZATIONAL FLYWHEEL
(HEALTHCARE FLYWHEEL®)

The Hub: Purpose, Worthwhile Work, and Making a Difference

Let's take a look at the very center of the flywheel shown in Figure 5.1. The central values at the core are to do work that has purpose, is worthwhile, and makes a difference. Professionals in service-oriented fields are driven by their core values, which keep them on target.

> Professionals in service-oriented fields are driven by their core values, which keep them on target.

But sometimes we bog down in daily tasks and forget why we chose our profession. As educators, we are lucky because our purpose sits in front of us every day. However, we live and work in an environment that's focused on diagnosing learning gaps so we can teach to close the gaps, which means we're more likely to focus on what's wrong than what's right. We forget how passionate we felt when we started in this field and how much of a difference we really do make.

Many of us have experiences that can jog our memories about why we got into education in the first place. As leaders, we need to take the time to remind employees, faculty, and key stakeholders that what they do has purpose, is worthwhile, and makes a difference. At Studer Education team meetings, in order to keep focused on why we do what we do, we start each meeting with a story that helps us remember our purpose.

Stopping We/They

Sometimes leaders act in ways that slow down the flywheel. For example, when a leader says, "Well, I wish we could all have raises, but Administration says no," that's we/they behavior. It's very common, and it's very damaging. We engage in we/they behavior when we throw somebody else under the bus for our own benefit. All of us have done it at one time or another. For example, when we were leaders, we'd sometimes communicate a mandate to our leadership teams by saying something like, "Building 10 [administration building] said we had to do it." This made our teams like us but dislike the senior leaders of the organization. Today, we do not allow ourselves to use we/they because it destroys any opportunity for creating a healthy systems culture.

We engage in we/they behavior when we throw somebody else under the bus for our own benefit.

For organizations to be high performing, employees need to have confidence that senior leaders have the skills to lead. When any leader criticizes a senior leader, he or she gains favor with the employees at the expense of the senior leader. Employees begin to lose trust in the direction the organization is going. The next time the senior leader needs employees to be responsive, they may resist, which jeopardizes the organization's ability to achieve its goals. In a school district, this may mean a decline in student achievement, which means the biggest loss occurs for students—the very people we are most passionate about.

Two actions help reduce we/they: transparency and effective communication. Transparency is another way of describing what Jim Collins calls "facing the brutal facts." It means leaders start with an honest approach to viewing data and then engage others to identify barriers and determine solutions. Leaders then present a common message about why the results are important and how the facts drove new solutions. Education leaders have plenty of data to work with, but it's what we do with the data that makes a difference. Sometimes leaders massage unfavorable data in a favorable way, or they fail to use data to make informed decisions. Both practices reduce transparency and eat away at the trust that employees and stakeholders have in their leaders.

Effective communication is communication that's accurate and consistent. It also starts with explaining the *why*. Here's what we mean. When a change is introduced, employees instinctively resist. Simply telling them what the change is and how the change is going to occur does little to motivate them to modify their behavior or to understand the decision behind a difficult situation. "Answering Tough Questions" is a story about preparing leaders to handle tough questions and not send mixed messages.

Quint's Story: Answering Tough Questions

I worked with a small community hospital in Indiana that was close to a large metropolitan city. Admissions were down, staffing needs were down, and a reduction in force had already been made. The hospital's leaders realized that too many potential patients were self-diagnosing and driving an hour to seek care rather than starting their care at their local hospital and being referred to the larger hospital system if needed. They assumed that the larger urban hospital would have more services.

A few weeks after the reduction in force, I happened to be speaking at a leadership session for the community hospital. A leader in the audience asked, "What are we going to do to attract more patients?" This question allowed the CEO to introduce the new marketing campaign set to launch. Its purpose was to explain the hospital's services and to urge the community to come to the local hospital first. Essentially, the hospital was promising that if people came there, it would get them to the right place for the care they needed.

The CEO described the marketing campaign, which would include aggressive use of radio, direct mail, and billboards. The marketing executive explained the campaign a bit further, and then the CEO asked everyone to give the marketing department a nice round of applause for all their work.

I was next on the agenda. I asked the room how many of them had had to let someone go or had a position they could not afford to fill. Many hands went up. Then I asked, "When these billboards, banners, direct mail, and radio advertisements start appearing, what are some of the questions your employees might ask?"

People suggested, "I had to let some good people go, so why are we starting an expensive new marketing campaign?" and "If we're so tight on money, how are we paying for these advertisements?"

I then said, "Now, how would you answer those questions?" We then addressed how to answer in a way that created consistent communication throughout the organization. The marketing campaign was certainly needed, but we had to make sure that when we answered the tough questions, we weren't sending mixed messages.

If leaders aren't provided the information and skills they need to answer tough questions from staff members, it's easy to end up with we/they answers that are incomplete and inconsistent. This situation weakens the organization. Even if a question involves sensitive issues such as spending money or cutting resources, we need a good and honest answer. We just need to equip our leaders to share it properly. This will keep the flywheel turning.

Turning the Flywheel

Edward Goldberg, former head of St. Alexius Medical Center in Hoffman Estates, Illinois, was a CEO who truly "got" the power of the flywheel. Ed took his leaders outside one day and asked them to get in a circle and turn like a flywheel.

The first time he said, "Go!" the group was in complete disarray; they didn't know which way to turn. After they had spent some time trying to figure it out, Ed said, "To make a flywheel work, you have to have a leader." So one person was chosen to be leader and got in the middle.

Now the group had strategic direction. The leader asked everyone to start at this time, move in this direction, take this many steps with this length of stride, and so forth. Even with the directions, it took a little time to get the flywheel going. People had to make sure they didn't go too fast or too slow. But soon enough, they got the flywheel going smoothly.

Next, Ed asked one person to stop in her tracks and see what happened. The flywheel immediately stopped moving, and there was confusion again. The lesson was clear: all it takes to stop the flywheel and bring progress to a halt is for one leader to be out of alignment with the organization.

All it takes to stop the flywheel and bring progress to a halt is for one leader to be out of alignment with the organization.

When just one leader practices we/they, it can disrupt the culture of high performance we're trying to achieve. For too many years in our past leadership positions in healthcare and education, we fell into the habit of being we/they leaders. It wasn't malicious. For the most part, our employees really liked us and I'm sure even felt sorry for us since we had to deal with those people in Administration. And why wouldn't they? The way we positioned it, anything that was positive was our doing, and anything negative was their fault.

We don't think anyone means for this to happen. We have either learned to use we/they behavior by watching others, or we haven't been taught not to do it, or the organization has been too accepting of it.

We have heard some superintendents and executives say, "Well, I'm okay being the heavy." But it really isn't okay. It creates dislike in the organization for those who take the blame. All leaders need to take ownership and stop creating a culture in which we/they is acceptable.

We have heard some superintendents and executives say, "Well, I'm okay being the heavy." But it really isn't okay. It creates dislike in the organization for those who take the blame.

We/They in Action

Here's an example of we/they behavior in action. A teacher (we'll call her Jessica) wants to leave early to attend her daughter's play. She has written down the wrong date for this family obligation. She thought it was to be held on Saturday, but actually it's Friday. So Jessica finds herself needing to leave work two hours earlier than usual.

The school where Jessica works is tightly staffed. There's really no one there to take her place, so her leaving early would impose on the rest of the staff and, in fact, could be detrimental to her students. The principal would have to divide her students and send them to other teachers' classrooms. Still, Jessica really wants to go to this family event, so she approaches the principal, Ellen, and explains the situation.

Ellen could say to Jessica, "You go right ahead. I'll take care of your work here for the next two hours." Jessica would be very grateful. As a leader, this is a great deposit in Ellen's emotional bank account.

But what if the answer were, "Sorry, Jessica, but you can't leave early"? Chances are Ellen would not be so eager to take ownership of the decision. If Ellen is not comfortable denying Jessica's request, she is likely to say, "Let me ask my director." Then she'll go to her director and say, "Jessica wants to leave early on Friday." It's possible that the director might figure out a way to make it happen, but it's more likely that she'll say, "I wish we could do something, but we can't set a precedent, so the answer is no."

When Ellen comes back with a no, she says, "I want you to know I really fought for you, but the answer is no." Now Jessica still feels good about Ellen, but she's none too happy with Administration, and division is created between employees and leadership.

This is the kind of thing we used to do all the time. Was it good leadership on our part? No, it was terrible leadership, but it's what we learned from others, and it's what we practiced until we found a better way.

We always coach leaders that if they're in a supervisory role, they're part of Administration. It's not just the people part of the senior leadership team—it's anybody who leads anybody. But leaders who have not been trained may not realize this. So what are leaders to do when they don't know an answer? They say, "Let me research it. Let me look into it. Let me study it, and I'll get back to you." Name a time when you will follow up. If you come back with a no, explain the *why* behind it so that you aren't pointing the finger at someone else.

We've worked with organizations that were tremendously dependent on blaming others. The behavior was so prevalent that the organization was semi-paralyzed. We had each leader fill out a piece of paper that read, "I, _____ [fill in name], resign my leadership position if I cannot quit we/they."

Eliminating we/they is one of the hardest parts of embracing the flywheel. When we do trainings, after the first day we ask people what they intend to take away. Eliminating we/they always shows up at or near the top of the list.

Passion and Self-Motivation

The next part of the flywheel is passion. In Jim Collins's book *Good to Great*, he describes a Level 5 leader as someone who leads with passion. Level 5 leaders are not only extremely passionate about what they do, they also are not afraid to show it. One could even call this passion "courage." Collins describes passion as demonstrating a relentlessness to achieve the desired outcomes.

Passion is demonstrating a relentlessness to achieve the desired outcomes.

Most people in education care passionately about their work. Sometimes things erode that natural passion, so we need to rebuild it or recreate it. One way to do this is to get leaders in the habit of complimenting people.

Many believe that in order for people to create positive relationships with others, compliments and criticism should be balanced. Several studies indicate that a higher compliment-to-criticism ratio works better. Through study, trial, and error, Studer Group and its partners have found the best ratio of compliments to criticism.

FIGURE 5.2 | CRITICISM-TO-COMPLIMENT RATIO

- If someone receives one compliment for every criticism, a negative relationship results.
- If someone receives two compliments for every criticism, a neutral relationship results.
- If someone receives three compliments per criticism, a positive relationship results.

Have you ever received a message that your supervisor wanted you to call as soon as possible? Was your first thought "Oh, good—more recognition!" or was it "Oh my goodness, what did I do?" Immediately thinking something is wrong may mean that you don't get complimented and recognized enough.

It is easy to fall into the trap of missing the positive. Although we may not realize it, we tend to spend so much time looking for things that are wrong that we don't see what is right. In K–12 systems, we tend to focus on the negative. Both of us have fallen into this trap when leading others. Rather than first looking for the positive, we immediately go to the problem. Both of us have learned the value of starting with the positives.

> Although we may not realize it, we tend to spend so much time looking for things that are wrong that we don't see what is right.

Janet's Story:
Starting with Wins

Every 90 days, I hold a strategic planning session with my team. At the end of the session, the team evaluates the day, including what could be done to improve the session. On one occasion early on, all members of the team suggested we start with the positives before we dive into the details for the day. From that point on, the first item on each session's agenda is "Start with the WINS!"

Quint's Story:
The Lesson of the Crooked Banner

When I worked at Holy Cross Hospital in Chicago, I had to drop by an open house at the new outpatient clinic. Clinic employees had stayed late the night before and showed up early that morning to set up the event. When I walked in, I noticed that the banner was just a little crooked. So I immediately found someone and told that person about the crooked banner.

A few days later, the leader told me that my comments had completely sucked the energy out of all the employees. They had worked so hard, and all I did was notice what was wrong. I was not proud of what I'd done, but I did learn a lesson that day. From that point on, I've always praised what was good and asked employees their opinion on what they did well. Only then do I ask, "By the way, if you were to do it over again, would you have any opportunities for improvement?" If I had done this at the open house, the employees themselves might have even mentioned that the banner could have been straighter.

In education, it is important to actively look for what is right. This does not mean ignoring what needs to be improved in order to run a better organization. We've found that we get there more effectively by focusing first on what's right. Rewarded and recognized behavior gets repeated, which fuels the passion that brought people into this field.

Rewarded and recognized behavior gets repeated, which fuels the passion that brought people into this field.

Principles and Prescriptive To-Dos

The next part of the flywheel is the prescriptive to-dos. This is where passion moves to skill. Prescriptive to-dos are the techniques, tools, and behaviors that will achieve the outcomes you want.

Prescriptive to-dos are the techniques, tools, and behaviors that will achieve the outcomes you want.

"Attitude is everything" might be a great poster slogan, but some people who have great attitudes lack the necessary skills. One of the most heartbreaking tasks is to tell somebody who has a great attitude that it's just not working out, that the organization is not the right place for him, or that he simply doesn't have the required skill set.

Quint's Story: The Right Skill Set Matters

On the Pensacola Blue Wahoos team, there is a player now who is probably one of the nicest young men you'd ever meet in your life. He's always signing autographs and always has young kids in the dugout, and when you hear him talk about Mother's Day on the radio, you want to take this kid home. Yet he's hitting .197. In baseball that's not good. He just doesn't have the skills for the job. And if he doesn't improve, he will be released and his dream of playing baseball at the highest level will be gone.

We need more than attitude. Attitude can be the foundation, but we also need skills. The best way to acquire those skills is to work for the right organization—one that gives us the opportunity for training and development. Yet if you work for an organization that doesn't offer development, you're not off the hook. Go out and see how to get better.

> If you work for an organization that doesn't offer development, you're not off the hook. Go out and see how to get better.

As a parent, you probably don't need a parenting class. However, if a doctor tells you that your child could have diabetes or autism, you immediately want to learn everything you can about the condition. So there's directed development and there's self-directed development. Both are needed if an individual is going to be successful as a leader. Throughout the rest of the book, we will talk about the prescriptions that really drive performance when they're combined with passion and the right attitude. In fact, sometimes when we carry out the prescriptions simply by going through the motions, we can get the outcomes and even regain our passion.

Our colleague Liz Jazwiec says that when she ran a hospital emergency department, she had employees implementing tactics they really didn't think were going to work. Sometimes the employees even did them in a way that was a little bit over the top, just to drive Liz crazy. For example, after Liz told the staff to be friendly to patients and walk them to where they needed to go, they'd ask patients, "How can I help you?" in a syrupy-sweet tone or "Let me take you to where you're going" in a loud, obnoxious voice. Though they exaggerated the tactics at first, they discovered that patients really liked the changes. Patients' reactions to them were much, much more positive. They saw the outcome and recaptured their passion.

On the flywheel, the to-dos feed into the Nine Principles®. In the book *Hardwiring Excellence*, the chapters align with the Nine Principles we focus on with partner organizations. These Nine Principles drive the decisions that leaders make when determining the best tactics to apply to achieve high-priority goals. Since that first book was written, the Evidence-Based Leadership framework has been more thoroughly defined using evidence that Studer Group has gathered from our thousand or so partners around the world. Think of the Nine Principles as the philosophy behind good leadership decision-making.

We apply the Nine Principles to assist school districts with their journey toward excellence. Because the Nine Principles are fundamental to our work with Evidence-Based Leadership in schools, we devote the next chapter to them, but we introduce them here.

Pillar Results

The third part of the flywheel is pillar results. When the techniques, tools, and behaviors are well executed, pillar results are achieved. The pillars are the foundation for setting organizational goals and direction, providing consistency, and maintaining focus. Chapter 8 digs deeper into the goal-setting process for K–12 systems.

> The pillars are the foundation for setting organizational goals and direction, providing consistency, and maintaining focus.

In the book *Creating the New American Hospital: A Time for Greatness*, author Clay Sherman introduced the term *pillars*, which stood for the organization's broad goals. While working in healthcare, Studer Group adapted this model by introducing five pillars (quality, growth, finance, people, and service).

We've found that the five pillars also work in education, with a slight twist. The learning experience and student results are the highest priority of all educational systems. So we've added the **Student Achievement Pillar**, which sits at the center of all other pillars. The **Quality Pillar** focuses on departmental metrics that indirectly affect student achievement. K–12 systems focus on service in two ways, both of which are important to measure under the **Service Pillar**. The first service area represents the service provided to those paying for services or those who have a stake in the services provided, such as parents and community members. The second area represents the service that departments provide to schools. The main focus of the **People Pillar** is to measure the engagement level of employees, which defines the quality of the workforce environment facilitated by leaders. The **Finance Pillar** includes metrics associated with cost savings, revenue generated, and return on investments made with allocated resources. The underlying measure for finance for K–12 systems is how well public institutions spend taxpayer dollars. The **Growth Pillar** usually includes measures related to student enrollment.

If an organization wants to add other pillars, that's fine. Jackson Public Schools in Jackson, Michigan, added a safety pillar because schools had reported an escalated number of fighting incidents. By focusing on this pillar, the district was able to reduce the number of such incidents each year.

Though a school system's emphasis is on the Student Achievement Pillar more than the others, when employees and key stakeholders look at all pillars, they see that the organization never loses sight of the big picture. Defining the measures aligned to each pillar focuses leaders' attention and sets the priorities of an organization in a way that's easily visible to all employees. The pillars reinforce the fact that all employees have skin in the game. Chapter 8 spells out the process of setting goals aligned to pillars as part of the Evidence-Based Leadership framework.

> When employees and key stakeholders look at the pillars, they see that the organization never loses sight of the big picture.

Summary

The Organizational Flywheel is the conceptual foundation of Evidence-Based Leadership—the approach we use with leaders to maximize organizational performance. At its center are the reasons we work in education: to have purpose, do worthwhile work, and make a difference. For most of us, education is a calling, not just a job, so the flywheel begins with our passion or self-motivation to do meaningful work. We call this part of the flywheel the *will*. The next part is the *skill*. Skills align with the leadership indicators associated with the Nine Principles.

The remaining third of the flywheel is *results*. Every leadership team member in a school district contributes in some way to the construction of a learning environment that gives every student the chance to achieve success. Teams contribute to the results (defined by the pillars) and carry out the prescriptions that position the school district for success. The remainder of this book focuses on how to do both.

CHAPTER SIX:

THE NINE PRINCIPLES®: A COMMITMENT

I n our effort to help organizations implement the Evidence-Based Leadership℠ approach, we've found that the concepts associated with the Nine Principles and the clear focus created by the pillars provide the structured approach that organizations need in order to achieve results. Years ago, the Nine Principles were developed to give organizations a process to attain the desired results—a road map to help them develop a success-based culture using evidence. The Nine Principles are the guiding concepts of Evidence-Based Leadership.

The Nine Principles are the guiding concepts of Evidence-Based Leadership.

Educational systems have made an unprecedented commitment to the pursuit of performance excellence. More and more K–12 leaders and boards of education express interest in applying for the Malcolm Baldrige National Quality Award (MBNQA) as well as state and local quality awards. The Baldrige Award recognizes public and private U.S. organizations for making great progress on several measures of quality and is awarded by the president of the United States. The next section in this chapter summarizes the criteria associated with the award.

Dr. JoAnne Sternke, superintendent of Pewaukee School District in Wisconsin, led her district to achieve the national award this past year. We've been fortunate to partner with her team. Dr. Sternke is a key resource, teacher, and speaker for districts that want to achieve similar results. The two other organizations that received the MBNQA this past year were healthcare organizations that partner with Studer Group. Our company itself was a 2010 recipient of the MBNQA. All of this is to say that we connect school districts to a network of leaders of high-performing organizations.

Quint's Thoughts: Baldrige Alignment

A few years back, while I was president of Baptist Hospital in Pensacola, Florida, I received a call from a CEO. He asked if I had ever worked with the Baldrige Award. I said no and asked why. He explained that he thought the Nine Principles were very much in alignment with the Baldrige criteria. Later I received a call from a Baldrige examiner who consulted with hospitals to help them prepare for site visits. The examiner made a similar comment. Are they 100 percent in alignment? No, but we have found that organizations that have implemented the Nine Principles, goals by pillars, and prescriptive practices have achieved very good results in many of the Baldrige categories, which makes preparation for the Baldrige a natural segue from our process.

Drive for Quality and Focus on Results

The Malcolm Baldrige Education Criteria for Performance Excellence are part of an outcome-focused, validated management model based on the characteristics of high-performing organizations. The ultimate goal of the MBNQA is to improve the quality and productivity of American business. Originally designed only for business, the criteria have evolved from a quality system model to an overall organizational management and improvement model. In addition, the criteria have been adapted to include a healthcare model and an education model (Figure 6.1).

FIGURE 6.1 | MALCOLM BALDRIGE EDUCATION CRITERIA FOR PERFORMANCE EXCELLENCE, 2013–2014

· **Leadership:** How senior leaders' personal actions and the organization's governance system guide and sustain the organization.

· **Strategic Planning:** How the organization develops strategic objectives and action plans, implements them, changes them if circumstances require, and measures progress.

· **Customer Focus:** How the organization engages its students and other customers for long-term marketplace success, including how it listens to the customer's voice, builds customer relationships, and uses customer information to improve and to identify opportunities for innovation.

· **Measurement, Analysis, and Knowledge Management:** A collection of all key information about effectively measuring, analyzing, and improving performance and managing organizational knowledge to drive improvement, innovation, and organizational competitiveness.

· **Workforce Focus:** Key workforce practices, including those directed toward creating and maintaining a high-performance work environment and toward engaging the workforce to enable workers and the organization to adapt to change and to succeed.

· **Operations Focus:** How the organization focuses on its work, educational program and service design and delivery, and operational effectiveness to achieve success and organizational sustainability.

· **Results:** A systems focus that encompasses all results necessary to sustaining an educational organization, including key student learning and process results, student- and other customer-focused results, workforce results, leadership and governance system results, and overall budgetary, financial, and market performance.

The Baldrige Criteria determine how an organization demonstrates well-deployed, systematic processes leading to a balanced set of results. We are finding that a growing number of school districts want to know how organizations have applied these criteria effectively. Leaders and boards of education are also looking for more advice and feedback on each category as they navigate the road to performance excellence. The Baldrige Criteria ask for systematic processes and results; the Evidence-Based Leadership framework in healthcare and education provides many of the answers to the criteria to hardwire excellence. That is, the behaviors and processes embedded in Evidence-Based Leadership become ingrained in the organizational culture.

The Evidence-Based Leadership framework is guided by the Nine Principles that we use within our own organization as the conceptual basis for applying the Baldrige Criteria to our work. We've taken our own learnings and successes and applied them to education and healthcare. Figure 6.2 provides an overview of the Nine Principles, the alignment of the Baldrige Criteria to the principles, and several descriptive items for each principle. Whether or not the Baldrige Award is the target, the bulleted items zero in on specific behaviors that leaders can apply to maximize performance in educational systems. These behaviors align closely with the Evidence-Based Leadership framework described in Chapter 7. The chart serves as a guide for our work with educational systems as we hardwire excellence and achieve important measurable results.

FIGURE 6.2	THE NINE PRINCIPLES® APPLIED TO K–12 SYSTEMS WITH BALDRIGE ALIGNMENT		
	NINE PRINCIPLES	**BALDRIGE CRITERIA**	**DESCRIPTION**
1	**Commit to excellence:** Improve the bottom line while living out mission and values.	Leadership, Strategic Planning, Measurement, Analysis and Knowledge Management, Results	· Models well-defined standards · Creates service excellence so employees, students, and parents feel valued · Merits a ranking for which any employee or parent recommends the school district to others
2	**Measure the important things:** Objectively assess the current status and track progress toward goals.	Leadership, Strategic Planning, Customer, Measurement, Analysis and Knowledge Management, Workforce, Operations, Results	· Identifies what the school district values · Defines specific targets · Determines aligned tools and processes · Maintains responsibility to public spending by calculating return on dollars/time invested to outcomes
3	**Build a culture around service:** Connect services to organizational values.	Leadership, Customer, Measurement, Analysis and Knowledge Management, Workforce, Process Management	· Ensures that thoughtful processes and procedures become the norm · Ensures high-quality, caring environment for employees, students, and parents · Invests in building relationships with employees and stakeholders
4	**Create and develop leaders:** Make leadership development a number one priority.	Leadership, Measurement, Analysis and Knowledge Management, Customer, Workforce Focus, Results	· Hires top-performing leaders · Develops aspiring new and existing leaders on well-defined and aligned expectations · Holds leaders accountable for defined outcomes

	NINE PRINCIPLES®	BALDRIGE CRITERIA	DESCRIPTION
5	**Focus on employee satisfaction:** Build a top-performing workforce.	Leadership, Measurement, Analysis and Knowledge Management, Workforce Focus, Results	· Gives employees opportunity for input · Engages in professional conversations to improve performance · Recognizes improved and high performance
6	**Build individual accountability:** Create a self-motivated workforce.	Leadership, Measurement, Analysis and Knowledge Management, Results	· Aligns individual goals and measures to those of the organization · Moves the hockey stick curve to a bell curve to represent performance
7	**Align behaviors with goals and values:** Align leadership and resources.	Leadership, Strategic Planning, Measurement, Analysis and Knowledge Management, Process Management, Results	· Creates transparency of results to develop trust · Creates leadership report cards using aligned scorecards · Aligns short-cycle actions to results
8	**Communicate at all levels:** Show why, then describe what and how.	Leadership, Measurement, Analysis and Knowledge Management, Process Management	· Speeds up the decision-making process · Creates proactive behavior · Improves working relationships
9	**Recognize and reward success:** Everyone makes a difference.	Leadership, Measurement, Analysis and Knowledge Management, Workforce Focus, Process Management	· Creates win-win situations · Never lets great work go unnoticed · Recognizes behavior that merits following

Principle 1: Commit to Excellence.

As we commit to excellence, we're going to set goals, improve accountability to achieve the desired results, and align processes. When we say we are committing to excellence, we're really asking, Where do we want to be in student achievement? Where do we want to be in service? Where do we want to be in quality? Where do we want to be in finance? In people? In growth? Those who add pillars such as safety or community will ask the same question for those areas.

Committing to excellence is based on a combination of where we are and where we'd like to be. This may not mean where we're going to be in one year. In fact, we have worked with several organizations that we just love because they set their ultimate benchmark and then figure out where they are and where they need to be each year in order to get there. They truly understand that we can't go from one level to another overnight—at least not if progress is to be sustained.

> Committing to excellence is based on a combination of where we are and where we'd like to be.

Principle 2: Measure the Important Things.

There is no lack of data in education. The key is to figure out the most vital data. Sometimes we see extensive measurement in one area and scant measurement in an area that's far more vital. In most school districts we work with, leaders express confusion about how to select the most important measures and how to know which ones represent overall results and which ones represent a predictive type of measure that informs decision-making.

Of course, student achievement is an essential measure for school districts, but organizations may not be measuring vital things such as teacher and staff engagement and parent satisfaction. If organizations do measure these factors, they don't have a process for sharing the results and gathering input for the purpose of improvement.

Years of research show that teachers tend to make a decision about their abilities to teach *within their first 90 days*, which indicates that they need the strongest support from their leaders at this critical time. We find that when people leave in the first year, the problem is typically one of selection and orientation. If they leave between one and three years, something has gone wrong with their adjustment period to the organization, perhaps in teamwork and employee development. If it's four to five years, the issue is usually compensation. Employees who stay for five years are pretty much going to stay for most of their careers. But if turnover criteria are not measured, leaders won't know which problems to fix. When we ask leaders how long the average person stays before leaving, they can't tell us turnover numbers by school or department.

The same thing happens with employee engagement. When we discuss engagement levels, we ask leaders if they have data on how satisfied employees are with their jobs. In most instances, leaders can't provide data in that format. And we know that engagement levels change over time. For instance, in general we find that at one and two years, teachers are highly satisfied, and at six and above, they are pretty satisfied—the key is to work hard to engage those three-, four-, and five-year teachers. But, again, without employment longevity data, we can't target people at critical times.

In summary, measures help us focus on the most critical elements that influence the success of a school district. What we measure, we value, and therefore, it's what we address.

What we measure, we value, and therefore, it's what we address.

Principle 3: Build a Culture around Service.

When we work with district partners, we focus on building a culture around service by defining what service looks like for students, their parents, and our employees. We make sure we have best-place-to-work standards that define the way people are expected to behave in their work environment. This also makes it clear which behaviors we won't tolerate, namely, those that don't fit with what we've all agreed will make the school district a great place for students to learn, teachers to teach, staff to work, and parents to send their children for a great education.

We also include parent satisfaction as a core measure under the Service Pillar, and we administer our parent satisfaction survey to partner districts. All of this is to say that the K–12 Evidence-Based Leadership framework reinforces service to parents and community stakeholders as well as to the district workforce.

A Service Excellence Team

Several years ago, we began working with Oklahoma City Public Schools on improving customer service. The leaders asked us to apply a train-the-trainers professional development model for frontline staff to train their peers. As a first step, we asked the superintendent and executive team to identify 20 high-performing frontline staff to work together with us to create a set of standards that would define a best-place-to-work environment. The team created the draft standards. We then sent the draft to the entire staff via an online survey tool asking for input. The standards were finalized and then used to create learning modules. We applied the train-the-trainers approach by training staff teams of high performers. We also trained the leaders on the standards and the modules. The staff members who volunteered to serve as trainers have done a remarkable job. The high marks they received on the evaluations for each training session reflect the employees' level of satisfaction with their colleagues as trainers. Also, the majority of frontline staff in schools and departments attended the sessions. As a follow-up, we also track how well department leaders provide high levels of service to others to stay in line with leaders modeling the expected behaviors.

Principle 4: Create and Develop Leaders.

This principle is vital because, as leaders, we can take someone only as far as we've taken ourselves. We need to develop leaders so they can develop others. As we train leaders on creating best-place-to-work environments, we promote the idea of leaders spending about 80 percent of their time supporting and coaching those they lead to achieve their highest potential. What we've found is that leaders have limited skills in this area and, in some instances, an absence of the mind-set needed to make coaching and support a priority. Developing high-performing leaders is so important that it became a major part of the Evidence-Based Leadership framework. Chapter 10 discusses this principle in detail.

We need to develop leaders so they can develop others.

Principle 5: Focus on Employee Satisfaction and Engagement.

People don't leave their jobs—they leave their leaders. The better the employees feel about their work environment, the greater the opportunity they have to create effective learning environments. And so we hardwire certain actions that leaders need to take: leader rounding with employees to gain input on areas working well and processes to be improved; rewarding and recognizing people, such as by writing thank-you notes; involving employees in selection of new staff; involving employees in generating new ideas; providing employees with development opportunities; and making sure employees have systems that work and the tools and equipment to do their jobs. Chapter 11 covers this principle.

People don't leave their jobs—they leave their leaders.

Principle 5 has become the centerpiece of the professional development we offer to leaders. Our employee engagement survey measures development outcomes with ten questions focused on the type of environment the supervisor provides for employees, three questions about the superintendent's leadership, and one question that assesses employees' loyalty to the school district. The superintendent and supervisor items give the leaders a pulse check on the level of we/they behavior in the educational system. For example, if a leader's scores are high and the superintendent's are low, it may be that the leader is communicating decisions that position senior leadership in a bad light. Remember, we said that we/they is one of the biggest barriers to achieving and hardwiring excellence.

Principle 6: Build Individual Accountability.

Principle 6 is where leaders ask, "What do I need from everyone in order for this to be a successful department, school, or district?" What we're talking about here is ownership—it's how well people live the values. Individual accountability means employees take ownership of modeling and living the standards. It's making sure that when someone asks an employee a question that needs to be redirected to someone else, the employee follows the person to ensure that the question gets answered. It's making sure people leave their work area in good condition so those who come in afterward will have an easy transition. It means people are willing to help in the hiring process because they want to have good coworkers. It also means that employees come up with ideas about how to improve the organization and are deeply engaged in process improvement. Individual accountability means people maximize their own performance for the good of the organization.

> What we're talking about here is ownership—it's how well people live the values. Individual accountability means employees take ownership of modeling and living the standards.

Individual accountability starts with senior leadership and school boards. Senior leaders model what they expect of others and engage with the board in a transparent and open manner. School board members model behaviors they expect of the organization. They expect the school district to achieve measurable results, spend money in the most efficient ways, and report progress to them so they know how to communicate to their constituencies. Board members also model how to interact with each other, with the district's education professionals, and with community stakeholders. To achieve and sustain excellence, both groups need to demonstrate high levels of individual accountability.

The school board members and the superintendent of Arlington Independent School District in Arlington, Texas, provide a great model for how boards and superintendents live this principle. In fact, they received the 2014 Outstanding School Board of Texas Award from the Texas Association of School Administrators. We've had the pleasure of providing some board development sessions for them and have seen how their actions demonstrate high performance to school district leaders, teachers, and staff. This does not mean that they agree at all times—it means they engage in professional discussions with the right end in mind. In fact, we've found most boards to be dedicated to producing excellent school districts.

Principle 7: Align Behaviors with Goals and Values.

Principle 7 is connected to organizational and individual measurement systems. It is important to make sure that the behaviors we're looking for truly connect with our values and are designed to meet the goals we've set. We call this one the accountability principle; it is highlighted in Chapter 8. We make sure we're setting the right goals for people and assigning them the weights that define our highest priorities and focus our attention.

It is important to make sure that the behaviors we're looking for truly connect with our values and are designed to meet the goals we've set.

Principle 8: Communicate at All Levels.

This principle falls under leadership development. Communication is a big part of the skill set leaders need in order to achieve results. Why? Because communication connects the dots for people—it ties all the other principles together. When leaders build their communication skills, employees are aware of the organization's commitment to excellence. They know what's being measured; they know the standards that create the culture. They know they have effective leaders, systems that work, and the resources needed to do the job. Because they understand what's going on and their role in it, employees take ownership of their own performance. Finally, they clearly see how behaviors connect to the values and goals of the organization.

Communication is a big part of the skill set leaders need in order to achieve results. Why? Because communication connects the dots for people—it ties all the other principles together.

Principle 9: Reward and Recognize Success.

When we recognize and reward behavior, we're not just being nice. We're trying to ensure that the behavior gets repeated—not just by the employee who originally performed the behavior, but also by those around that person who observe the reward and recognition. Recognizing people encourages others to do the right thing, and ultimately, it encourages the consistency we need in order to create a culture of excellence.

> Recognizing people encourages others to do the right thing, and ultimately, it encourages the consistency we need in order to create a culture of excellence.

Summary

It's clear that the Nine Principles are as vital today as they were years ago when they were introduced in *Hardwiring Excellence*. In fact, they are the glue that holds Evidence-Based Leadership together and connects passion to results on the Organizational Flywheel. They are probably the easiest way to demonstrate to department leaders, staff, and key stakeholders what it takes to maximize performance.

> The Nine Principles are the glue that holds Evidence-Based Leadership together. They are probably the easiest way to communicate to every department what it takes to create a culture of high performance.

If the Nine Principles are displayed on a department wall, it's easy to write underneath them what our commitments to excellence are and how they translate into goals. We can write down what we're going to measure, how we're going to live the standards, and what behaviors make up the school district's culture.

The list of principles makes it clear that leaders need to be able to run good meetings, communicate well, and explain concepts that are difficult to grasp. Employees understand what they need to do and what they need from their leaders in order to achieve goals that demonstrate a commitment to excellence.

As we discuss later in the book, individual accountability makes great process improvement possible. For leaders, it says: You can count on me. So, we're going to live the standards, which means living our values. We're going to align our goals and values to make sure we have that commitment to excellence. We're going to communicate our progress along the way, including what we do well and what we can do better. We're going to recognize and reward success, and the greatest success we can have is truly making a difference in people's lives.

These Nine Principles—which began in 1993, which became the foundation of *Hardwiring Excellence*, and which we've practiced and refined in hundreds of organizations since then—are still alive and well. They work at the school and department levels. They work at the system level. We integrate them into Evidence-Based Leadership, which ties into the operational framework of the pillars, which drives that flywheel that perpetuates a sense of purpose, worthwhile work, and making a difference, which drives us to hardwire the prescriptive to-dos, which gets the outcomes we need—all of which adds up to higher-quality student achievement, greater consistency and reliability, and greater efficiency and effectiveness. In the end, we find we've hardwired excellence throughout the organization and, in the process, have maximized leadership performance.

Chapter Seven:

The Execution Flywheel^{SM}: Hardwiring Educational Excellence

O ne of the greatest obstacles to getting results is poor execution. The Organizational Flywheel presented in Chapter 5 showed us that we need well-defined goals and measures, the right strategy, and leadership development. If our leaders don't apply the strategy with high levels of performance, the likelihood of success diminishes. So besides living the concepts of the Organizational Flywheel, which are reinforced by the Nine Principles®, leaders also need to execute with fidelity. Regardless of the strategy, tactic, or process we apply to achieve results, leaders should hardwire the behaviors associated with the Execution Flywheel.

This chapter is about diagnosing a problem and its causes before determining a solution. It is about validating that 100 percent of leaders comply with a decision and gain the skill set needed to execute strategic actions with fidelity. As K–12 leaders, we can be too quick to implement a program or initiative because we are eager to achieve results. This isn't surprising, considering today's pressure to perform faster and better in education. We've found, however, that without proper diagnosis, people cannot treat the problem or sustain good results. Also, without a systematic process for validating compliance and quality of execution, it's difficult to know why something is not working. We blame the program or product rather than conducting an in-depth review of our own actions.

Studer Education is known for helping organizational leaders hard-wire behaviors to achieve results, and the Execution Flywheel is the process we use. Most school districts seek to improve the current performance of their leaders, teachers, and staff while achieving desired outcomes. What keeps them from improving and sustaining results? As we have coached partner school districts, we've found answers to this question. We created the Execution Flywheel (Figure 7.1) to provide a visual for working with leaders to apply and sustain a continuous systems-improvement process.

FIGURE 7.1 | EXECUTION FLYWHEELSM

At the center of the flywheel is the word *excellence*, which means school district leaders acknowledge that in order to maximize performance, every school and every department in a school district is to be excellent. The inner circle of the flywheel is the same inner circle of the Organizational Flywheel, which represents the core components for hardwiring excellence. The outer circle represents the continuous improvement process we apply with leaders and their teams to achieve and sustain results and to reflect on how their individual performance influences overall system results.

When district leadership and boards consider partnering with Studer Education, they tend to ask, "How is Evidence-Based Leadership^{SM} not just one more thing our leaders will have to add to their already-full schedules?" The Execution Flywheel is the answer to this question. Our goal is not to add more to the plate, but rather to apply the process represented in the Execution Flywheel to determine if what's on the plate is really helping school districts achieve the key outcomes. If so, are leaders complying with the defined expectations and doing so with high quality?

Our goal is not to add more to the plate, but rather to apply the process represented in the Execution Flywheel to determine if what's on the plate is really helping school districts achieve the key outcomes.

Our starting point in any district is the executive leadership level. If the executive team is resistant to change, K–12 systems have little or no chance of achieving at a high level and sustaining that level over time. The Evidence-Based Leadership framework described in Section 3 of the book lays out the approach for leaders to follow. Leaders can use the framework to continuously assess how system-wide decisions and aligned individual performance and compliance influence results.

Think of the Execution Flywheel as the engine that drives the Evidence-Based Leadership framework. The leader is the driver behind the wheel. The framework and flywheel create a well-oiled machine. The leader determines the precision and speed on a constantly changing road to success. The leader also constantly checks the gauges and makes adjustments to keep the machine running smoothly.

Let's look at each part of the outer circle of the Execution Flywheel.

Diagnose

When we engage in initial conversations with district leaders, either the leaders do not have data at their fingertips to help diagnose the current state of affairs, or they have massive amounts of data points stored in their systems and sometimes also on software-supported dashboards. At times we've seen 50 or more measures on district dashboards, as well as narrative information from observations and classroom walkthroughs. With glazed eyes, the leaders ask, "What do we do with all this data, and how do we make sense of it?"

Diagnosing the problem accurately is the first step. As we review the data, we first ask leaders to determine the key measures that define success. Some measures on the existing dashboards are identified as key measures, others as progress-monitoring measures, and still others as measures that are "nice to have."

Regardless of the situation, the purpose of our initial work with leaders is to determine the key drivers that define success and to identify aligned, progress-monitoring measures. To reach this point, we work with leaders to gather and review data to diagnose the current state of affairs in the school district. We ask probing questions of leaders, and often of the board, to determine which key factors define success for their district.

From there, we begin to create a district or system scorecard, which documents the key drivers for success as well as progress measures toward achieving the goals. The end-of-year results inform the next year's diagnostics. Therefore, the cycle of the Execution Flywheel is continuous and evaluative.

The Execution Flywheel provides the needed structure for leaders to make good, informed decisions rather than letting emotion or intuition drive decisions that merely add to their burdens. The diagnostic part of the flywheel is critical if leaders are to set clear, evidence-based directions.

Diagnosing the current state and comparing it to the final goal is the first step toward making strategic and thoughtful decisions. From the diagnosis, we set goals that determine where to focus attention. Each leadership decision affects the daily work of teachers and staff. Moving forward without applying an intensive diagnostic process to the current reality is unfair to those who live with the actions that follow from decisions.

Moving forward without applying an intensive diagnostic process to the current reality is unfair to those who live with the actions that follow from decisions.

Sometimes leaders put a positive slant on their data rather than viewing it critically. During diagnosis, however, we talk to leaders about the value in facing the "brutal facts." To progress positively, school system leaders can examine the current reality and pay close attention to these facts, however disturbing they may be. The goal is for leaders to view the data honestly and critically. Jim Collins found that most successful leaders made a conscientious effort to use evidence to guide their decision-making. Equally important, these leaders had an unwavering faith in the organization's future success. Being critical was essential, and failure or lack of improvement was not an option.

The evidence from the diagnostic phase becomes transparent to others, thus providing opportunities for leaders and staff to share input about the system's circumstances. The Evidence-Based Leadership Scorecard offers a transparent communication and strategic planning tool for all system stakeholders to use to continuously improve. (More about the scorecard in Chapter 8.)

Facing the Brutal Facts

The School District of Janesville, Wisconsin, was our pilot site for applying the Evidence-Based Leadership framework in school systems. Years ago at one of our initial planning sessions, we asked the Janesville board and superintendent, "How would you rate your district on student achievement?" Most leaders and board members gave it a high rating. We then showed them a slide demonstrating that student achievement scores on the state tests were below the state average and close to the bottom in relation to comparable districts. That day was a turning point for the Janesville district, as leaders had to face the brutal facts. Five years later, the district student achievement scores rank above the state average and are at the top relative to districts they use as comparison districts. Janesville has also received several student achievement awards. It all started with using evidence to diagnose the current state of affairs.

Act

As we diagnose the current state, we begin to establish key goals and measures that define success and track progress. Next, we decide on the actions that will help our team achieve the overall goals.

Here's where we engage in collective conversations with our teams to gain insight on best-practice strategies. Our goal is to apply the 80/20 Rule (Pareto's Principle) by answering this question with the team: What strategic actions will make up the 20 percent of our time that will accomplish 80 percent of the results? The point here is that the relationship between effort and results is rarely, if ever, balanced. Approximately 20 percent of our efforts will produce 80 percent of the results. Learning to recognize and then focus on that 20 percent is the key to making the most effective use of our time. For example, an elementary school principal chooses to spend one day a week meeting with grade-level teams of teachers to review student achievement results for each of their students. At the meeting, weekly interventions are assigned to students failing to achieve the expected outcomes. Over the course of the year, the principal and teachers discover that this one action results in a substantial gain in overall student achievement for the school.

We also apply Stephen Covey's first discipline in this part of the Execution Flywheel: *People are naturally wired to focus on only one or two things at a time.* According to research, people have an 80 percent chance of achieving results when doing one thing to achieve those results. Add a second goal, and the success rate drops to 64 percent. As we keep adding, the likelihood of success nosedives. We've found that school improvement plans have five or more actions for teachers to apply in classrooms to achieve results. In these cases, school teams have only a 33 percent chance of getting excellent results.

People have an 80 percent chance of achieving results when doing one thing to achieve those results. Add a second goal, and the success rate drops to 64 percent.

For each goal, we advise leaders to work with their teams to determine the one—or, at most, two—strategic actions they can apply in order to get excellent results. This means leaders are disciplined and focused to achieve specifically defined results.

Coach

When referring to employees, we often use the word *team*. Teams are the building blocks of any organization. An effective leader knows how to coach teams to success. So leaders should also know how to select, build, and guide teams of people to apply a strategic action to achieve a defined outcome.

When we have this conversation with leaders, here's how it might go:

Janet: What are teams trying to do?

Leaders: Win.

Janet: How do teams know when they win?

Leaders: They outperform another team or reach the target score.

Janet: What happens if the teams come to work every day and they don't know what the target is or what it means to win? Or they don't get enough quick wins toward a bigger target?

Leaders: They wouldn't want to show up and continue.

Janet: Now, think of your team. Do they know the targets and what it takes to get quick wins? Let's say they do—what then?

Leaders: We have to give them a game plan and give them time to practice.

Janet: What do you do while they are practicing?

Leaders: Give them feedback and make sure the game plan is the right one.

Janet: Bingo! That's what this part of the Execution Flywheel is all about.

Coaching includes teaching, supporting, and facilitating teams to gain the skills they need to execute the strategic action to achieve results. Working with our partner districts, we call ourselves coaches. Our job is to coach leaders to coach their teams, so our success depends on the leadership. Who coaches whom in school systems? Superintendents coach their senior leaders. Senior leaders coach principals and department leaders. Principals coach teachers. Department leaders coach managers. Here's what's so great: coaching directly flows down, or cascades, to the classrooms. An effort that starts at the top results in teachers coaching students to achieve their highest potential.

Our job is to coach leaders to coach their teams.

Janet's Story:
From the Tennis Court to the Classroom

When I started teaching math at Woodham High School in Florida, I was excited that I was also chosen to coach the tennis team. I loved to coach—coaching tennis was about communicating why we are practicing today, how the practice session relates to the match play, and what we are going to do each day to build the players' skill sets so the team can be successful. The team or school that won the best out of seven matches won the school competition. Each player had to be coached both as part of a team and as an individual so he or she could contribute to a winning team.

I would teach math for five periods a day and then host a weight and conditioning class for athletes during the last period. One day I walked from my math classroom to the tennis courts, eager to coach the team. I had not had a good day with my math students. As I watched, encouraged, and coached the tennis players, it dawned on me that if I applied this same approach in my classroom, my math students might be as eager to perform and engage in math class as the tennis players were in practice sessions. I realized my math class was also a place of practice: practicing new math skills every day for the purpose of achieving a well-defined goal. From that day on, my math students and I found a way to recognize successes in class that was similar to the way my players achieved goals on the tennis courts.

Validate

At this phase of the Execution Flywheel, leaders know the expected goals and actions and have been coached on the necessary skills. Validation is one of the most slighted phases, but it is equally important. Validation entails 100 percent (or almost 100 percent) compliance on behavior as well as the highest quality. Ensuring compliance and quality is critical to improving both individual and system-wide performance.

After years of work, we now know that if people practice a certain behavior with a certain frequency, they will get the outcome they want. If they don't, they are either doing something wrong or they are doing it right but not often enough—they are not doing it *always*. What we call Always Behaviors[SM] are what we expect people to do almost all the time. If we strive for perfection, we will fail; if we strive for excellence, however, we will succeed. With that in mind, *always* actually means that leaders apply expected behaviors 97 to 98 percent of the time, which takes into account the few circumstances that get in the way of compliance.

If we strive for perfection, we will fail; if we strive for excellence, however, we will succeed.

Validation, as part of the Execution Flywheel, takes place when every leader consistently applies a well-defined and clearly communicated process. When leaders are always compliant, attention is focused on the quality of execution. We celebrate high performance and address any performance gaps that may interfere with people achieving at their highest potential. It is difficult to judge performance without monitoring compliance. Are there performance gaps? Do the gaps relate to noncompliance with the expected behaviors? Compliance relates to frequency, and frequency helps us improve performance.

Who validates whom? The validator is the person who performs an individual's evaluation. School boards validate superintendents, superintendents validate senior teams, senior team members validate principals and department leaders, department leaders validate managers, and so on. This process keeps leaders from making excuses for low performance and blaming mishaps on system malfunctions rather than first looking in the mirror. Validation is about holding up the mirror to determine if we are always complying and executing with high quality.

Positive Phone Calls: A Priority

In all our partner school districts, one of the lowest-scored items on the parent satisfaction survey is "I receive positive phone calls home about my child." Most people in school systems agree that it's a worthwhile action to take, but it's easy to postpone. Mary Jo Raczkowski-Shannon, principal at Hunt Elementary School in Jackson, Michigan, expects her teachers to make five positive phone calls home a week, with the goal of calling every parent at least once a semester. She validates this by checking a phone log in which teachers record the student's name, the time the call was made, and a summary of the call. The school's score on the parent satisfaction survey has increased, and so has the parent satisfaction with that item (Figures 7.2 and 7.3). Most importantly, the teachers themselves report feeling that the calls have great value.

What a win! The students feel good, the parents are elated (some parents are just relieved it's not a negative phone call), and the teachers feel proud.

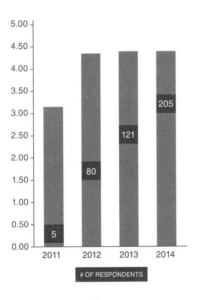

FIGURE 7.2 | TEACHER PHONE CALLS TO PARENTS
Hunt Elementary School, Jackson, MI:
Overall Parent Satisfaction Results and
Number of Parents Completing Survey

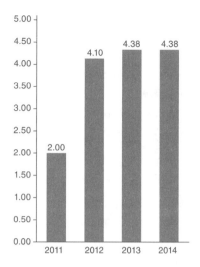

FIGURE 7.3 | TEACHER PHONE CALLS TO PARENTS
Hunt Elementary School, Jackson, MI:
Overall Results on Positive Communication
about Child to Parents

Assess

Assessment on the Execution Flywheel connects an end to a new be-ginning—it's where we use measures to establish a new starting point. We assess progress in two ways. First are the *summative* or *lag* measures, which represent the result we are trying to achieve. The initial pillar measures that define success are lag measures. Second, we continuously assess progress-monitoring measures, usually identified in the form of *lead* measures, which determine the value of the actions we take toward achieving measurable goals. These measures predict how well we will do in achieving results, and they are directly influenced by people work-ing toward the goal.

Here's a simple example to show the difference between lag and lead measures. Let's say we want to lose 20 pounds in 10 weeks. Our **lag measure** is the 20-pound weight-loss goal within the given time. What **lead measures** will help predict and influence our ability to hit that goal? The trainer tells us we must exercise for 45 minutes at a time for three days a week, expending 150 calories at each session, and reduce our caloric intake to 1,500 calories a day. These lead measures are gauged along the way. If we are moving toward the goal by losing an average of two pounds a week, we continue. If we fall behind, we need to adjust our activity.

During the assessment phase, we determine how well the progress-monitoring measures predicted the overall success of achieving the annual measures. We mark our achievement levels for each goal using a green, yellow, red (GYR) process (green equals achieve goal; yellow equals stay the same or slightly improve; red equals decline from the starting point). We also assess the extent to which our core strategic actions helped the school district achieve the overall goals. For goals achieved, we celebrate success; for those not achieved, we reflect on why not. We ask questions such as these: "Did everyone execute the strategy with fidelity?" "Did we provide the training, support, and resources for people to be successful?" "What parts of the strategy worked?" "What parts failed?"

As coaches to our partners, we provide an external lens to the assessment process that informs leadership of how to make the best decisions to maximize performance. We engage leaders to use the results to celebrate wins, identify gaps, and share their own mistakes. Before we shift blame for why something is not working or why we haven't achieved a goal, we have to hold up the mirror and reflect on our own behaviors. Leaders become better when they use evidence and research to help them get better.

Before we shift blame for why something is not working or why we haven't achieved a goal, we have to hold up the mirror and reflect on our own behaviors.

Building Motivation for Change

For most districts we partner with, reading achievement at the elementary school level is a priority student-achievement outcome measure. We've witnessed millions of dollars being spent on program after program with little, if any, improvement as a result. School districts buy programs and accompanying training but do little follow-up to ensure compliance and quality execution by leaders and teachers. Leaders may not know the program well enough to determine what it looks like when applied with high fidelity, and they may not have communicated the reason for the change or selection. For that matter, all the leaders may not even buy into the decision. Teachers don't understand why they need to change, so they may not comply. If they comply, they might have only a lukewarm commitment to the new program, or they may simply continue with their usual, familiar practices. However, we find that most teachers apply a new strategy or approach well when they know why the new strategy is important, when they see that the results will be positive for students, and when they understand why the approach was chosen. Therefore, creating and communicating a measurable goal with aligned actions accompanied by lead measures builds the motivation to enact change.

Summary

Driving performance depends on the extent to which leaders execute the strategic actions well. The Execution Flywheel starts with diagnosis. If we start with the correct diagnosis and then act, coach, validate, and assess, we end up with a system with high consistency, reliability, efficiency, and effectiveness that achieves key results. This is what it means to hardwire excellence—to create a truly sustainable culture of excellence in which leaders apply a process that maximizes performance.

We end this chapter with a short scenario to illustrate how the Execution Flywheel works in practice. Let's say a school district is getting numerous complaints about buses not picking up children on time in the morning.

Diagnose: The Transportation Supervisor reviews the route maps and pickup times and completes an analysis to determine which buses have late pickups. A more thorough analysis takes place when the supervisor asks various groups to determine why it's happening. It is determined that late pickups over the past 90 days averaged 22 percent. The goal this year is to reduce this number to 5 percent.

Act: Using the evidence gathered, the supervisor and his team determine a specific action they believe will reduce the number of late pickups. Also, the Transportation Department implements a system to continuously monitor on-time morning pickups. A person in the department is charged with monitoring the system. Most of the late pickups are found to be associated with bus drivers starting late and the use of substitute bus drivers.

Coach: Using a team of high-performing bus drivers, the Transportation Department creates a standard of practice for starting and ending times and trains each bus driver. More experienced bus drivers with good on-time bus driving records coach those with less experience or with poor on-time statistics. They coach those drivers on best practices to achieve the target and give them plenty of practice opportunities to demonstrate their performance levels.

Validate: All bus drivers are required to enter start times into a new mobile GPS that tracks the bus routes for each pickup. At the end of the routes, the bus drivers receive a report indicating late morning pickup times.

Assess: For each late pickup, the bus driver records why it occurred so that at the end of certain time periods, this information can be assessed to determine if routes or times should be adjusted. At the end of each 45-day cycle, overall measures are compared to the 5 percent goal, and at year end, the annual average is calculated to determine if the goal has been achieved.

SECTION THREE:

APPLICATION

Leaders use the Evidence-Based Leadership^SM framework to apply the performance-maximizing concepts presented in earlier sections of the book. The framework focuses on three areas: aligned goals, aligned behaviors, and aligned processes. Chapters 8 through 13 address these areas. The organizer below highlights what's ahead in each chapter.

SECTION 3 CHAPTER HIGHLIGHTS		
ALIGNED GOALS: GOALS AND SKILLS		
CHAPTER 8	Organizational Performance	Chapter 8 describes how leaders create system EBL scorecards. Our first step is working with superintendents, senior executive teams, and the school board to create an EBL district scorecard. School and department leaders use that scorecard to create their unit scorecards in a three-step process. Leaders first collectively define six to eight key measures that define system-wide success and that align to the pillar areas. Second, leaders identify progress-monitoring measures for each pillar measure. Third, they determine one or two strategic actions for each measure. The actions are used to determine development needs for leaders and staff.
CHAPTER 9	Individual Performance	The selected key measures on the scorecard are used to determine how leaders will be held accountable and evaluated. Chapter 9 provides an overview of how to select the right goals, measures, weights, and scales when creating leader evaluations.
CHAPTER 10	Leader Development	Chapter 10 provides an overview of a leadership development structure that has proven successful over the years. We discuss why and how to apply Leadership Development Institutes to engage leaders in continuous learning aligned to the key measures and strategies.

ALIGNED BEHAVIOR: PERFORMANCE MANAGEMENT

CHAPTER 11	Always Behaviors[SM]	Chapters 11 and 12 focus on essential skills leaders must gain to create a work environment that supports teachers and staff in achieving their highest potential. Chapter 11 introduces behaviors that foster employee engagement.
CHAPTER 12	Performance Management	Chapter 12 focuses on how leaders conduct performance conversations with employees. The chapter covers conversations for three performance levels: high, solid, and low or subpar performance. This is the breakthrough part of the framework. If subpar performance is not addressed, people lose their momentum and the organization's performance declines.

ALIGNED PROCESSES: PROGRAMS, PROCESSES, AND TECHNOLOGY

CHAPTER 13	Process Improvement	Chapter 13 only touches on approaches for improving processes, but it reinforces the need for process improvement to maximize performance. One key theme of the book is stressed as part of process improvement: to sustain results, it's essential that leaders validate compliance and the quality of selected strategic actions.

Chapter Eight:

Organizational Performance: The Organizational Scorecard

FIGURE 8.1 | EVIDENCE-BASED LEADERSHIP^{SM} EDUCATIONAL FRAMEWORK

Chapters 8 through 13 focus on how leaders apply the Evidence-Based Leadership[SM] framework in school systems. This chapter and the next two focus on the aligned goals component of the framework. As shown in Figure 8.1, organizations achieve high performance when leaders: (1) create the right goals with the right accountability and the right leadership development, (2) apply the right approach for managing individual human performance, and (3) select the right processes, programs, and technology to accelerate the continuous systems-improvement process. Let's start with best practices for planning and setting goals.

Most leaders of school systems work with their teams to develop strategic plans that include mission, vision, core values, and goals. Any strategic plan's value depends on the level of definition, precision, and direction it offers for achieving the most important results. How does your district use a strategic plan to determine the outcomes that define success? How does the district align leadership to strategic actions to achieve these outcomes? And how is progress measured along the way?

The K–12 Evidence-Based Leadership framework helps leaders refine strategic plans and create district, school, and department scorecards that include core pillar goals and measures. To begin, school board members, the superintendent, and the senior team create the district scorecard by determining six to eight core measures aligned to student achievement, workforce engagement, service to employees and families, and financial efficiencies for supporting student achievement. Scorecards include annual results measures (lag measures) aligned to the core pillars, few and focused strategic actions for each measurable goal, and progress-monitoring measures (lead measures) to determine the success of actions applied to achieve goals. The district scorecard is then used to create aligned district, department, and school scorecards.

Figure 8.2 outlines the aligned goals part of the Evidence-Based Leadership framework. This part of the framework considers goal setting, planning, and accountability at the organizational level and the individual level. Chapter 8 focuses on the organization and Chapter 9 on the individual.

FIGURE 8.2 | EVIDENCE-BASED LEADERSHIP K–12 FRAMEWORK SYSTEM AND INDIVIDUAL FLOW

SYSTEM LEVEL	INDIVIDUAL LEVEL
Results Measures (Lag Measures Aligned to Pillars)	→ Individual Performance Evaluations (Weights and Measures)
Progress-Monitoring Measures (Lead Measures) Green · Yellow · Red Priority Strategic Actions per Measure Short-Cycle Strategies and Execution Plans	→ Individual Action Plans Goals · Actions Progress (Green · Yellow · Red)
Professional Development (Aligned to Actions)	→ Individual Development Plan

Let's start with the organizational scorecard. Here's how it works. The superintendent, the leadership team, and the board offer input into the development of the district scorecard. School and department leaders then use it to work with their teams to create unit (school and department) scorecards. The district scorecard is applied to all leaders, including those in academic and operational units. As previously noted, the core pillars for school districts are student achievement, people, service, and finance. Most executive team leaders contribute to the results associated with these four pillars. Since student achievement is the core business of school districts, we suggest that all leaders own a portion of the student achievement goals. For example, a cafeteria manager at an elementary school would include measures associated with elementary student achievement. The work of cafeteria employees has an indirect yet important influence on student achievement. The majority of the operational leaders' scorecards will include core measures that directly align to their job responsibilities, which are measured on the Quality Indicator Pillar. In transportation, for example, the most important results may be buses arriving on time to school in the morning. So the transportation director's scorecard would include this measure under the Quality Indicator Pillar.

Let's take a closer look at how operational areas complete the Quality Indicator portion of the scorecard. Figure 8.3 shows a sample scorecard for a director of human resources. There are two core measures under Quality Indicators. Each has a progress-monitoring measure used to track short-cycle results and one strategic action that employees can take to achieve the goals. So, leaders use this tool to make sure employees have the skill sets and the resources needed to do the job.

FIGURE 8.3	QUALITY INDICATORS ON A SAMPLE SCORECARD FOR A HUMAN RESOURCES DIRECTOR		
	QUALITY (INDICATORS)	**EXAMPLE**	
RESULT MEASURES	· Metrics aligned to each department's job responsibilities that represent efficient and effective services that provide the operational efficiencies to influence student achievement.	· Improve vacancy-to-hire rate by 20%. · Paperwork processing turnaround time reduced from 4 weeks to 2 weeks.	
PROGRESS MONITORING MEASURES	· Lead measures aligned to department metrics.	· Daily tracking of vacancy to hire with monthly rates reported. · Daily tracking of paperwork processing time with monthly rates reported.	
STRATEGIC ACTIONS	· Strategic actions aligned to department metrics.	· Assign a team to report to the director to oversee vacancy-to-hire rate and apply the improvement plan as well as include in the team's personnel evaluation. · Apply the new software paperless system (train summer with full implementation in fall).	

Menomonee Falls: Taco Nacho Day

Ruth Ann Kiley-Wiedmeyer is the director of food services in Menomonee Falls School District in Wisconsin. As part of the food service team's short-cycle planning and results process, Ruth Ann's team focused on meals-per-man-hour, meaning that the team wanted to reduce man-hours and be more efficient. The cafeteria team found that Taco Nacho Day seemed to take more man-hours than other menu options. It was a popular option, however, so the team wanted to keep the day. They identified the time-consuming part as scraping cheese off the lunch trays, so they decided to put the cheese in a small paper boat, which reduced cleanup time. The cost of the boats was far less than the cost of the time needed to scrape the trays. Ruth Ann then reallocated the man-hours to other areas, which reduced overall costs. She did not have to replace or hire additional help, and no one lost hours of work. The district's goal is to reallocate cost savings into classrooms with teachers and students.

Now let's focus our attention on a sample district scorecard.

Sample District Scorecard

Figure 8.4 is a sample district scorecard that shows alignment of three major components. The first component shows the six to eight key drivers or results measures that define success for a given year, which most likely align with three- to five-year district goals. As we are developing scorecards with district leaders, we ask, "What single measure will define success for the district three years out?" A common answer is, "We strive for all our students to be college- and career-ready." Then we ask, "What do we need to measure to determine if we achieve success?" "How do we define success in a given year; in other words, what moves the district closer to the overall goal?" We then explore the pillar areas that influence success: people, service, and finance. Our goal is to agree on six to eight key measures that drive decision-making throughout the year.

The second component focuses on progress-monitoring measures (lead measures). For each result measure, leadership teams define the most important measures that track performance every 60 to 75 days. These measures should serve as the best predictors for achieving the results measures. Remember Covey's dictum: The fewer, the better. Less is more as we create our scorecards. The same holds true as leaders select the most important strategic actions to achieve the measurable goals. These actions help determine where development needs to occur for leaders and others.

> The fewer, the better. Less is more as we create our scorecards.

The district scorecard is used to create scorecards for all schools and departments. The department directors and school leaders will look at the district expectations and align their unit's goals and actions to the district scorecard. All leaders will be working with their teams to achieve their goals, which in turn will help the district. Therefore, leaders and staff know what it takes to achieve success, how progress will be tracked, and what teams and individuals will do to maximize performance.

FIGURE 8.4 | SAMPLE SCHOOL DISTRICT SCORECARD

STUDENT ACHIEVEMENT	SERVICE	PEOPLE	FINANCE
Every student will be college- and career-ready.	Provide high-quality service to internal and external "customers."	Provide a high-quality work environment so every employee can perform at the highest levels.	Gain the highest return on dollars invested and create operational efficiencies.

ANNUAL RESULTS MEASURES

STUDENT ACHIEVEMENT	SERVICE	PEOPLE	FINANCE
· Increase from 0% to 25% of schools in the district that will achieve the "significantly exceeds" level on the state report card (3-year goal is 100%). · Increase average ACT score from 20.2 to 21.4 (3-year goal is 23.2).	· Improve parent satisfaction from 4.28 to 4.33. · Improve district support services from 4.21 to 4.31.	· Improve employee engagement from 3.99 to 4.09. · Realize 20% improvement in employee attendance.	· Gain a return on student achievement at schools scoring in the lowest 25% in third-grade reading and eighth-grade math to the dollars invested in a teacher coach at each school (reading for elementary and math for middle school). · Improve operational efficiencies to reinvest savings into instruction (from $75,000 to $175,000).

STUDENT ACHIEVEMENT	SERVICE	PEOPLE	FINANCE
Every student will be college- and career-ready.	Provide high-quality service to internal and external "customers."	Provide a high-quality work environment so every employee can perform at the highest levels.	Gain the highest return on dollars invested and create operational efficiencies.

PROGRESS MONITORING MEASURES			
· Implement 60-day benchmark tests. · Monitor failures at each grading cycle for all students. · Improve attendance from 88% to 92%.	· Every 60 days, survey random parents on three questions; focus on positive feedback to parents. · Document the number of positive phone calls home made by leaders and teachers. · Collect district support services survey scores every 45 days.	· Rounding logs—total number of employees rounding with. · Attendance of employees. · Retention of employees.	· Dollars spent aligned to academic progress-monitoring measures every 45 days. · Quarterly cost savings by department.

STRATEGIC ACTIONS			
· Implement Plan, Do, Study, Act (PDSA) for all grades; apply a common process for data retreats by leaders at all schools. · Assign math and literacy coaches for lowest-performing/high-risk schools	· Teacher calls every parent before school year, before winter break, and before end of year. · School makes 3 to 5 positive phone calls home each week. · Senior leadership team rounds on district department leaders.	· Round with employee monthly. · Schedule performance conversations for all employees throughout the year. · Apply the process for writing and sending thank-you notes.	· Select high-performing teachers, certify their skills through training, and monitor each coach's progress by evaluating student achievement every 60 days through benchmark assessments. · Cascade specific efficiency actions to departments.

Now we'll take a closer look at each pillar for this school district.

Student Achievement Pillar Sample

The superintendent and executive team decided that over the next three years, they wanted every school to achieve the Exceeds Expectations category on the state report card. Currently, all schools are at the level below that. For the first year, the goal is for 25 percent of the schools to achieve the target level. For this district, the goal was determined to be a challenging yet reasonable one, with the understanding that more aggressive growth will occur in years two and three. In addition, district leaders and the board made raising ACT scores a district priority.

The leadership team then decided on the best progress-monitoring measures, or predictive indicators, of student achievement. The three measures include a student achievement benchmark test, documented student failures, and attendance. The triangulation of these three data points gives the leaders a quick check of how the district is trending toward the overall goal.

The team spent considerable time deciding on the best strategies to produce the highest results—the 20 percent of actions that would yield 80 percent of the results. They answered the question, What do we want standardized across the district that will help us achieve our goals?

Finally, they focused on supporting middle and high school students in their quest to attend college. The focus on improvement areas, such as closing the performance gap and focusing attention on solid and high-performing students achieving higher ACT scores, positions the district for achieving its overall goal: all students being ready for college and career.

The School District of Janesville's "Exceeds Expectations" Press Release

Each year Wisconsin schools receive one of five accountability ratings on their state report cards. These ratings are based on a score from these four priority areas: Student Achievement, Student Growth, Closing Gaps, and On Track to Graduation and Postsecondary Readiness.

The School District of Janesville (SDJ) scored in the Exceeds Expectations category, with a 74.8 overall accountability score on the first Wisconsin District Report Card in 2012–2013 (Figure 8.5). Based on how well schools perform in priority areas, schools and districts receive an accountability score on a scale of 0 to 100. The district report card is calculated for the district as a whole.

The 2012–2013 school report cards were also impressive. Two SDJ schools rated Meets Expectations, fourteen were classified as Exceeded Expectations, and one rated Significantly Exceeded Expectations. It was Harrison Elementary School's second year scoring in the Significantly Exceeds Expectations category, the highest distinction available. The report cards signal a new era of school accountability that honors the complex work of schools and focuses on making sure students graduate ready for college and career.

School report cards place a high value on integrating information. They are used to show the public the progress schools are making, and they give direction to schools about ways they can improve student learning. In short, the new system is designed to be both informative and useful.

SIGNIFICANTLY EXCEEDS EXPECTATIONS	83–100
EXCEEDS EXPECTATIONS	73–82.9
MEETS EXPECTATIONS	63–72.9
MEETS FEW EXPECTATIONS	53–62.9
FAILS TO MEET EXPECTATIONS	0–52.9

FIGURE 8.5 | ACCOUNTABILITY RATING—
　　　　　　 SAMPLE FOR THE STATE OF WISCONSIN

Service Pillar Sample

The district leadership is committed to providing superior service to employees and parents. The two key results measures on the district scorecard are parent satisfaction and school leader satisfaction with services offered by district departments. The sample district applies our annual parent satisfaction survey and a district support services survey three times a year. The ultimate goal is for departments to score 4.50 or higher and to set an improvement goal to get there. In this example, the district departments are continuing to improve services, so an improved score represents a measurable goal.

Typically, one of the lowest-scored items on the parent satisfaction survey links to parents receiving positive feedback about their children. Therefore, the specific action and progress-monitoring measures on the scorecard focus on this area. We find that when leaders and staff focus on one thing, it has a multiplier effect. In other words, improvement in one area leads to improvement in other areas.

Parent Satisfaction at Hunt Elementary School, Jackson, Michigan

Principal Raczkowski-Shannon talks about how she led her teachers to better serve parents.

"Our lowest score on the [parent satisfaction] survey was on sending positive notes or making phone calls to parents. It's true—the only time we called home was if there was a problem; there were only negative phone calls. So we asked ourselves, 'What can we do different?'"

Teachers are now required to make five positive phone calls to parents per week. The calls are logged, and the call logs are part of teachers' evaluations.

Identifying a Junior Viking of the Month is one way Hunt Elementary rewards and recognizes students. Posted in every classroom are the expectations for students: "What a Hunt Viking Is" and how to achieve it (a Hunt Viking is a good citizen, has a good academic record, and does certain things at school). When awards are made, parents are invited to the reception.

"We let students and their parents know that we do care about their children," says Principal Raczkowski-Shannon. "We have a flyer posted outside of every classroom or on the door, signed by each teacher, that says, 'Dear Students, I believe in you. I trust in you. You are listened to. You are cared for. You are important. You will succeed. Love, [teacher name].' Parents appreciate this attitude and seeing these signs."

It is evident that Principal Raczkowski-Shannon and the teachers at Hunt Elementary School care about and value their students. They make a difference in the lives of students and their parents.

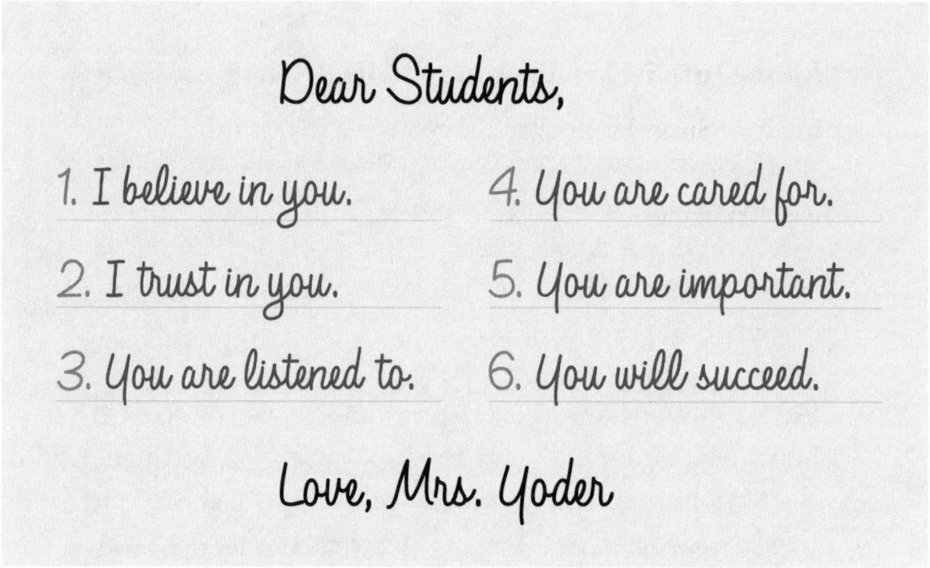

Dear Students,

1. *I believe in you.*   4. *You are cared for.*

2. *I trust in you.*   5. *You are important.*

3. *You are listened to.*   6. *You will succeed.*

Love, Mrs. Yoder

FIGURE 8.6 | SAMPLE COMMITMENT TO STUDENT AND PARENTS FROM HUNT ELEMENTARY SCHOOL, JACKSON, MI

People Pillar Sample

The People Pillar measures leaders' skills in making the workplace environment a "best place to work," so the sample district uses the employee engagement survey to measure this outcome. On this survey, teachers and staff members can provide feedback to leaders about the extent to which they have the resources to do their jobs, how much feedback they receive to help them improve their performance, and whether they are recognized for performing in ways that produce good results.

In the past three years, the district has seen a rise in employee absenteeism. As leaders improve the workplace environment, standardize certain practices, and commit to professional development, the rate of employees showing up for work should improve.

Shout-Outs in Menomonee Falls

One way Superintendent Greco of the Menomonee Falls School District, Menomonee Falls, Wisconsin, improved the workplace environment was by introducing "shout-outs" in monthly newsletters.

Dr. Greco writes, "Enjoy the shout-outs.☺ And thanks for ALL THE SUBMISSIONS!"

- Here's a shout-out to a teacher from a parent:

  "☺ I had no expectation that you would look at and especially reply to work emails while you were on vacation. That's above and beyond. You should have been leaving all this and all of us behind for at least a little while. If the sunset picture is any indication, looks like you had beautiful weather in a gorgeous location. I bet it went by much too quickly. My child really missed you. He hoped he would see you every day. Tonight when he remembered he'd see you tomorrow, he literally jumped for joy. What a wonderful feeling for learning, for school, and for his teacher that you have instilled/inspired in these children! Not an easy task, yet you make it look effortless. Hope you got some rest because my child is FULL of joyful energy waiting to see you tomorrow."

- Here's a shout-out from one staff member to another:

  "☺ Thank you for dropping everything and fixing the fire alarm. The secretary said every time she sees you, you're right on top of everything, quick, and reliable. Thank you!!!!!"

- Here's a shout-out from a principal to two teachers after having a conversation with a school board member:

  "☺ I was talking with one of our school board members today, and she made it a point to compliment both of you on the amazing work you have done developing our FBLA chapter. She also noted your statewide leadership with this association. I share her pride in our FBLA team and our incredible advisors. Thank you both."

- Here's a shout-out to the grounds crew after a long, cold winter in Wisconsin:

  "☺ A big shout-out to the grounds crew team. They have battled the elements in the limited time they have had and made the fields look great. Not only the day-to-day mowing, lining, and putting up nets, but cleanup after games has been the best ever. Thanks, guys, for all you do behind the scenes for Falls soccer and all the sports teams and playing sites."

- A senior team member posted a shout-out to the superintendent:

  "☺ Pat, thank you for your leadership. A lot of good things happening at tonight's board meeting. Great meeting . . . a testament to your leadership in, and around, the whole organization. You continue to IMPRESS, your leadership is APPRECIATED, and I thought you should know!"

Finance Pillar Sample

The finance goal for our sample district focuses on two areas. First, the school board members made a decision to support the investment in reading and math coaches in high-need schools. They want to know if this decision affects student achievement positively. Second, operational leaders set a cost-saving goal so that savings can be reinvested into classrooms with teachers and students. The departments will own this goal (remember Taco Nacho Day!).

Optional Health and Safety Pillar

Some of our partner districts include a Health and Safety Pillar and have adopted the Positive Behavior Intervention and Supports approach. The superintendent establishes an overall district goal that rolls down to all schools. All leaders and teachers are trained to apply a district-wide process for improving behavior.

Scorecards as Communication Tools

Scorecards are the central communication tool that lets everyone know the district's priorities. The department and school scorecards show the unit priorities, and people can see how their actions help the district maximize performance. They can also see how other units focus their attention. This tool shows that we are all in this together and every person has a part.

Scorecards are the central communication tool that lets everyone know the district's priorities.

Parents and community members want to see district and school priorities. Most districts place scorecards on their websites, including goals, measures, actions, and results. In other words, they let people know the *why*, *what*, and *how* of school and department improvement efforts.

The scorecards are the "we're all in it together" tool. They're road maps created with teams. As we track progress, teams celebrate the wins and act to close the performance gaps. Everything is transparent because the name of the game is improvement.

Scorecards as Drivers of a Systems Planning Process

School systems create district scorecards (results measures, progress-monitoring measures, and system-wide strategic actions) and cascade the process to schools and departments. Now the focus turns to leaders, teachers, and staff executing the plan. They know the measurable outcomes and targets to hit along the way.

Planning is nothing new to school districts. Here's what usually occurs. Before the school year, leaders work with their teams to create an annual plan that can be used as a short-cycle planning tool during the year. In some cases, schools have called these types of plans school improvement plans.

Some district departments and schools have their own unique tools and processes for planning. But there's a problem with that: the unit plans may not align to the district ones. This type of planning process tends to cause schools and departments to work in silos (i.e., in isolation, without communication between units). This gets in the way of good organizations becoming great ones. Aligned scorecards offer a process for setting a clear and aligned focus; all arrows point in a common direction. Think of the scorecard as the advance organizer of the school improvement plan.

Planning may be a waste of time unless we use it to continuously review our progress, or do what we call short-cycle planning. Here's our philosophy about short-cycle planning—the time when leaders review progress measures and assess how well the strategic actions are working. Every day counts in schools. Therefore, the greatest value of planning rests with how leaders approach short-cycle planning. We find that 60- to 75-day planning cycles seem to work best, because **every day** within that 60-day window counts. It's essential to have weekly debriefs with teams on which areas are working well and which are trending in the wrong direction. These debriefs don't have to be long and can be done in various ways. Whatever approach leaders use, we always suggest that they give team members the chance to speak. Often, 20- to 30-minute weekly debrief sessions with content teams or grade-level teams work well.

> Planning may be a waste of time unless we use it to continuously review our progress, or do what we call short-cycle planning.

We could write another book simply on short-cycle planning strategies, but that's not the purpose here. Here's the point to remember: **every day** counts, and if we don't have a process for reviewing our goals and evidence showing our progress along the way, too many days will get away from us.

For now, here are a few quick tips on short-cycle planning.

(1) Determine how progress-monitoring measures align with weekly progress toward measurable goals.

(2) Use the results to help you decide on strategies.

(3) Use results on the progress-monitoring measures to report at the end of a short cycle.

(4) Apply a green-yellow-red (GYR) assessment (the Stoplight process) for each goal.

(5) Describe areas that are working well and look for what's causing improvement.

(6) Describe areas not hitting the target and find out why they're not.

(7) Determine if or how areas need adjusting.

(8) Define the next short-cycle priorities and focused measures.

The short-cycle planning process shows where we need to focus our efforts, and it also highlights leadership gaps. In Chapter 10, we focus on a process for developing leaders called Leadership Development Institutes, which we suggest should be used alongside every short-cycle planning session. The most successful leaders have a strong desire to adjust plans when needed and engage in development opportunities to make them better leaders. A model example is the Menomonee Falls School District in Wisconsin. The superintendent, department leaders, and principals come to Leadership Development Institutes ready and eager to reflect, reset, and learn every 45 days during the school year.

School Board Role

School boards play an integral role in setting the organizational direction and defining performance indicators in three major ways. First, they provide insight into the annual results measures as well as long-term goals and measures. Second, they translate these measures into the superintendent's evaluation so that his or her evaluation aligns with the school system results. Third, boards want to know if the funding decisions they made produced student achievement results. Therefore, the superintendent and senior leadership team are responsible for reporting short-cycle results and next-cycle direction to the board.

In addition, we find that board members also want to be developed to be their best. In many of our partner districts, we provide board development sessions focused on Evidence-Based Leadership. We also work with boards as they self-evaluate their contribution to the district and community as well as their productivity as board members. When a school board has a clear picture and has opportunities to view results, even those that are unfavorable, the board becomes a vital member of the school system team. The focus becomes continuous systems improvement every year. As we say, "No matter how well we have achieved, we can always do better." Superintendents, leaders, and boards simply need the right kind of urgency and a deep commitment to excellence.

Summary

This chapter focuses on getting the organizational direction and flow to achieve results. Here are the keys to doing so:

(1) Superintendents and senior leaders, along with school boards, create district scorecards that define the six to eight critical results measures. They serve as the key drivers for defining success in school districts.

(2) Alongside these drivers, leaders create progress-monitoring measures to track system-wide performance. These measures serve as the best predictors we have for achieving results.

(3) Leaders apply a thoughtful, reflective process to define one or two key strategic actions for achieving in each pillar area.

(4) The district scorecard is communicated to all leaders, teachers, and staff in the school district so that everyone knows the direction for the year.

(5) The school and department leaders work with their teams to develop aligned scorecards and cascade the communication of scorecard components to their staff. The scorecards serve as the transparent communication tool for everyone in the school system as well as parents and community members.

(6) District scorecards serve as catalysts for short-cycle planning, which usually occurs every 60 to 75 days. Short-cycle planning focuses on the quality of execution and addresses how teams work together to achieve measurable goals.

The goal development and planning process includes all divisions, departments, and schools in a school system. We work with leaders to align goals and measures that put great focus on fewer strategic actions. The best part is that it makes our work more meaningful and worthwhile.

CHAPTER NINE:

INDIVIDUAL PERFORMANCE: LEADER EVALUATION SYSTEM

FIGURE 9.1 | EVIDENCE-BASED LEADERSHIP^{SM} EDUCATIONAL FRAMEWORK

In this chapter, we continue to examine the key components of the Evidence-Based Leadership^{SM} (EBL) framework and explore how each leader is held accountable for system-wide performance. In the framework (Figure 9.1), we are still focused on goals, but now we are translating organizational goals into individual accountability. Along with leader development (the subject of the next chapter), individual accountability is instrumental in obtaining system-wide outcomes.

The One Thing: Advice from a Baldrige Winner

When it comes to high performance, one of our most striking experiences occurred at the 2010 Malcolm Baldrige Award ceremony. Advocate Good Samaritan Hospital (Downers Grove, Illinois) was a winner that year, and its CEO, Dave Fox, appeared on a panel. Someone asked him, "If you could do only one thing to achieve the high performance that led you to winning the Malcolm Baldrige Award, what would it be?" Without a pause, Dave Fox said, "Making sure you have an objective, metric-driven, weighted evaluation tool."

Dave went on to explain that his senior executive team spent well over 40 hours making sure they chose the right goals for the right individuals, the right metrics, and the right weights. Although that seems like a lot of time, Dave felt they gained back that time throughout the year by establishing a tightly aligned team.

Like Dave Fox, Superintendent JoAnn Sternke of the Pewaukee School District in Wisconsin led her team to win the Malcolm Baldrige Award (in 2013). To show her continued commitment to excellence, she and three other Wisconsin school districts (Kettle Moraine, Muskego Norway, and Oconomowoc) became Studer Education partners during the spring of 2014, working in a collaborative model. To sustain the level of excellence attained in the Pewaukee School District, Dr. Sternke and the other three superintendents know that each leader needs aligned goals and metrics with the right weights to drive continued success.

All organizations want to achieve high performance. As we proved in the high-performing organization study highlighted earlier in the book, when leaders are asked, "What is the key to sustaining high results?" the answer is the alignment of a measurable leader evaluation tool.

Leaders Welcome Objectivity

We estimate that about 99 percent of leaders receive an evaluation that they meet, exceed, or substantially exceed expectations. If leaders are already meeting expectations, why would they want to move to an evaluation tool that could mean their rating will drop?

The willingness to change evaluation systems depends on the performance level of the individual leader. When we work with organizations to apply the EBL evaluation system, we often find that high-performing leaders actually celebrate the fact that they now have an evaluation system that is more objective and weighted.

They particularly like the objective part. Why? Because they know they have been performing at a high level, but too often their evaluation rating is about the same as coworkers who are not achieving comparable results. With an objective, weighted tool, finally they will be clearly recognized for their accomplishments.

So, high performers are excited about the new evaluation tool. A solid performer may have some anxiety, but this quickly dissipates when the metrics are set and the skill set is developed to achieve the metrics. Those who are not achieving results aren't happy, because under an objective and weighted system, they'll no longer be able to get a good evaluation without producing needed outcomes.

Senior leaders might also be nervous. It takes a courageous and value-oriented organization to install an objective evaluation system. Why? Because it shines a blinding spotlight on how well an organization is meeting its goals and living up to its mission. *There is no way to sustain a culture of high performance without having an objective, weighted evaluation system in place.*

> It takes a courageous and value-oriented organization to install an objective evaluation system. It shines a blinding spotlight on how well an organization is meeting its goals and living up to its mission—and it forces people to achieve high performance.

Well-Designed Evaluations Lead to Better Outcomes

As reported in Chapter 2, Studer Group gave our Straight A Leadership survey to more than 34,000 healthcare leaders across the nation and found that organizations with more objective evaluation tools outperform those without such methods. Objective, weighted evaluations drive better outcomes across the board.

The research also showed that leaders identified two barriers or challenges that keep them from achieving results. First, leaders feel they have too many things to do at once. Second, they feel they have too many priorities or are confused about which priorities are highest. In other words, if everything is important, nothing is important. Getting the right number of measurable outcomes a leader needs to address and aligning actions to them allows for prioritization, which is a substantial factor in success.

An evaluation tool that is both objective and weighted remedies both concerns. It ensures that people know *exactly* what they are supposed to accomplish. Not only does this clarity make meeting your organizational goals more likely, but it also relieves anxiety in leaders and staff. Engaged employees at every level want and appreciate clear expectations and priorities.

All too often, leaders can get good evaluations simply by employing certain tactics or behaviors. These tactics may produce results in the short term, but leaders need to be held accountable for outcomes if they are to sustain their success. Objective, weighted evaluations provide the incentive for accountability: by aligning the outcome to the evaluation, leaders get the behavior right.

As a leader, if I'm accountable for the results, I'll not only have to engage in the behavior, but I'll also have to do it effectively and consistently. And if my evaluation is tied to outcomes, I'll figure out a way to sustain the behavior. That is why organizations that implement the right kind of evaluation system achieve the best long-term results.

Setting and Cascading Objective Goals

As described in Chapter 8, effective goal cascading starts with organizational goals, not individual ones. Now we move from organizational goals to individual leader accountability for achieving the goals. In working with organizations around the country, we find hundreds of goals that could be placed on individual leader evaluations. When we look at them all together, however, only six to ten key metrics are critical to achieve in a given performance period (typically the fiscal year). These goals are the key drivers, and from them, subset goals cascade to school and department leaders.

We find that while an organization may have six to ten key metrics, individual leaders should carry between four and eight metrics on their evaluations. This allows them to focus on the most important things via weighting, which we address as one of the best strategies a senior leadership team can use to drive outcomes.

The sample goals included in this chapter show a school district with a system cascade that begins with the superintendent, moves divisionally to the senior leadership team, and ends with school and department leaders. With each level of leadership, the cascading process breaks down the organizational goals into unit goals that are relevant to the leader in each area. Right leader, right goal, right weight. This ensures that the organization's focus carries from senior leaders to their direct reports and so on down the chain of command. Before showing an example of how a superintendent's evaluation cascades to a senior team member and then a principal, let's look at the components of the EBL leader evaluation system.

Goals

As Peter Senge (author of *The Fifth Discipline* and an expert on creating learning organizations) writes, the goal should be difficult enough that people know they have to change, which generates the creative tension necessary to make adjustments. If the goal is too low, people might think they don't really have to change or they can wait until the last minute to start. If it's too high, though, leaders could think it's unattainable.

The organization's leadership ensures that goals are set at the top level and then cascaded down in a relevant and meaningful way to the leaders of each area. First, the organizational goals are set; they should become the superintendent's goals. Then the senior team's goals are set. The school leader's and director's goals are set after that, and finally, the managers' and supervisors' goals are set.

A rule of thumb learned from years of working with school districts is that the closer a leader's evaluation is to 100 percent use of metrics, the greater the chance that the school system will achieve the overall results. Here's what we suggest as we coach partner districts: **no less than 90 percent of the superintendent's and senior team's evaluations should be based on measures aligned to goals.** For others, we recommend no less than 75 percent of the evaluation be based on measurable goals. The challenge of shifting to 100 percent metrics lies in overreliance on supervisor assessments using competencies. Competency assessment is what got us into inflated evaluations of leaders and misalignment of leader evaluation results with student achievement results; that is, more than 90 percent of leaders received the highest level of evaluation when the school district student achievement results were subpar. The EBL leader evaluation system corrects this problem and aligns evaluations with school system goals and measures.

> Competency assessment is what got us into inflated evaluations of leaders and misalignment of leader evaluation results with student achievement results; that is, more than 90 percent of leaders received the highest level of evaluation when the school district student achievement results were subpar.

Competencies and standards are important for leadership, but we have seen that competency-based evaluations don't drive results. An organization has to hold leaders accountable for metrics and outcomes to sustain good results and move the mark.

The Metrics

Once we've completed the first step in setting the measurable and objective goals for individual evaluations, we identify the associated numeric values and the scale for those goals. Over the past three decades, several studies, including one by Studer Group in healthcare organizations, have analyzed typical levels of performance in organizations. Like the other studies, the Studer Group research showed that 34 percent of people are high performers, 58 percent are solid performers, and 8 percent are subpar or low performers. Our recommended approach to manage and drive performance aligns to the findings about how performance plays out in most organizations. We use a 5-point scale and define the range of metrics at each level for leaders who are trying to improve performance as well as for those already achieving at high levels who want to sustain high performance. For each goal, a leader creates an associated scale using the guidelines in Figure 9.2.

FIGURE 9.2 | GUIDELINES FOR CREATING SCALES

	IMPROVING PRINCIPLES	SUSTAINING HIGH PERFORMANCE
5	Super stretch goal	Exceptionally exceeding high performance
4	Stretch goal	Exceeding high performance
3	Challenging goal	High performance
2	Stay the same or higher but not hitting goal	Below expected performance
1	Declining from prior year's performance	Well below expected performance

At the end of a performance period, it's typical for an organization to have an overall evaluation score of 3 to 3.5. Achieving this level of performance means the goal setting was probably accurate—achievable and not too low. If the organization is hitting the high 4s at the conclusion of the performance period, either (a) continued spectacular growth was achieved, or (b) the goals were not set correctly.

The nice part about this process is that leaders can keep getting great evaluations for sustained high performance. It's okay if they score a 5 year after year if their school or department is achieving measurable results. When you're performing well, sometimes it's acceptable—even great—to maintain your current performance. This process is just as much about recognition for sustained performance as it is about moving the mark in areas in which your organization isn't doing well.

Prioritization

When we look at organizations that struggle with too many priorities, we find that *"weighting"* goals is usually what's missing.

When we look at organizations that struggle with too many priorities, we find that *"weighting"* goals is usually what's missing.

Weighting the goals is the real magic of this process. Our experience shows that a leader who has eight unweighted goals will achieve six of them well and the other two not at all.

Most likely the two goals that are not achieved are still extremely important to the organization; otherwise, they wouldn't be part of the eight in the first place. However, at evaluation time, the leader will receive an evaluation that's "good" or even one that shows goals have been exceeded to some extent. Six out of eight isn't bad, right? But what if those two missed goals are vitally important?

Organizations that don't apply weighting can send the wrong message about priorities. If a leader hits six out of eight goals yet is given a good evaluation at year end, the message can be that it's okay to miss two goals. So in the future, the leader might focus on the six goals that resulted in the good evaluation and not so much on the two that were not met—even if they were told to focus more on those two over time.

Now let's adjust the scenario by applying weights. If one of the eight goals is weighted 30 percent out of 100 percent, and the other seven are weighted at 10 percent each, that leader knows for certain which one is the most important goal. Let's say a leader has five goals: one is weighted 30 percent, one is 20 percent, and the other three goals are divided up to equal the remaining 50 percent. In this case, too, the leader knows which metrics will most powerfully drive the overall evaluation score.

Not every leader's evaluation will look the same, even when their goals are aligned. As indicated earlier, a key leverage point in the leader evaluation process is the movement of the weights by leader and metric (Figure 9.3). Here's a typical rule of thumb for weights: a goal weighted at 10 percent means you are aware of it; a goal weighted at 20 percent means you focus on it, and a goal with a weight of 30 percent is perceived as urgent.

FIGURE 9.3	WEIGHTING OF GOALS		
10%	**20%**	**30%**
Awareness	Focus	Urgency

Consider applying more or less weight based on a leader's skills or past performance. If a leader has a high-volume unit and her turnover is very high, the weight on her turnover metric would be higher than that of another leader with a small unit and lower turnover.

Figure 9.4 shows the weighting of the same goal for three leaders. Leader A has a turnover of 20.5 percent, which is considerably higher than Leader C, whose turnover is 12 percent. One could apply a higher weight (30 percent) to the turnover metric for Leader A because of the need for improvement in this area. In addition to baseline, a leader might also take into account the size of the department or volume when creating these weights.

FIGURE 9.4	SETTING WEIGHTS		
ORGANIZATIONAL GOAL: Decrease organizational turnover from 18% to 14% as measured by HR report by FY end.			
	LEADER A	**LEADER B**	**LEADER C**
CURRENT DEPARTMENTAL TURNOVER	20.5%	16.2%	12%
WEIGHT	30%	20%	10%

Prioritization matters in evaluating leader performance. Using heavy weights with evaluation metrics is one of the largest levers organizational leadership can pull to move performance on a leadership team.

Once the metrics and weights for each goal are set, the priorities become clear to the leader. The end-of-year annual evaluation will be a score between 1 and 5 and will be calculated by multiplying that score by the weight and adding to get the total evaluation score. Assuming challenging goals are set at level 3, leaders who achieve the goals and are performing at a solid level could receive a score between 2.75 and 3.50. As scores go up, the achievement moves toward hitting the stretch goals. Overall leader scores lower than a 2.0 average need some prescriptive attention.

We illustrate with a sample superintendent evaluation, showing how the goals and weights cascade to the senior leader who supervises high school principals and then to a high school principal. Let's take the student achievement goal as an example. The superintendent's evaluation includes one overall district student achievement score from the state report card grade for the district. The director of high schools owns three core measures that influence the state report card grade at the high school level. The director then owns the average of the three district high schools in the school system, whereas each high school principal owns the three measures associated with his or her school and with varying weights assigned to the measures. The highest weights are assigned to areas of greatest need for each principal. Figure 9.5 shows the alignment of the EBL leader evaluation system from superintendent to high school director to one of the high school principals for the Student Achievement Pillar. The total weight of this pillar ranges from 50 to 60 percent. The remaining pillars (service, people, and finance) would carry weights that bring the total to 100 percent.

LEADER	GOAL AND MEASURE FOR STUDENT ACHIEVEMENT PILLAR	WEIGHT	SCALE
FIGURE 9.5 SAMPLE LEADER EVALUATION CASCADED			
Superintendent	Increase number of schools exceeding expectations on state report card from 9 to 11 schools (out of 15 total schools)	50%	5 = 15 schools 4 = 13 to 14 3 = 11 to 12 2 = 9 to 10 1 = Below 9
Director of high schools	Improve average district ACT scores from 21.8 to 22.5	20%	5 = Above 23.6 4 = 23.1 to 23.6 3 = 22.5 to 23 2 = 21.8 to 22.4 1 = Below 21.8
	Increase average graduation rate from 82% to 84%	30%	5 = Above 86% 4 = 85.1% to 86% 3 = 84% to 85% 2 = 82% to 83.9% 1 = Below 82%
	Increase average passage rate of end-of-course tests from 74% to 78%	10%	5 = Above 82% 4 = 80.1% to 84% 3 = 78% to 80% 2 = 74% to 77.9% 1 = Below 74%
Jebson High School principal	Improve school ACT scores from 19.2 to 20	30%	5 = Above 21.6 4 = 21.1 to 21.6 3 = 20 to 21 2 = 19.2 to 19.9 1 = Below 19.2
	Increase average graduation rate from 83% to 85%	10%	5 = Above 87% 4 = 86.1% to 87% 3 = 85% to 86% 2 = 83% to 84.9% 1 = Below 83%
	Increase school passage rate of end-of-course tests from 72% to 76%	20%	5 = Above 82% 4 = 80.1% to 84% 3 = 76% to 80% 2 = 72% to 75.9% 1 = Below 72%

Equity Review and Goal Auditing

It's important to ensure alignment across the entire organization. The equity review process validates that the right goals are in place with the right weights for the right leaders and that the individual goals work toward the larger good of the organization. In Phase 1 of the equity review, it is recommended that the superintendent review all evaluations and metrics with the senior leadership team so that each senior leader sees the others' goals and discusses them together, asking questions such as, "What are the priority metrics for each person?" "What level of urgency are they communicating to their division?" "What cross-division support is needed to achieve the outcomes?"

After this work, it's time to cascade goals across the organization through middle management. Also, if this piece is completed first, senior leaders have their metrics and weights set, thus their prioritization and urgency can cascade appropriately to those in their divisions who will help drive the outcomes.

Phase 2 of the equity review incorporates the senior leader review of the layers under them to ensure alignment and focus. This type of transparent communication and review will begin to break down silos (divisions between departments) and reveal issues that need addressing.

Let's say that during the review it is noted that one of the department directors responsible for hiring does not have a goal of managing processing time for hiring new teachers, and this is a known barrier to attracting high-quality people. The HR director knows that without this goal, the quality of the teaching workforce could be jeopardized, ultimately affecting student achievement goals. By reviewing the goals, the HR director includes this goal on her evaluation and presents it to her team as a focus of the upcoming performance period.

The equity review gives the senior leadership team the opportunity to address not only what's there but also what's missing. They understand the items they are expected to achieve as a senior leadership team—those items were determined before the equity review—so now they know where to spend time ensuring that the individual goals of the leaders support the senior leaders' larger objectives and goals. The equity review shows clear goals and measures for which senior leaders, directors, principals, and managers are accountable, as well as the weighted priorities.

Individual Action Plans: The Key to Development

Monitoring progress is one thing, but we in education are what we call "full-plate people." Our plates were full a few years ago, and since then, somehow even more responsibilities have been piled on. The fact is that anyone who works in education will always have more than enough responsibilities. The individual action plan focuses on how individual leaders can map out their actions to achieve the specified goals, so they know where to focus. It also helps supervisors engage in meaningful conversations with individuals that focus on their performance aligned to the measurable goals that define success.

We learned about action plans when we were high school teachers working with special education students. As you know, we call them individual education plans (IEPs). Every 90 days, we would sit down with the parents and talk about goals for the student to meet during the next 90 days. Obviously, if one waits for a one-time meeting at the end of the year, it's too late to help the student. Likewise, if there was only a beginning-of-the-year meeting, there would be no way to adjust the plan based on how well it was working in practice to successfully meet the goals.

An individual action plan (sometimes called an interim review) is a tool designed to manage dialogue between a leader and his or her supervisor on progress toward goals and to specify actions to achieve those goals. Remember, we're talking about consistent execution of the tactic—*always*, not *sometimes* or *usually*. The interim review allows leaders to identify what's in place to achieve the results on the evaluation and helps them maintain awareness of their priorities. It also serves as a planning tool for the leader, so that efforts to achieve annual goals do not become a last-minute scramble. Finally, the individual action plan facilitates the establishment of interim goals to create results and generate excitement to help the leader push to the next level.

An individual action plan, which is created at the beginning of each semester, lists the annual goals, short-cycle goals, and specific action steps (or tactics) needed to achieve results as defined by the goals.

Leaders start by planning with the end in mind. To achieve level 3, 4, or 5 performance for a particular metric, they work with their supervisors to create individual goals that set them up to exceed the anticipated target by year's end. At the end of the semester, leaders and supervisors meet to review the progress of the semester. From there, they work together to revise the individual action plan for the next semester and define the next goals and tactics. In school districts, we recommend that senior leaders hold a meeting every year in August or September, December or January, and May or June to monitor progress and set the stage for the next semester. The structure of this meeting includes the supervisor hearing from leaders on performance areas that are working well and those needing improvement. The trending results on their unit's scorecards and their individual evaluations inform the discussion. These meetings help leaders know what is expected, gain support where needed, and keep their actions focused on achieving the goals.

Summary

It takes a courageous team to do what we have outlined in this chapter. Objective, weighted evaluation systems truly challenge leaders and leave little room for guesswork on how well they are performing. However, once such a system has been installed, the organization has accomplished a tremendous amount (Figure 9.6).

FIGURE 9.6 │ OBJECTIVE EVALUATION ACCOMPLISHMENTS
WEIGHTED, OBJECTIVE EVALUATION SYSTEMS HELP ORGANIZATIONS DO THE FOLLOWING:

• Create a clear set of objective goals that are understood by all leaders	• Break down silos
• Weight the goals in a way that aligns with organizational priorities	• Connect clearly on what outcomes are to be achieved
• Align the goals so there is consistency throughout the organization	• Cascade goals through the entire organization
	• Develop leaders through individual action plans

Once the leader evaluation tools are set, we've really opened up a clear path to where we want to go next, which is leadership skill development. When leaders know how they are going to be held accountable, they tend to get extremely hungry for information on how to improve their skills and what best practices they can implement to achieve these goals.

We've all heard the saying that when the student is ready, the teacher appears. The objective evaluation system gets the student ready.

When the student is ready, the teacher appears. The objective evaluation system gets the student ready.

CHAPTER TEN:

LEADER DEVELOPMENT: CREATING STRONG LEADERS TO KEEP US UNSETTLED

FIGURE 10.1 | EVIDENCE-BASED LEADERSHIP℠ EDUCATIONAL FRAMEWORK

Leader development is the next foundational element of the EBL framework. Successful organizations need a dependable process for educating their leaders and enhancing the skills needed to drive organizational outcomes. Once the objective evaluation system is in place, leaders will be trying to acquire the skills they need to achieve their goals and improve their leadership performance.

The Straight A Leadership Assessment asks, "How well does your current leader training prepare you to lead for success in your organization today?" The data from our study show that leaders typically answer with a "fair" response, and fair just isn't good enough for creating a culture of high performance.

As the external environment becomes increasingly difficult, leaders *must* enhance their skills. At the end of the last chapter, we repeated the famous saying, "When the student is ready, the teacher appears." Well, the ever-changing external environment is forcing more and more "students" into readiness—and it's up to organizations to step in and fill the role of teacher.

As the external environment becomes increasingly difficult, leaders must enhance their skills.

Factors such as technology changes, state accountability, and the rising cost of labor make it imperative that organizations continuously assess what leaders need to know to stay out in front of change. There is no perfect way to build skills. In fact, an organization needs to provide an array of skill development options for leaders and employees at all levels. However, there are fundamentals to be aware of, and this chapter will explore them.

One of the challenges we all face is to stay close to the external environment and to know what is coming (also expressed as "seeing around corners"). The corner we saw around years ago was state grading systems for school districts and schools. The vision of old is today's reality. Here's an example.

As we go into the next school year, our partner districts are challenged by not knowing how states are going to compare state tests from past years to newly developed tests that align to a different set of standards influenced by the Common Core Standards. Whether or not a state adopts the Common Core Standards, all states are modifying their assessments. We've shifted from focusing on state tests to guide student achievement outcomes to asking this question of leaders, "In the next three years, what measure will determine if your school district is successful?" We hear a consistent answer: "We want our students to be ready for college and careers." So we talk about variables of student achievement that serve as the best measures to get districts closer to this goal.

A good understanding of the changing external environment is vital to skill development. All school systems need to prepare leaders and staff to operate effectively in the new world that waits around the corner.

A good understanding of the changing external environment is vital to skill development.

Fundamental Leadership Skills

Leader development begins with the senior leadership team looking closely at the desired outcomes and goals of their organization. Based on what they want to achieve, they can determine what skills are needed from every leader in order to attain those outcomes.

Most leaders need certain fundamental skills. We share an exercise based on those skills, which was developed by working with senior leaders and guiding them through a leadership skill gap and opportunity analysis. It is a quick, easy, and cost-effective way to identify the skill gaps in an organization and to build awareness of the need for investment in training and development.

Using a blank Foundational Leadership Skill Matrix like the one in Figure 10.2, the senior leadership team discusses leader skills and ranks themselves on a scale of 1 to 10 in their proficiency at each skill listed:

FIGURE 10.2 | FOUNDATIONAL LEADERSHIP SKILL MATRIX

SKILL SET DESCRIPTION	EXECUTIVE TEAM	PRINCIPAL AND DIRECTOR	MANAGER SUPERVISOR
Managing change	7	6	6
Running effective meetings	9	7	7
Managing financial resources	8	8	7
Answering tough questions so as to not create a we/they culture	10	7	5
Selection of talent	9	7	6
Development of talent	6	7	7
Critical thinking	9	8	8
Removing underperforming employees	6	6	6
Understanding the external environment	10	8	7
Managing up the positive, the solution, and the decision	9	6	6
Improving processes	9	8	8
Communicating	7	7	7

In the example in Figure 10.2, the senior leadership team members give themselves a 10 in the area of understanding the external environment. This makes sense because the skill is so vital to their job. On the other hand, they do not rank themselves as high in development of talent. Next, the senior leadership team ranks the leadership layers who report to them. (Depending on the size of the organization, there may be more or fewer layers than identified on the matrix provided.)

The exercise allows the senior executives to clearly see the areas where they're weaker—recall the "development of talent" example—

than those who report to them. Since senior leaders are role models, they'll know it's time to reduce that skill gap and become more effective and consistent in this vital area.

The matrix will also show where leaders below the senior level need to focus. Let's say that senior leaders ranked themselves high in talent selection, but the supervisors were weak in that area. Because the supervisors and managers do most of the hiring, this is a red flag. Now selection of talent has been identified as a critical focus area for supervisors and managers.

Along with the fundamentals, we've found that, across the board, education leaders seem to need skill development in two areas: creating best-place-to-work environments and applying service excellence with employees, students, parents, and community members. As a core offering, we provide tactical leader development to focus on these deficiencies. Chapter 11 briefly summarizes several tactics.

Leadership Development Institutes

Once the skill gaps are identified, a system will be needed for teaching the appropriate skills and closing the gaps. If you've read *Hardwiring Excellence*, it is clear that one solution is to conduct Leadership Development Institutes, or LDIs. The purpose of LDIs is to develop leaders' skills in order to enable the achievement of organizational goals as well as improve individual leadership performance.

Recall that in Chapter 7 we described the Execution Flywheel[SM], which outlines the process that leaders use to create consistent and reliable school systems. We're trying to create a school district in which parents could send their child to any school and classroom, and be equally satisfied. Consistent leadership practices assist with this outcome. Since consistency is important, so too is leadership development.

Investing in leader development also saves money for school districts. Districts have invested millions of dollars in what seems to be the next solution, only to again experience disappointment. It's usually not the program that failed, although that's where we pinpoint the problem. When people are unclear about expectations or lack skills, an organization reduces the likelihood of achieving desired outcomes regardless of the program, tool, or process in place.

LDIs are regularly scheduled skill development sessions (held three or four times a year) during which the entire leadership team comes together for two days of intense training. These sessions focus exclusively on the skills identified as needing improvement to meet organizational goals.

The time between LDI sessions allows for the feedback, coaching, and practice that leaders need to successfully integrate new skills into their daily work lives. If possible, holding an LDI off-site is tremendously valuable; it gives leaders a chance to get away from their regular work environment and concentrate on development.

These training sessions may not always make leaders experts in a particular skill, but they are an important step for gaining experience, increasing awareness, and sending consistent messages about the organization's overall goals.

Referencing *Hardwiring Excellence*, we propose that leaders use LDIs as well as the teams that come together to help make each institute happen. Some organizations adapt the LDI structure to fit the scope or size of the leadership group or organization. The key is to develop a structure that is appropriate for an organization and to ensure that all LDI responsibilities are covered.

We recommend that leadership teams do the legwork of the LDIs. Following are some functions for teams to consider.

Curriculum. Design the content of each training session to fulfill the learning objectives set forth by the senior leadership team. Because the learning objectives of an LDI are so closely aligned to organizational outcomes, people who serve as content designers remain very aware of what is happening in the organization.

Communication. Develop and cascade key information about the LDI to leaders, teachers, and staff. Keep everyone informed about actions to be taken pre- and post-LDI.

Social. Energize the sessions and make sure people have fun. One LDI had a ship theme to help participants focus on the "voyage they were undertaking, the calm and rocky water they may encounter, and the need for all the leaders to steer together throughout the process." The analogy was a very effective way to enhance the learning that took place.

Logistics. Make sure parking, food, audiovisual components, and room setup are in place for the session.

Linkage. Coordinate the learning that needs to occur between LDIs, and ensure that follow-up and validation occur.

Let's look at a sample agenda for an LDI. This school district focused on recognizing employees. The responsibilities of the teams and the outline of agenda topics show the typical structure of an LDI.

The team responsibilities were:

- Curriculum: Prepared the agenda, invited speakers, and organized the curriculum for the event.

- Communications: Developed a communication plan for the LDI, created the publications and website content, and cascaded LDI information to the school district employees.

- Social: Planned and created the social events aligned to the theme and content.

- Logistics: Secured the venue, handled the technology, and decorated the venue aligned to the theme.

- Linkage: Created the homework assignments and worked with the curriculum team to apply online learning between LDIs.

The prework, learning objectives, curriculum for the sessions, and linkage assignments shaped the agenda as follows:

Title: *Superheroes Academy:*
What Gets Recognized Gets Repeated

Prework: Read the recognition tool kit and respond to the reflection questions.

Learning Objectives:

- Explain why recognition is important in the workplace.

- Apply recognition strategies that have sustaining results.

- Apply specific ways to recognize employees using key words at key times.

Agenda Topics:

(1) The meaning of the theme for creating a best-place-to-work environment

(2) Connect to Purpose:

　　(a) Appreciation letter from a parent to a teacher

　　(b) Appreciation letter from a teacher to a maintenance worker

(3) Superintendent State of the School District
     (60-day results cycle)

(4) Recognitions:

     (a) Student achievement results for this
          60-day cycle

          (i)   Overall student achievement results

          (ii) Improvement results

     (b) Department recognitions for this 60-day cycle

          (i)   Overall district services survey results

          (ii) Improvement results

(5) Superhero Skit

(6) Speaker: *Why Recognize?*

(7) Group activity on the speaker topic

(8) Speaker: *When to Recognize*

(9) Group activity on the speaker topic

(10) Speaker: *How to Recognize*

(11) Group activity on the speaker topic

(12) Superhero Rollout: How the leaders' superheroes
     of choice relate to what they learned

(13) School and Department Teams Work Sessions:
Create 60-day action plans for recognizing
employees

(14) Roll out action plans to the group

(15) Recognition of leaders achieving pillar results

(16) Superintendent Closing: *A Pebble in a Pond*

Linkage:

(1) Apply the action plans.

(2) Complete the validation matrix.

(3) Senior leaders round with leaders to determine
areas working well and barriers with action plans
and to validate the quality of execution of the new
behavior.

(4) Complete the online reflection activities.

General Tips for Leadership Development

As we've watched healthcare and educational organizations take a
stab at hardwiring best practices, we've learned—from our own and
others' experiences—the successes and failures involved in developing
high-performing leaders. We encourage leaders to include these tips in
the LDIs as a way to help leaders manage change. Leadership development topics focus on change to align to John Kotter's observation:
change is no longer episodic—it's continuous. Therefore change should
be integrated into leadership development in a continuous way. The
tips help leaders do that.

Before we dive into the tips, recall the phases of individual and organizational change described in Chapter 4. Individuals move through the four phases of change: unconsciously unskilled, consciously unskilled, consciously skilled, and unconsciously skilled. We move from not knowing what we don't know to doing something so often that it becomes second nature. Organizational change happens much the same way—it gets tougher before it gets better.

Tip 1: Ask Yourself if Your Organization Values Skill Development and Training.

An organization with the right culture of high performance is going to make sure its people get the skill development needed to be successful. Over the years, we've found that people can tell the values of an organization by the amount of training it supports. Skill development and training are key. If an organization falls short in this area, perhaps its values should be rethought as well.

People can tell the values of an organization by the amount of training it supports.

Tip 2: Take Frequency into Consideration When Learning New Skills.

The more often we do something, the more comfortable we get with it. That's why it's important to provide enough opportunities for practice that tasks become second nature for leaders. Just think about when a family has a third or fourth child.

Practice Makes Perfect

When a couple have their first baby, they may think they know what they're doing from everything they learned in their childbirth classes. When the pain gets to a certain level, however, all bets are off. Some women can tough it out with the breathing exercises they learned in class, but many others go through a period of anxiety. Eventually, after a lot of suffering, the woman gets an epidural.

After the baby is born, things settle down, and the couple realize that what they read about baby care doesn't prepare them—at all—for the reality. When the baby is bathed for the first time, it may take two adults to get the job done. They bring an overabundance of towels and a number of the latest lotions lined up prepared for use. Meanwhile, both parents are terrified of drowning the baby.

Now, jump to the couple's fourth child. By then, the couple may ask for the epidural at the first sign of a contraction—and when it's time for the first bath, the baby is practically hosed off outside.

Sometimes we have to do things that we don't often do. For example, letting someone go is so hard in part because it's done so infrequently that it's tough to get really good at it. Whenever we have to let someone go, we must do more preparation and study than we would for something we do on a daily basis. Some events happen so infrequently that we may never become unconsciously skilled at them. Most likely we will always have to study just to be consciously skilled.

Some events happen so infrequently that we may never become unconsciously skilled at them. Most likely we will always have to study just to be consciously skilled.

Tip 3: Take Care to Find the Right Mentoring Match.

It may seem normal to ask someone who's in that fourth phase (unconsciously skilled) and who performs a skill naturally to mentor and train somebody in the second phase, who really just figured out what she doesn't know. And it may work—but be careful. The Phase 4 person can make a skill look so easy that he intimidates the person in Phase 2.

Janet's Story: The Right Match

Going into this year, I wanted to make tweeting a priority in my work. It may seem simple to some, but I needed help. So I decided to ask someone who was very skilled with Twitter to help me. I located a colleague who was very good at it and asked her for help. However, I found out that she was so skilled that she moved too quickly for me to gain an understanding of the *why*, *what*, and *how* of Twitter. What I needed was someone who would go slowly, explain each step, and give me a chance to practice. The highly skilled Twitter user was not the right mentoring match for me.

Tip 4: Teach the Fine Art of Explanation.

If a task is made to look too easy, the person learning it can get discouraged. He may compare his skill level (as a novice) to the skill level of the person training him (an expert) and feel negatively about himself. That's why extreme proficiency at something isn't enough to make someone a good teacher or mentor. Just mastering the skill itself doesn't mean one has mastered the art of explaining how to do it.

In professional sports, sometimes the greatest coaches were not the greatest athletes. Why? Because they had to work and study and figure out how to play the sport since the skills didn't come naturally. That process creates understanding of and empathy for others like them.

Tip 5: Deal with Pushback—the Toughest Part of Change.

Let's say that a person or group of people you lead have moved from unconsciously unskilled to consciously unskilled to consciously skilled, and finally to unconsciously skilled. Now you're going to implement something brand new, such as a new writing curriculum, a new piece of software, or a new teacher evaluation method because of the new state accountability requirements.

Let's say it's the new teacher evaluation system, which uses a mobile application. The system will focus principals' attention on identifying effective classroom instruction. Principals will be in classrooms more often and will be having performance-improvement conversations with teachers.

Here's the challenge: getting to that point is a difficult journey. Someone once told us that when God closes one door, He opens up another one, but there's hell in the hallways. Well, implementing a new teacher evaluation system can be a little bit of hell in the hallways—and the person feeling the most heat is the leader having to implement the new system, especially when that person may not really want to change.

Quint's Story: The Old Hammer Works

My dad liked to use an old hammer with electrical tape on it because it was easy to use, it fit his hand, and he was used to it. So when he received a brand-new hammer, he'd use it, develop a blister, and get frustrated. The next time he really needed a hammer, he'd go back to the old one with the electrical tape. That old hammer worked for him.

Janet's Story: It Just Takes a Little Practice

My dad loves to fish. After having his johnboat for over 30 years, he decided he was ready for a new boat. However, when he got into his brand-new boat, instead of feeling excited about the experience, he felt uncomfortable and apprehensive. It sounded silly to me, but ironically, when I rode in the boat, I felt the same way. In fact, he and I both felt it for months as we went out on the water. But time passed and several months later, when we were both out in the boat, my dad felt such great confidence in driving it that he turned the driving over to me so I could become more comfortable with it. It just took both of us a little practice.

Today's leaders are like our dads. Even though there's a new way to do something, learning the new way is going to take longer, and they're going to get frustrated and say, "I like the old way better." Then the organization is frustrated because teachers and staff may feel that the leader is not being helpful.

As we coach them, leaders find shifting unconsciously skilled people into a new situation can be quite challenging. Unconsciously skilled people push back because they don't want to experience discomfort. This is the moment of creative tension that moves leaders from good to great. Some people will have to go all the way back to unconsciously unskilled. Some are going to go back to consciously skilled, but it's going to take them longer. If we don't manage the change process by explaining *why*, *what*, and *how*; if we don't fix everything around them; and if we don't explain that things might get worse before they get better, we're going to get pushback.

Now, the person who's resisting is not going to say, "Hey, I'm pushing back because I'm feeling nervous and anxious." You won't hear, "I don't like the feeling of not being as competent as I used to be." Instead, people say things like, "The software is not good," "I have too much to do already," or simply, "This won't work." In reality, people are expressing the fear that they might not be able to make the change.

Going Backward in Order to Go Forward

We live in an area of the country that many talented golfers call home, including Bubba Watson, Boo Weekley, Joe Durant, Heath Slocum, and Jerry Pate. Each one of them goes through ups and downs. Many times they hit a certain level, and they have to make a change. To get to the next level, golfers may have to redo their swing or change the way they're putting. Often they get worse before they get better. If they can't handle going backward in order to go forward, they quickly revert to the way they used to do it, and there's no improvement.

This is why we have to validate the change and let people know they can expect to go backward for a time—and that it's definitely going to be uncomfortable.

Tip 6: Communicate the Challenges of Change.

Make sure every leader in the organization understands the phases of change described in Chapter 4 and that it may get uncomfortable at times. Some leaders will be more apprehensive than others. To keep the right amount of anxiety in the leadership ranks, communicate what will be done to make the change process as easy as possible. Also communicate that leaders are to be the role models of change.

We believe education and healthcare are two of the most challenging fields in which to manage change. Think about it: both are filled with highly competent professionals, and few industries can equal our percentage of high performers and perfectionists. These people take things so seriously, they just can't stand not being the best they can be.

However, these pluses pose difficulties as we hardwire excellence and create accountable leaders. If we can't accept the struggles that come with the change process, we'll never reach the level where we need to be—a high-performing organization that is consistent, reliable, effective, and efficient.

Tip 7: Emphasize Mentoring.

Skill development and mentoring go hand in hand. When people are asked who or what has had the biggest impact on them, they often mention a mentor. That's why it's so unfortunate that mentoring is not as common today as it was years ago.

The trend is toward a more intense focus on group skill development and a decrease in individual mentoring. School systems seem to be providing more professional development and training than ever before, which is a positive step. However, by implementing a formal training activity or tapping one person to be in charge of professional development, we need to be careful that we are not signaling that everyone else can back off and let that person do the job.

Many organizations put someone in charge of aspiring school leader development. These people are typically engaged, talented, and valuable leaders. However, an organization must watch to make sure people don't depend too much on this person or position and stop mentoring aspiring leaders. If this happens, the results may actually decline, not get better.

By the way, a mentor is someone who individualizes skill development by working one-on-one to nurture a leader or staff member. In a personal setting, the mentor can teach and talk about skills, share learning and experiences, and help prioritize and sequence activities.

Janet's Story: My Mentor

In my first leadership position at the University of West Florida, I was blessed to have the dean of the college, Wes Little, as my mentor. Dean Little met with me faithfully at 9:00 every Monday morning. We would go over the week and talk about the prior week. What worked well? What are the concerns? Dean Little was there to teach me, but he also made me feel valued because he asked for and was open to my input. And beyond the work and tasks, I knew Dr. Little cared about me as a person, and we had some good times and laughs along the way.

Years later, Dr. Little retired from the position, and I had the honor of taking over from him. His mentoring ensured that I was ready to lead and had the confidence and the skills to lead. He showed me what true mentorship was about, and his example gave me a road map to mentor others along my journey.

While anyone can be a mentor, your leader or supervisor may be a good person to fill that role. Having your leader as a mentor bestows transparency. It means we're going to be really serious about what we think we do well, what gaps we have, and what we can do to be better. We suggest the practice of frequently asking your boss, "What am I doing well?" "Are my priorities in place?" "What can I do better?" "What skills would you recommend that I refine and develop?"

Having individualized mentoring meetings is extremely important. The best thing leaders can do is to develop the people who work for them. As we tell people around the country, if you're a CEO or superintendent, develop the people who report to you; their job is to develop the people who report to them.

The best thing leaders can do is to develop the people who work for them.

Our goal is to mentor and develop people to be the best they can be. If someone can't meet expectations, they must be removed from the position because they're just not going to be helpful to the rest of the organization. It is also not fair to the person to leave him in a role in which he will not be successful.

Whatever our titles, we all lead somebody sometimes. And helping others live up to their leadership potential is a great gift to give as well as to receive.

Summary

This chapter reinforces that high-performing organizations have leadership development as a top priority. To create a culture of high performance that hardwires excellence, we need to have the most skilled senior leadership team we possibly can. We achieve that only by making sure we do everything we can to let all employees maximize their human potential.

The beauty of this approach is that it's the best succession plan an organization could have. Several superintendents have told us that one of their biggest worries is the loss of leadership from retirement. They don't feel they've done a good job creating a solid leadership bench, so they ask us for help. The best way to build a bench is to provide leadership development on the important skills noted in this chapter and the next, and to make good mentor selections for aspiring leaders.

Leadership development has become such a high priority that we've created LDIs for teachers and instructional coaches who want to become assistant principals and then principals. Why? School districts want a pipeline of future leaders who hardwire the leadership skills we describe in this book.

We continue to come back to one theme—that the cornerstone of being a good leader is the ability to manage change. This subject can be taught effectively in LDIs and held consistent in future leadership training. This valuable skill, as well as the other skills fundamental to leadership, can be reinforced through mentorship. In fact, how to be a good mentor is a great topic to include in LDIs.

Life is about change. When we can learn to manage it well, we become powerful leaders at work, at home, and in every interaction we have in our communities.

CHAPTER ELEVEN:

ALWAYS BEHAVIORS[SM]: COMMUNICATION, TRUST, AND TRANSPARENCY

FIGURE 11.1 | EVIDENCE-BASED LEADERSHIP[SM] EDUCATIONAL FRAMEWORK

Prior chapters have focused on aligned goals and skills, including the organizational scorecard, objective evaluation system, and leader development. Now it's time to examine the type of leadership behaviors that leaders need to apply for high performance on the job—what we call Always Behaviors[SM] (Figure 11.1). We've found that leaders are least proficient at what people call "soft skills," or dealing with people's emotional needs. We wonder, "If they are soft skills, why are they so hard to do?" This chapter introduces strategies for building environments in which teams want to work and succeed.

In March 2014, we and several of our partner districts presented and attended a conference hosted by the Carnegie Foundation for the Advancement of Teaching and Learning. Dan Heath, the coauthor of *Switch*, was another presenter. He displayed a picture of an elephant and rider similar to the one in Figure 11.2 as he talked about people's rational and emotional sides.

FIGURE 11.2 | ELEPHANT AND RIDER

Since then, we have shown the picture to school system leaders, explaining that the rider represents our rational side and the elephant represents our emotional side. We ask, "If the rider and the elephant got into an altercation, who would win?" Then we talk about how the Evidence-Based Leadership (EBL) framework helps leaders shape the path and direct the rider. In fact, we've talked a lot about this in the previous chapters. What we now suggest is that if we don't take care of the emotional side of all those who work for and with us, neither the path nor the qualifications of the rider will make much difference. We simply can't achieve excellence without attending to the emotional side of others in an organization.

We simply can't achieve excellence without attending to the emotional side of others in an organization.

This chapter describes tactics we coach leaders to use to create a best-place-to-work environment. Applying these tactics helps leaders build trust through transparent and effective communication.

In healthcare, Studer Group has referred to certain tactics aligned to patient experience and workplace environments as Must Haves®. Leaders choose the Must Haves they believe will help the organization achieve results. Years ago at Studer Education, we began to use the term "Always Actions," meaning actions that teachers should perform every day in their classrooms to help students achieve. These Always Actions are the foundation of the book *Who's Engaged? Climb the Learning Ladder to See* (by Janet). Complementary leader tactics associated with school leadership are described in *How to Lead Teachers to Become Great* (coauthored with Robin Largue).

As we've worked with leaders in schools, the term "Always Actions" has carried over. It describes how we define the expected compliance level. For these purposes, we define *always* as 97 to 100 percent of the time. It's also important to assess the quality of execution. In this chapter, we summarize desirable leader behaviors, whereas Chapter 12 focuses on individual performance of expected behaviors. Both make up the aligned behaviors part of EBL. From here on, we refer to things that leaders should always do as Always Behaviors. This chapter also includes prescriptions that leaders should follow to create best-place-to-work environments for their teams.

Leaders' Always Behaviors (Figure 11.3) are behaviors that leaders must always do in order to achieve the outcomes set by organizational leadership.

> Leaders' Always Behaviors are behaviors that leaders must always do in order to achieve the outcomes set by organizational leadership.

There's no prescribed sequence for teaching and coaching these behaviors. Rather, we use data from the current state of the school district to determine which to focus on first. Then we coach leaders to hardwire it—to consistently execute the behavior with the highest quality.

FIGURE 11.3 | LEADERSHIP ALWAYS BEHAVIORS^{SM}

- Leader rounding
- Survey perceptions on "customer" service (employee, parent, student services)
- Results rollout process
- Cascading communication; key words at key times (written and oral)
- Employee recognition such as thank-you notes and WOW cards
- Selection and the first 90 days
- Professional performance conversations
- Employee forums
- Best-place-to-work standards of practice

When superintendents and senior team leaders determine the core system-wide strategic actions aligned to each pillar, these leadership behaviors become hardwired throughout the leadership in a school district. That is, the superintendent makes these actions mandatory for the senior team and their direct reports and so on down the line. The expectation is not that employees sometimes or usually apply the defined actions; the superintendent expects these actions to *always* occur at all levels of the school district. The supervisors then become responsible for validating that their direct reports apply the behaviors 97 to 100 percent of the time and do so with high quality.

Our leadership Always Behaviors align to the Nine Principles® and are core to our work. There are two things to consider. First, the goal is not to introduce all the behaviors at one time; rather, we scaffold them so they become hardwired. Second, superintendents and leaders might come up with their own leadership Always Behaviors that add to the foundational behaviors. In all cases, leaders should be taught, they should have time to practice, and they must know the validation process for doing the behavior.

Leaders should be taught, they should have time to practice, and they must know the validation process for doing the behavior.

We have developed tool kits for each leadership behavior so that our partners can hardwire them in their school systems. As we tell our partners, each school district can tweak, modify, and adapt tactics to fit their environment. The most important aspect of applying any of the leadership behaviors goes back to the Execution Flywheel[SM]: We use data to diagnose the highest need in order to determine what to focus on. Then we select the right behavior to improve a result. From there we develop, coach, and support people to achieve to their highest potential. We then validate the Always Behaviors to ensure 97 to 100 percent compliance and high-quality execution. Finally, we assess to determine if the desired results were achieved.

Always Behavior: Leader Rounding

The number one reason people leave their jobs is their "boss." In our experience, leader rounding may be the most important tactic to help leaders engage individuals in the work environment. By *rounding*, we mean making the rounds, checking in with employees—but it's really much more than that.

> Leader rounding may be the most important tactic to help leaders engage individuals in the work environment.

If you are like us, you'll probably say that you're already rounding with employees. We would have said so, too, at one time. In fact, during that time, if people had asked us if we rounded, we would have said, "You bet! I can do the whole organization in less than 30 minutes." In fact, we would say to our assistants, "I'm going to go round. I'll be back in 18 minutes."

We would walk through the halls and flash a thumbs-up to employees as we passed by. We would ask people, "How you doing?" Usually they'd say, "Fine." We would say, "Great!" and keep up the pace. If someone responded with a problem, such as "We're understaffed," we would say, "Hang in there!" and move on.

Leader rounding is different from what we thought it was. First, we encourage all leaders to round with their direct reports. The first thing we do as leaders when we round is build relationships with our employees—get to know them, what they like, what they relate to, the people who are most important to them, and other things that define employees as individuals. When leaders round, they recognize employees' needs, which are to feel cared for, to develop their skills through training, and to have the resources they need to do their jobs.

Employees deserve to feel satisfied with their work. We've found that employees want three things, which are represented as the centerpiece of the Organizational Flywheel described in Chapter 5:

(1) They want to believe that the organization has the right purpose. That's why leaders who make themselves look good at the expense of the senior leadership do a disservice to all other employees—because the senior leadership represents "purpose" to the employees. And if employees don't feel good about senior

leaders, they don't feel good about the organization. A we/they culture breeds dissatisfaction.

(2) They want to know they are doing worthwhile work. That's why they got into education in the first place.

(3) Employees want to make a difference. The results are what fuel their passion. Getting results motivates people to persevere and seek more results.

Our experiences tell us that education leaders want to do all three of these things. But we also think that we sometimes forget to capture the "wins" because we have so much noise coming at us each day. In addition, we have been trained to focus on what's wrong.

Rounding is the most powerful leadership tactic that focuses on employee engagement and satisfaction. It helps us harvest wins and allows employees to provide feedback about their work environment.

So, let's dig a little deeper into the tactic. Rounding is a tactic that, first and foremost, helps us establish positive relationships with others. By doing so, we retain an engaged workforce. When leaders round, it is key for them to recognize employees' needs.

What are employees specifically looking for in their leaders?

- A good relationship

- Approachability

- Willingness to work side by side

- Efficient systems

- Training and development

- Resources to do the job

- Appreciation

Rounding is so powerful because it helps a leader meet these needs and gain an opportunity to learn what is occurring in people's lives. Rounding shows we have concern and care for our employees.

If we're principals, we're rounding with our teachers and staff. If we're district department leaders, we're rounding with our staff. If we're the superintendent, we're rounding with our senior team. If we know that the individual we're rounding with has a son who just entered his first year of high school, we ask how her son's day went. It shows we care and that we know about something meaningful in the mother's life.

If we're principals, we're rounding with our teachers and staff. If we're district department leaders, we're rounding with our staff. If we're the superintendent, we're rounding with our senior team.

It's always important to start with a personal question. Then we get more specific with our questions and drill down on the employees' needs.

Questions to Ask When Rounding

- What's working well?

- Are there any individuals who have been especially helpful to you whom I could recognize?

- Do you have the resources to do your job?

- If there anything that we could do better?

When we consistently ask employees what's working well for them, they tend to shift their focus from the negative to the positive. In education, we're accustomed to identifying performance gaps. Therefore, we've been trained to look for what's wrong. We also need to train ourselves to look for what's right. Start with the positive.

During rounding, Samantha may recognize that the technology coordinator helped her get a piece of equipment working. She might say, "John in technology was very helpful in getting my computer working so that I could start my lesson on time." Now we have a win. We recognize John in the technology department by telling him why Samantha recognized him. Three people win—John, Samantha, and the leader. How do you think the service in the technology department will be the next day? Even better. We're harvesting wins and bringing them back to the departments as well as to individuals. The positive feedback recognizes desired behaviors. Recognized behaviors get repeated.

In reality, we're trying to re-recruit our staff all the time. If we're not constantly doing so, we'll lose them and they will lose their level of engagement and satisfaction in the workplace.

We follow a positive first question with a second one, asking employees to identify someone who has been especially helpful to them this week. Another win.

Now we get into process-improvement questions. Employees tell us about resources needed and barriers to doing their best job. We transfer this information to Stoplight Reports, where green means completed, yellow means in process, and red means can't fix the problem and here's why. We update the Stoplight Report on a consistent basis so employees know what's being done to improve their workplace environment. Rather than only seeing their item, they now see additional requests being addressed. The Stoplight Report shows the work being done in the school or department to create a productive work environment. This communication tool provides a win for the leader as well as the employees. Most importantly, it creates a better place to work.

The Power of Rounding with Teachers

Dr. Reggie Lipnick is a middle school principal in the Escambia County School District in Pensacola, Florida. In one of her first school leadership positions, she made rounding with teachers one of her top priorities. By doing so, she learned something from them. The sixth grade teachers told her that their students were losing about 20 minutes of instructional time a day because of where classrooms were located. To allow students time to get to places like the cafeteria and special areas, the teachers had to shorten the academic classes. Being new, Dr. Lipnick asked them how long that had been going on. The answer ended up being about 15 years! Dr. Lipnick then did a great thing. She asked the teachers how they believed the problem should be solved. In the middle of the school year, the teachers made a decision to change classrooms to accommodate the students' needs. We've found that when we ask teachers to solve problems, they will do what's right for students every time.

That's leader rounding. It serves many purposes. We are likely to retain employees, recognize more people, create an engaged work environment, and apply process-improvement strategies. This is one of the most important tactics leaders apply to turn the Organizational Flywheel. It's a single approach with a multiple focus. It's not easy, because at first we are overwhelmed by the number of systems that have not been fixed in a long time. Plus, we have to do more to improve processes while also increasing the time we spend on recognition. So at first, rounding actually creates more work.

But once we've been at it for four to six months—once the processes have been improved, systems are working well, and staff have the resources they need—rounding takes much less time and, in fact, becomes one of the most enjoyable aspects of a leader's job. Instead of rounding to react, we are now able to round in a proactive way to look for additional process improvement. Our work is more satisfying. Employees feel valued and satisfied. Leaders make a difference in the lives of those they lead.

Another nice thing about rounding is that we can apply it with others as well. Here are a few examples:

- School leaders can round with parents and students to retrieve information about the school learning environment.

- Teachers can round with students and their parents to harvest wins and improve classroom processes.

- District leaders who provide services to schools can round with school leaders to gain a better understanding about the quality of their services to schools.

- Superintendents can round with community members to gain insight into how they perceive the quality of the school district.

- The school board can round with the superintendent as well as their respective communities.

Rounding establishes genuine relationships with others. It lets people know that their input is important and ensures that they have the resources to do their jobs. Our workforce becomes engaged and satisfied.

Always Behavior: Surveys

There's another important tool, in addition to rounding, that drives employee engagement and results. It is a system-wide employee engagement survey. The key to this survey, or any others we use, is not the score itself—it's how well we, as leaders, share the results with staff and how we communicate actions based on their feedback. This rollout process is described in the next section of the chapter.

Measurement supports the alignment of desired behaviors. It excites the organization when results are achieved. Measurement also holds individuals accountable for results and helps determine if things are working. We are not just measuring to measure. We are measuring to align to specific leadership and employee behaviors that cascade throughout the organization to drive results. The better the organization can align these behaviors, the more quickly it will achieve desired results and create opportunities to recognize staff. Recognized behavior gets repeated, which turns the Organizational Flywheel.

Sometimes a leader will ask us, "Don't you think we are focusing too much on the numbers?" We remind them that 4s and 5s (higher scores) represent employees' appreciation of the work environment and parents' satisfaction with their child's education. Most agree that those things are worth measuring.

Survey tools measure people's perceptions of how well they are served by our school district. We define customers in school districts as employees, students, parents, and community members. We contend that focusing on service improves an organization's chance of being successful. Our results over the years show that people's perceptions matter if we want to maximize school district performance.

We recommend that education leaders use three surveys as tools to measure several important factors. First, we suggest using an *employee engagement tool*. We've worked with school districts to design an employee engagement survey that focuses on a specific definition of employee engagement: the extent to which leaders provide a workforce environment that supports employees in achieving their highest potential. Second, we administer a *parent satisfaction survey* for our partner districts. Parents of children attending all schools in a district are given the chance to complete the survey and provide input to the school staff. Third, school leaders as well as other leaders, as applicable, complete a *district support services survey*. It measures the extent to which school leaders perceive that departments provide good services to support their schools. In addition, some of our partners gain insight from students through a student engagement survey.

For our partners who use these surveys, we compare the results with other districts. We also generate a report that summarizes the results for the district, its departments, and its schools. The surveys provide perception data that inform us, but the most important part of surveys is what we do with the results.

The surveys provide perception data that inform us, but the most important part of surveys is what we do with the results.

Always Behavior: Results Rollout Process

We teach a results rollout process to our school district partners that leaders use to present survey results. The process also applies to any results that schools and departments receive that are important to communicate to teachers and staff. The better we communicate the results, the greater the opportunity we have to create a team approach to problem-solving.

> The better we communicate the results, the greater the opportunity we have to create a team approach to problem-solving.

We train leaders to explain the results of the survey to their employees, celebrate the wins, and ask for input on ways to improve. The survey rollout process teaches leaders to develop key words and actions for the survey rollout meeting they will have with their staff.

As part of the rollout process, leaders hold meetings with staff to present the highest-scored items and for leaders to ask staff why those items yielded the best results. Then, leaders present the lowest-scored items, ask why staff members think the items showed the least improvement, and invite suggestions for improving those areas. The leaders complete the meeting by gaining input on one or two action items to apply over the next 60 to 75 days.

We've found that about 95 percent of the time, when leaders have the proper training in using key words during the rollout process, employees rank the leaders highly on items related to communication, feedback, and input. This boosts leaders' self-confidence as they continue to engage with employees to work toward achieving their unit goals.

Some news from the survey results unsettles us. Our own experiences tell us it's difficult to roll out unfavorable results. The problems seem overwhelming, and the negative information is upsetting. However, once rolled out, everyone sees that many problems have been narrowed down to two or three that can be solved with a good action plan. For example, the top two issues may be work pressure and communication issues. After the rollout meeting, we have insight into how employees define these two barriers and what they expect to see. Also, the employees' input determines the top priorities that need to be addressed.

If leaders receive bad results, they might say something like:

"The employee engagement results are back. Thank you for completing the survey. I want to tell you that I'm disappointed. Obviously I'm not the leader I want to be. But I want you to know that I'm committed to making this a better school and to being a good leader. I hope you'll help me."

Once you say, "I hope you'll help me," most will be on your side. A big part of the results rollout discussion is our ability to be open about the results.

At the end of the meeting, we administer an evaluation of the meeting. Our teams provide us with feedback on the results rollout meeting. The entire rollout process is about improvement.

We use the results rollout process with all surveys. This same process can be used with any results, including student achievement. Schools usually use data to monitor student achievement progress every 45 to 60 days. Similar to surveys, the key is to explore these results with teachers in order to celebrate the wins and close student performance gaps.

Achieving the Results

Remember Mary Jo Raczkowski-Shannon, principal of Hunt Elementary School in Jackson, Michigan? She started with low scores on the parent survey as well as low scores on the employee engagement survey. Once she decided to change her behavior and apply the tactics associated with improving the workforce environment and parent satisfaction, however, she moved from being a low-performing leader to a high-performing one.

In the first year of our partnership, Mary Jo sat in the back of the room and rolled her eyes during the training sessions. As part of the EBL partnership with the school district, we administered employee engagement and parent satisfaction surveys. During that year, Mary Jo's school reported some of the lowest scores of any school we have worked with (3.16 on the parent survey and 3.28 on the employee engagement survey on a 5-point scale).

At the end of that first year and going into the second, Mary Jo did not like the idea of being the lowest-scored school in the district, so she reluctantly began to apply the tactics we were teaching. She rolled out the survey results and faithfully applied the leader rounding process. She mandated that teachers make five positive phone calls to parents each week. At the end of the year, Mary Jo's scores soared to 4.41 on the parent survey and 4.01 on the employee engagement survey. Most importantly, after being principal of her school for 12 years, Mary Jo rekindled her sense of purpose in her work. She was happier, her staff members were happier, and the parents were much more engaged with their children's education. Why? Mary Jo did more than the required tactics—she changed the school's culture. This past year, hers was one of the only schools in the district to make significant student achievement gains, even as accountability standards became more rigorous. Mary Jo is making a difference in the lives of her faculty, staff, students, and their parents— and she's achieving results.

Always Behavior: Cascading Communication Using Key Words at Key Times

Through our organizational assessment and the various surveys and focus groups we employ in school districts, we have found that good communication is one of leaders' biggest obstacles to overcome.

Here's what we focus on with leaders. First, leaders want to be better communicators. This means leaders value transparency of decision-making practices and know how to support decisions with evidence.

Second, superintendents and their senior leadership teams need to create a specific way to cascade information throughout the district. When information comes from the top, the senior leadership team members cascade the message to their direct reports within 24 to 48 hours. Their direct reports pass the message to their direct reports within the next 24 to 48 hours, and so on. Why? If leaders wait until the next scheduled meeting, some meetings might occur within the week, but others might be two or three weeks away. Employees receive information at different times, so some messages are old news by the time employees get them. Or employees could hear the message from a colleague, who may not present it as it was intended.

Third, when leaders communicate with their staff, other leaders, or various stakeholders, using key words reduces the possibility of misrepresenting a message. We coach leaders to first identify the outcome they want to achieve from any communication and then intentionally deliver a message using thoughtful language that invites a response. This means that the communicator also has to be an excellent listener. In most instances, the goal of communication is not to get your way or to get your point across. Rather, it's to engage in a mutual conversation to make the best possible decisions.

Finding the right words at the right time builds a culture of service and operational excellence. It is critical to let others know why we do things. People want to know what is going on and want us to connect the dots to let them know why we need to take a particular action or change a behavior.

For example, if a principal decides to start observing a teacher and walks into a classroom unannounced, the teacher wonders what this new behavior is all about. She might think he is rude, is trying to find something wrong, has heard something that was alarming, and so on.

Think of how much more productive the interaction between the two would be if the principal introduced the new behavior using key words at key times. Prior to the observation, he could say something like, "Next week, I am going to go into classrooms to observe ways in which students are engaged in their lessons. Since we are focusing on student engagement this year, I want to learn what teachers are doing and talk about areas working well and those that can be improved to better engage students. I value the work you do with your students and look forward to this opportunity to be in your classroom. I'm going to jot down some notes so that at our meeting, we can have a conversation about student engagement."

Now the teacher may still be a little nervous, but she understands why the principal is applying a new behavior. In fact, the teacher looks forward to learning ways to improve.

Using key words at key times with key behaviors makes all the difference in the world. It's best for leaders to develop their own key words that make sense to them and their situation. The survey tools help in this development. The content of the items leads us to an outcome we want to achieve, and effective communication helps us all work in a positive direction to achieve a common outcome.

It's All About Communication

On one of our site visits to Jackson Public Schools in Jackson, Michigan, we rounded with principals. Jackson Public Schools is a district with eight elementary schools, one middle school, one high school, and one alternative high school. All the principals report directly to the superintendent. The principals identified communication as an obstacle, so we probed into the specifics. The principals reported that they did not know what was discussed at the superintendent's cabinet meetings and felt left out of the communication loop. They would discover what had been decided when someone—let's say a crew from buildings and grounds—would show up at their school to do something. Or maybe Human Resources would send out some new paperwork for schools and departments to complete or even start a whole new process without any advance notice.

When we brought this up with Superintendent Evans, he initiated a process for cascading communications and sharing summaries of cabinet meeting minutes. When we went back to the principals, they told us that that single action was extremely helpful and had improved communication. As we continued to talk with Superintendent Evans over the years, he realized that when he failed to follow this process, communication became a problem. All of us have to commit to a process and be consistent with follow-through. When Evans consistently communicated with a defined process, the principals were better informed and felt good about the communications from central office.

Always Behavior: Employee Recognition

We find that three tools are particularly effective in recognizing people for the work they do. First, we promote creating a process to manage up other people. We teach that managing up is a specific type of recognition that positions people well with others. It promotes people recognizing other people for good work. We recommend that leaders manage up people when they do things well. Managing up helps everyone know "what right looks like." Also, we know that what is recognized gets repeated. The reason for managing up is to create the habit of focusing on the positive. Our goal as leaders is to build a manage-up culture. Here are several ways to manage up:

(1) Coleaders manage up leaders.

(2) Leaders manage up teachers and staff.

(3) Teachers and staff manage up leaders.

(4) Coworkers manage up coworkers and other departments.

We teach that when someone is managed up to leaders, a leader then manages up that person to senior leadership by giving credit to both people. For example, we managed up a Studer Education staff member, Paul, to the president of Studer Group, B.G. Porter, who wrote Paul a thank-you note mentioning that we had promoted the work he had done on a project. Who wins in this situation? Paul and us.

We also provide the WOW Card (Figure 11.4). The card simply says, "You WOWED me when you . . ." Another option is a pack of "Give Me Five" sticky notes. These are quick, simple ways to recognize performance.

FIGURE 11.4 | SAMPLE WOW CARD

One of the most important ways we have found to recognize people is by sending them a thank-you note, preferably handwritten and sent to the person's home by mail. Over the years, Studer Group has discovered that leader rounding and employee thank-you notes have the greatest effect on employee retention.

Three important notes about recognition: First, no matter which tool is used to recognize, remember that it takes three compliments to one criticism to yield a positive outcome. Second, praise should be descriptive and contextual so that the individual receiving the praise and others know "what right looks like." Third, leaders need to be trained to use the tool, and a process for applying and validating should be in place. Some people say that we may lose the meaning of specific praise using agreed-upon tools when we mandate it to occur, but sometimes we have to mandate a behavior in order to change an attitude.

> No matter which tool is used to recognize, remember that it takes three compliments to one criticism to yield a positive outcome.

Always Behavior: Selection and the First Ninety Days

Jim Collins and his research team discovered that great leaders know that in order to make an organization great, they have to begin with *who* (the employees) rather than *what* (curriculum materials, teaching programs, and so forth). Selecting the right teachers and staff is one of the most important decisions that school and department leaders make.

> Selecting the right teachers and staff is one of the most important decisions that school and department leaders make.

We recommend that leaders hardwire certain actions for the selection and onboarding process. First, we train leaders to apply a peer interviewing process, which includes a peer review team and an objective review process. Second, we train peer interview teams to apply both behavior-based and performance-based questions when interviewing candidates. Third, we train leaders to use 30- and 90-day meeting protocols with new employees. Why? Because organizations tend to lose employees in the first 90 days if they are not supported, coached, and heard. As leaders, we need to hire with this in mind. The worst thing that could occur in the first 90 days of school is for a new teacher or staff member to decide to leave. Peer interviewing tends to help leaders retain staff because the employees who participate become invested in the new hire. Also, the leader and the peer interview team co-own the hire and, therefore, co-own the task of providing support.

When scheduling the 30- and 90-day meetings with new hires, we make sure they know this is "business as usual." Too often when leaders ask to meet with employees, they are sharing bad news or identifying a problem that needs to be corrected. When a leader calls employees into the office, they begin to wonder what they've done wrong. By letting employees know up-front that these meetings will be occurring, leaders can reduce that anxiety.

We suggest leaders ask the following questions in the first 30 days and then at 90 days:

- How do we compare to what we said we would be like?

- Tell me what you like. What is going well?

- I noticed you came to us from _____. Are there things you did there that might be helpful to us?

- Is there anything here you are uncomfortable with?

On the 90th day, we suggest that leaders ask the same questions and also add two others to their conversation:

- [If hiring] Is there anyone you know who might be a valuable addition to our team?

- As your supervisor, how can I be helpful?

The 30- and 90-day meetings reinforce that leaders are committed to retaining the new hire they and the peer interview team selected. The leader can share appropriate information with the peer interview team so that they can be supportive and helpful. In fact, the peer interview team's job isn't over on the new hire's first day. Creating ways for the peer interview team to stay engaged with the new hire further strengthens the stake they feel they have in the new hire's success.

The 30- and 90-day meetings, along with leader rounding with staff, build a supportive workforce culture in which problems are proactively addressed and individuals are recognized for work that produces results.

Always Behavior: Professional Performance Conversations

Conducting professional performance conversations is such a complex and critical behavior that it can't be addressed here. It determines whether a school district will break through to excellence or hit a wall. The next chapter, on performance management, treats the subject fully.

Always Behavior: Employee Forums

One way for senior leaders to communicate at all levels is through employee forums. We find that as senior leaders, we are pretty good at making decisions, but we don't always think about how we are going to communicate those decisions.

> One way for senior leaders to communicate at all levels is through employee forums. We find that as senior leaders, we are pretty good at making decisions, but we don't always think about how we are going to communicate those decisions.

Employee forums are quarterly employee meetings led by senior leaders. The meetings can be held in person, in groups, or virtually. They offer senior leaders a chance to communicate a consistent message to all employees and an opportunity to learn about and celebrate their workplaces. Employee forums should occur at set intervals and follow a predetermined agenda that is tied to the organization's designated pillars. Forums are usually built on a theme that ties together the session, supports the mission, and creates an enjoyable opportunity for teamwork. All employees should attend or view these sessions, with leaders setting this expectation.

Many organizations already have employee forums. We've heard leaders say that attendance tends to be low. How do we encourage employees to attend?

- Set a tone that conveys the importance of the forums. Choose a theme or key concept for the forum and make sure to communicate the relevance of the theme to employees.

- Align the meeting agenda to the organizational outcomes or what we have defined as the pillars. This communicates the strategic direction of the school district.

- Solicit questions prior to the forum so that the superintendent can share answers to questions at the end of the session.

- Hold a meeting with leaders prior to the forum to educate the leadership team on information that will be presented to employees. Promote ownership by allowing leaders to offer input and feedback to improve the meeting. Also, prepare leaders to reinforce the information and answer questions after employees return from the forum.

- Offer employee forums at a time that makes it easy for staff to attend.

- After each forum, ask employees to complete an evaluation of the forum in addition to asking any questions that were not addressed. The results of these evaluations are used to improve the next forum. Along with the answered questions, they are also shared with the staff.

Always Behavior: Best-Place-to-Work Standards of Practice

Most people want to feel proud of where they work. We find that they also want leaders to hold people accountable to high standards in the workplace. The goal in creating standards is to get faculty and staff input on defining the way people engage in the workplace environment so that it becomes a pleasant, satisfying, and productive place to work. The standards create awareness, which affects daily behavior. The standards are created by staff members and shared with leadership for input and direction.

The goal in creating standards is to get faculty and staff input on defining the way people engage in the workplace environment so that it becomes a pleasant, satisfying, and productive place to work.

We recommend that organizations assemble a team to develop an initial draft standards document. They use the standards to align to the outcomes the school district wants to achieve. Sometimes looking at items on the surveys can be helpful to teams as they draft the standards. We've also found that applying a brainstorming activity with the team by asking them to describe "model" behaviors in the work environment works well.

This draft is then sent to organizational employees for additional input, which is used to revise the standards. Leaders use the final document as a communication, support, and accountability tool that defines what employees want when they come to work each day. The standards also guide employee training priorities and set expectations for new employees.

We've worked with a lot of staff members over the years and have marveled at the high expectations they have for themselves and their peers. The sample standards from Menomonee Falls School District (Figure 11.5) provide a good example. In fact, employees tend to create higher standards than leadership expects. Leaders feel good about their employees when they see these high expectations. It helps them model "what right looks like" in the workforce.

By involving staff, we are not only establishing consistent standards, but we're also creating buy-in from the school district. Employees are invested in the standards they are asked to model.

FIGURE 11.5	**SAMPLE STANDARDS OF PRACTICE FOR BEST-PLACE-TO-WORK ENVIRONMENTS, FROM MENOMONEE FALLS SCHOOL DISTRICT, WI**
ACCOUNTABILITY	· Be responsible and follow through with important actions. · Own each problem that comes to you. · Look beyond your defined role to add value. · Act honestly and ethically. · Do the right thing, even when no one is looking. · Act like an owner: treat district resources as if they were your own and stakeholders as if they were your family.
COMMUNICATION	· Smile, make eye contact, and greet others in a positive manner. · Communicate with sincerity, honesty, and respect. · Actively listen without interrupting and without judgment. · Speak clearly without using terms that are unfamiliar to the customer.
PROFESSIONALISM	· Take personal ownership to improve. · Strive to be the best every day. · Model learning. · Recognize others for a job well done. · Maintain a strong work ethic.
RESPECT	· Appreciate diversity in others. · Display a positive and empathetic attitude toward others. · Maintain confidentiality and respect privacy at all times. · Value the opinion of others.
TEAMWORK	· Work with others to help the district achieve goals. · Work together in a supportive manner by being dependable, trustworthy, and flexible. · Celebrate success and have fun at work. · Help coworkers and customers feel valued by recognizing them for doing something that helps the school district achieve goals.

A side note: allowing employees with a bad attitude to work in the organization is a morale killer. When leaders begin to hold employees accountable for their attitudes and ask those who choose not to follow the standards to leave, organizations experience a boost in all pillar results. Why? Once we ask poor performers to leave the organization, teamwork and interdepartmental relationships improve. This leads to more efficient operations. More staff become willing to align their behaviors to pillar goals, which in turn leads to better bottom-line results.

We recommend that employees be required to read and sign a commitment to the standards of practice. Make it part of the employee application process. Likewise, the standards should also be used in the discipline process. If employees are not following the standards, their behaviors should be addressed.

For many leaders, the standards of practice are the first concrete process they've applied with employees who are technically good but are difficult to get along with. We've been asked, "What if someone has good skills on the job but is difficult for others to work with?" We respond, "That person is a low performer." Systems cannot be excellent when negative attitudes are affecting the work environment.

Not New—Better

All the change we discussed in Section 1 and the tactics we have introduced in Section 3 can feel overwhelming to people. That's why it's important to frame change in the right way. We need to make it clear to people that, nine times out of ten, something that may seem new actually isn't. Realizing this creates a psychological shift that can make the process much easier.

Sometimes people tell us that the features of EBL are just common sense. That may be true, but we sure have a difficult time applying common sense, and we think this is true for all of us. That's why a framework with evidence-based components, good structure, and tight processes helps us become better leaders.

Recognition – A Better Way

Mike Thorpe is the principal of Milton High School in the Santa Rosa County School District, Florida. His leadership has been highlighted in several publications. Mike applied some of the recognition tools we've described.

Here's one thing Mike and his assistant principals did at the school. They asked teachers to identify one student per week who performed well and to send the principal that student's name and a description of the performance. The principal and assistant principals then divided up the students and called their parents to promote the positive recognition.

At the beginning, they thought this was silly and would just end up being one more thing to do. In the end, they said it was something they should be doing every day. This recognition makes a difference for parents, students, and teachers. Why teachers? Because the leaders also told parents where the positive recognition came from.

The ideas in this book are not really new. We would love to say we are delivering breakthrough technology, but that's just not true.

Sometimes we joke about it. We'll say, "Now we're going to talk about rounding with employees, and nobody is going to say, 'That's brilliant! I would never have thought of talking to my employees!'" When we talk about reward and recognition, no one says, "You know what? I've always wondered what tool I was missing. You're right. I don't recognize people."

Goal setting is another example. We've always set goals in some way. But we haven't done so with focus and consistency—in other words, we haven't done it reliably. We haven't set goals frequently, and we haven't done it the same way every time. And we haven't performed the tasks as effectively or efficiently as we could.

So the parts of EBL are not new, but the way we use them is, and we've certainly seen improved results by focusing leadership coaching on executing goals and implementing behaviors and processes. We see improved quality outcomes, better workplace environments, and more satisfied stakeholders. As we coach, we support leaders who are taking current practices to the most up-to-date iterations or advances.

Figure 11.6 shows how EBL promotes taking current practices and making them better.

FIGURE 11.6	NOT NEW—BETTER	
CURRENT PRACTICE	**EFFECTIVE APPROACH**
Strategic plans	Operational alignment tools
Department meetings	Consistent agendas
Employee conversations	Rounding for outcomes
Employee reward and recognition	Recognition tools such as thank-you notes
Staff selection and orientation	Peer interviewing and 30- and 90-day meetings
Workforce retention	Individual performance conversations
Workforce and key stakeholder engagement	Survey rollout process
Staff policy	Standards
Communication	Key words at key times
Leader evaluation	Individual accountability
Leadership training	Data-driven leadership training

Let's review a few examples:

- Most school districts and postsecondary institutions create strategic plans. The question we get from boards and executive teams is this: how do we operationalize the plan to know where we are doing well and where we need to improve? The first step we take with leaders is to apply an alignment tool or the EBL Scorecard, which includes key measures, progress-monitoring measures, and strategic actions with short-cycle plans.

- There have always been departmental meetings, but they can be made far more efficient and effective. Here is one of the current practices we teach: instead of waiting until the last minute to figure out the agenda, we suggest using a consistent agenda based on the pillar approach. We also suggest including an evaluation to rate the meeting so that we can improve the process.

- Many leaders talk with their employees. However, when we're rounding for specific desired outcomes and making sure it is done with a certain frequency, we get a lot more "bang for the buck." With rounding, we're still having employee conversations—it's just that now we're being specific about what we're looking for and what outcomes we want.

- Organizations generally reward and recognize employees, but too often it has been the equivalent of a generic pat on the back. If we get specific about the behaviors we reward and recognize, we'll go much further toward encouraging others to practice those behaviors. Plus, it's important to create systems for recognition, such as making it a regular part of rounding and hardwiring a certain number of thank-you notes (handwritten notes sent to employees' homes can have a huge impact on their lives).

- We've always selected staff and provided employee orientation. Now we are doing performance-based and behavior-based interviewing using a matrix and involving peers. We're conducting 30- and 90-day meetings for new employees. All these improvements help us identify, select, and retain the best possible candidates for the job.

- Speaking of retention, the education sector has always used various methods to retain employees. But now we're improving the methodology by implementing individual employee meetings and rounding aimed at re-recruiting high performers and developing middle performers, both of which have proven very effective. We've also realized that if we don't deal with the people who aren't good team players and aren't pulling their weight, we'll lose the ones who *are*.

- Most leaders give lip service to the importance of having an engaged workforce and involved stakeholders. Employees, students, and our community deserve better than that. They deserve an opportunity to provide feedback on how well we are doing. Also, we now do something with that input by applying a results rollout process to celebrate our strengths and work on improving areas of need.

- Organizations have always set forth certain staff policies and guidelines. Now we are developing those into specific bottom-up standards aimed at making sure the organization has well-defined, consistent expectations.

- When we ask people to identify the number one breakdown point in the organization, they say poor communication. Every part of EBL integrates the cascading of messages using key words. Applying specific strategies to key word information allows leaders to disseminate consistent, reliable messages in a timely manner.

- We've found that many leader evaluations are unbelievably complex. It takes so long to do them that most people fall behind. To ensure that organizations achieve results, leaders have to own their part of the results. The leader evaluation is the way to reinforce this ownership, so we realized we had to make them more efficient. To be effective and hold leaders accountable, the leader evaluations have to include a few key measures and weighted priorities. Accountability means "you can count on me," which high-performing and solid-performing leaders welcome.

So, if none of these items are really new, then what *is* new? I'd say the one thing that's really new about what we do is leadership training specifically focused on creating best-place-to-work environments. Why? The data we've collected demonstrate this need. In most organizations, leaders might say they do training, and some of them do, but not in the area of leadership skill building. In K–12 systems, few leaders receive training on how to build an engaged workforce, hold effective meetings, engage in process-improvement strategies, recognize and provide feedback on individual performance, and communicate using key messaging strategies. Some of our most cherished moments come when leaders thank us for helping them gain these skills. By adding more focused time and much more commitment to developing skills in leaders, we really *are* doing something new to increase the efficiency, effectiveness, consistency, and reliability of educational systems. This connects right back to the values of the organizational leaders.

Janet's Story: It Just Makes Sense

After a leadership development session with one of our partners, I and one of my colleagues, Robin, received a note from an aspiring leader. The note said, "Thank you for your knowledge and expertise and the great session. I've learned more about being a good leader in four hours than I did in two years of graduate school."

Now, Robin and I didn't do anything especially new or innovative that day. But what we did do was focus on the values of the leaders. We looked at how leaders engage with teachers and staff to give them every opportunity to reach their highest potential. It just seemed to make more sense to the aspiring leaders in the session that day when the content connected back to tactics they could use to create a better place for teachers and staff to work.

Think about it like this: to manage change and better position what we're doing, we mainly need to capitalize on our current practices and improve them with the latest effective, efficient approaches. And while this book does address some specific approaches, it's really about improving educational systems and maximizing performance to create a culture that inspires and empowers people to implement these approaches.

Once we have EBL in place, we're using the Nine Principles, and we understand the pillars and flywheel, we can be very flexible in what we put into each of those arenas. The culture really works for all types of performance improvement.

The key in every organization is to create a culture with the agility to adjust to an ever-changing world in a positive, forward-moving manner. Such organizations and the people who work inside them run to meet the challenges that wait ahead. They run to the future.

Summary

This chapter focuses on the elephant, or the emotional side of our employees. Of the surveys we administer for school districts, the one on which districts usually score the lowest is the employee engagement survey. This survey measures the extent to which leaders give their teams a best-place-to-work environment. We suggest that leaders apply the behaviors summarized in this chapter to shift from low to high performance. The behaviors help leaders become more transparent and effective communicators. The outcome is that people gain trust because leaders listen carefully and hear people's needs and concerns. Better yet, employees see actions being taken to create productive workplace environments.

Studer Group has long advocated that leaders hardwire a set of key tactics, tools, and techniques to achieve an organization's goals. We call these Always Behaviors, meaning that leaders apply the behaviors 97 to 100 percent of the time. These leadership behaviors create best-place-to-work environments, which give leaders, teachers, and staff every opportunity to achieve at their highest potential. Leaders and their teams work every day to serve students, parents, and community stakeholders.

Chapter 11 summarizes our best-place-to-work Always Behaviors: (1) survey perceptions, (2) results rollout process, (3) leader rounding, (4) cascading communication using key words at key times, (5) employee recognition, (6) selection and 30- and 90-day meetings, (7) professional performance conversations, (8) Leadership Development Institutes, (9) employee forums, and (10) standards of practice.

When leaders in school districts apply these behaviors, they renew their sense of purpose and their joy in doing worthwhile work. A principal at an elementary school in Charleston County School District in South Carolina reluctantly (at first) sent a short survey to parents to gather insight; she rounded with several parents as well. She was stunned and excited to hear all the good things parents were saying about the school. We consistently find that people say more good things than negative things. Let's celebrate the good work we do and appreciate the people we work with as well as our students and their parents by creating a best-place-to-work environment for employees and best-place-to-be environment for students and families.

The good news is that we don't need to start from scratch to help people move through change. We simply tweak and refine many practices we're already familiar with. Even when something looks new, when we dig a little deeper, we find it probably isn't. Instead, it builds on the classic tactics we've always used in education.

In other words, it's not new—it's better. That's how leaders need to position change to achieve maximum buy-in and compliance as we strive to build better, more reliable, more consistent, more cost-effective educational systems.

CHAPTER TWELVE:

PERFORMANCE MANAGEMENT: HELPING EMPLOYEES LIVE UP TO THEIR HIGHEST POTENTIAL

FIGURE 12.1 | EVIDENCE-BASED LEADERSHIP^{SM} EDUCATIONAL FRAMEWORK

We've come to the performance management component of the Evidence-Based Leadership^{SM} framework (Figure 12.1). Many organizations struggle with performance management. And in an age of continuous change, it's more critical than ever to ensure that employees are doing what they need to be doing to meet the organization's goals. In fact, this is one of the five areas that organizations need to master if they are to truly improve their performance, along with accountability systems, leadership skill building, sequencing, managing performance, and communication (Figure 12.2).

FIGURE 12.2	QUESTIONS TO ASK IF YOUR ORGANIZATION IS STRUGGLING WITH HIGH PERFORMANCE
ACCOUNTABILITY SYSTEM	Is your leadership evaluation holding people accountable for outcomes?
LEADERSHIP SKILL BUILDING	Is leadership skill building happening continuously?
SEQUENCING	Is your sequencing right? Are you implementing the right steps in the right order?
MANAGING PERFORMANCE	Are you managing performance well?
COMMUNICATION	Are you communicating the *why* along with the *what* and the *how* behind what you are asking them to do?

Before we jump into the how-tos, let's take a look at the three levels of performance that exist inside most organizations.

The Three Levels of Performance

In any organization, employees can be categorized into three areas: (1) high performers, (2) medium/solid performers, and (3) low/subpar performers. Typically an organization has about 8 percent low/subpar performers, 58 percent middle/solid performers, and 34 percent high performers (Figure 12.3). Figure 12.4 summarizes the characteristics of each type of performer.

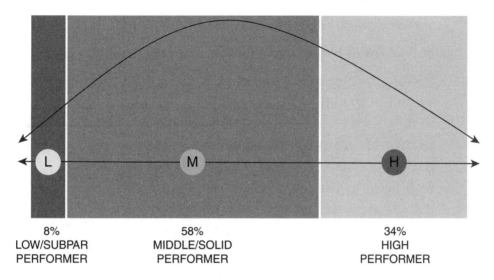

8% | 58% | 34%
LOW/SUBPAR | MIDDLE/SOLID | HIGH
PERFORMER | PERFORMER | PERFORMER

FIGURE 12.3 | THE PERFORMANCE CURVE

The High Performer

High performers are people we have the utmost confidence in. Why? They come to work on time. They have a positive attitude. They solve problems. We tend to relax when they are at work because we know that what needs to be done will be done.

High performers are good role models and good influences for others on the team. These are the people we ask to do peer interviews. They show ownership of the pillars, and if there is a problem, they bring a solution to it.

They are typically the experienced individuals in an organization. Sometimes new employees have the potential for high performance, but this may not be evident right away. New hires with a lot of experience may struggle at first because they're comparing their first days on their new jobs to their last days at their previous jobs. There is a learning curve, and it may take some time for people to adjust.

Role Model Superintendents

We had the pleasure of initiating a partnership with Arlington Independent School District in Arlington, Texas, in the year when Dr. Marcelo Cavazos became superintendent. Dr. Cavazos entered his first year as a good, solid performer. His ability and skill quickly moved him into high-performance status. Why? He is a problem solver and a good listener. He believes in people's input, intentionally works toward a good relationship with the board, and is not afraid to make difficult decisions.

Dr. JoAnn Sternke, superintendent of Pewaukee School District, a 2013 Malcolm Baldrige Award Recipient, is an experienced, high-performing superintendent. In 2014 she presented at our What's Right in Education conference. The evaluations from the audience showed that Dr. Sternke's presence and the evidence from her work as the executive leader made her a role model for other superintendents and leaders.

The Middle/Solid Performer

Solid performers have good attendance and demonstrate loyalty most of the time. They want to do a good job but may need additional experience and training to perform at a high level. They might waver a bit because their actions can be greatly influenced by either high or low/subpar performers. Although they do help identify problems, they may not have the confidence yet to present a solution (and risk rejection).

Basically, a middle/solid performer is someone who is progressing in the right direction. No organization can have all superstars, and that is okay. In fact, when there are too many high performers, there can be too much internal competition. We want good middle/solid performers, and, in fact, they are vital players. Balance is key for a team, and employees from both categories are needed for the organization to perform well.

As we mentioned, middle/solid performers may not be stellar problem solvers. This is why mentoring is so vital. Authors Susan and Peter Glaser, experts in the field of communication, wrote the book *Be Quiet, Be Heard: The Paradox of Persuasion*. Susan and Peter suggest that when someone brings you a problem, ask them what they suggest as a solution. If they don't know, follow with the question, "If you did know, what would you do?"

Making Problem Solvers: What Do You Think We Should Do?

One elementary school had a spike in student discipline referrals during its third 60-day planning cycle. Instead of jumping in to solve the issue, the principal asked the teacher leadership team, "What do you think we should do?"

At first the teachers said they didn't know. The principal followed up with, "Well, if you did know, what would be some of your ideas?" The teachers suggested that the number of indoor recess days had increased because of extreme winter weather and that the Positive Behavior Intervention Support approach was not being followed consistently by all teachers because of confusion about the process. This situation was an excellent opportunity to develop the teachers while gaining insight on possible problems to solve. At this point, the leader and teachers could do more research on the suggested solutions.

Encouraging solutions helps create a culture in which people feel comfortable sharing ideas. Middle/solid performers, like everyone, need this type of culture. They need to know we're committed to their development and that they aren't in the shadow of high performers. They need to know they are good, they have valuable ideas, and we want to retain them.

The Low/Subpar Performer

Subpar performers do not meet performance expectations. They have bad attitudes; they point out problems without offering solutions and do it in a negative way. They manage down leadership. They are masters of we/they and are the first to blame their leaders. To the low/subpar performer, the leader or someone else is always the problem. They are passive-aggressive, thinking they will outlast the leader.

Some low performers have good attitudes but simply lack the skill set to do the job, even when given additional support and resources. All of us who have been leaders know that these people are the most difficult to address because they have good attitudes. All our colleagues (leaders, teachers, and staff members) must have both good attitudes and the skill set to continue to work in our systems.

To be clear, here we are talking about how to deal with current employees (not new ones) who clearly aren't meeting performance expectations. Our first step is holding the mirror up to ourselves. Do low/subpar performers know they're not meeting expectations?

- Have we clearly identified "what right looks like"?

- Have we put them on a corrective action plan?

- Have we documented it?

Research from our Straight A Leadership Assessment shows that 52 percent of people who are not meeting performance expectations are aware of it, but 48 percent are not aware of it and have not been given a corrective action plan.

Research from our Straight A Leadership Assessment shows that 52 percent of the people who are not meeting performance expectations are aware of it, but 48 percent are not aware of it and do not have a corrective action plan.

We often hear excuses such as "Human Resources blocks corrective action" and "The union is going to protect them." Neither point is true. Human Resources wants good documentation. So do unions. No one wants to protect an employee who might be dangerous to coworkers and students, nor do they want to put them in a position in which they know they're not meeting expectations and coworkers are frustrated with them.

A low/subpar performer has one of two underlying issues. The first—and the easier one to deal with—is a person who has the skill to do the job but doesn't have the right attitude. We need to ask ourselves, "Could faulty processes and systems be causing their attitude?" If not—if other people seem to have good attitudes—then systems are not the problem.

A much tougher case is someone who really has the right attitude and is nice and helpful but doesn't have the skills to do the job right. These are the people who make performance management so challenging.

FIGURE 12.4 | CHARACTERISTICS OF PERFORMER TYPES

	HIGH PERFORMER	MIDDLE/SOLID PERFORMER	LOW/SUBPAR PERFORMER
DEFINITION	· Inspires the utmost confidence · Comes to work on time · Displays a positive attitude · Solves problems · Serves as a role model and is a good influence · Participates in peer interviews · Shows ownership of the pillars	· Maintains solid performance · Has good attendance · Demonstrates loyalty most of the time · Wants to do a good job · May need more experience · Influenced by high and low/subpar performers · Helps manager be aware of problems; not confident	· Points out problems without suggesting solutions · Manages down leadership · Master of we/they behavior · Blames leaders · Displays passive-aggressive attitude · Thinks they will outlast the leader
RESULTS	· Exceeds goals	· Achieves goals	· Does not achieve goals
PROFESSION-ALISM	· Adheres to unit policies concerning breaks, personal phone calls, leaving the work area, and other absences from work	· Usually adheres to unit policies concerning breaks, personal phone calls, leaving the work area, and other absences from work	· Does not communicate effectively about absences from work area; handles personal phone calls in a manner that interferes with work; takes breaks longer than allowed
TEAMWORK	· Demonstrates high commitment to making things better for the work unit and organization as a whole	· Committed to improving performance of the work unit and organization; may require coaching to fully execute a behavior	· Demonstrates little commitment to the work unit and the organization
KNOWLEDGE AND COMPETENCE	· Eager to change for the good of the organization; strives for continuous professional development	· Invested in own professional development; may require some coaching to fully execute a behavior	· Shows little interest in improving own performance or the performance of the organization; develops professional skills only when asked
COMMUNICA-TION	· Comes to work with a positive attitude	· Usually comes to work with a positive attitude; occasionally gets caught up in the negative attitudes of others	· Comes to work with a negative attitude; has a negative influence on the work environment

How to Deal with Each Type of Performer

After the team has been divided into the three categories, what comes next? For the most part, we've found that there are some proven ways to deal with each type of performer and to move the organization to the next level. And deal with them we must, because less-than-optimal performance can have a devastating effect on the organization as a whole.

Lessons From Peter Senge: It Matters

We really like Peter Senge's work in *The Fifth Discipline*. At one of his workshops, he talked about the impact that a small group of low/subpar performers can have—basically, they can endanger a larger group. We played a simple game that showed how a person who doesn't know how to manage inventory can bankrupt a company. It could be one person or an entire department. And as we've seen over the years with cases like Enron, the higher up in the organization the performance issues occur, the greater the harm done.

Peter also discussed a mountain-climbing technique. If a number of climbers are chained together, just one having an accident can take everyone down and possibly kill everyone on that team. In education, one low/subpar performer can cause enormous damage to other people and to the culture of an entire organization.

Let's begin with high performers. These people want to achieve so badly that when they see a new tool or technique, they quickly move to implement it. As a result, their frequency in the behavior is good, and they increase their performance quickly.

The middle/solid performers look at the high performer to see "what right looks like," or perhaps they're taught and then they implement the changes. Their performance is a bit more delayed, but they also want to be successful for all the right reasons, so middle performance goes up.

With low/subpar performers, whether it's "will or skill," they cannot improve their performance. If it's an attitude problem, they don't want to change. If it's a skill problem, they can't. Either way, maybe we can give them some solutions, but for now they're not moving.

At first the gap between low/subpar performers (about 8 percent of the population) and high/middle performers (about 92 percent) is pretty much hidden. Yet as the organization begins to improve—going from the lower quartile to the middle quartile, say—the gap won't stay hidden for long.

So, we're moving along. That critical mass of employees is improving and we're making good gains. And maybe that subpar 8 percent of the workforce can be carried for a while. But remember: we're also being compared to other organizations, so once "average" is hit, or a little better than average, it becomes clear that we can't carry the low/subpar performers any longer.

The Intolerable Gap Appears

In fulfilling our mission statement that says we're going to provide the highest quality, we're probably going to have to move up to that top-tier performance or top-tenth performance. This is when the gap between low/subpar performers and everyone else starts to become obvious (Figure 12.5). At first it's uncomfortable, but soon it's intolerable.

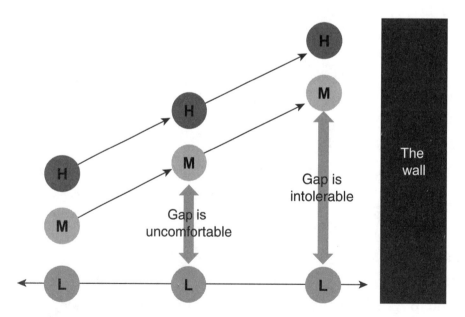

FIGURE 12.5 | THE GAP BECOMES INTOLERABLE

About this time, the high performers are getting a little frustrated because they now know what type of performance is expected, they see people not delivering it, and those people are still employed. How can this be?

The middle/solid performers are actually in the same boat, but something else is going on for them: they're starting to be targeted by the 8 percent. Many of the low/subpar performers, especially those with attitude issues, don't want the organization to change. They've been able to survive so far, but with a new evaluation system, new standards of behavior, and more consistency, they're going to have to make drastic changes. And so these low/subpar performers try to sabotage the effort.

As Ralph Waldo Emerson said, people wish to be settled. Low/subpar performers *really* wish to be settled. So do high and middle/solid performers, but they also get the second part of Emerson's observation, which is that only as far as they are unsettled is there any hope for them. The 92 percent of good performers feel hope and are moving forward. So the low/subpar performers latch on to some of the middle/solid performers and try to pull them backward, using we/they behavior and any other weapon they can find.

The low/subpar performers latch on to some of the middle/solid performers and try to pull them backward, using we/they behavior and any other weapon they can find.

Now the organization has an issue, and if we don't address it, things are going to start moving backward. Figure 12.6 shows how great progress can reverse.

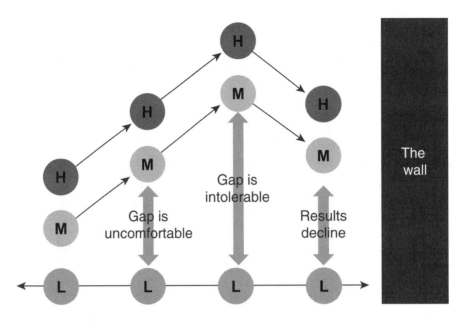

FIGURE 12.6 | THE EFFECT OF LOW/SUBPAR PERFORMERS ON ORGANIZATIONAL PERFORMANCE

When Studer Group first starts to work with organizations, leaders are excited. They're eager to measure things like student achievement, employee turnover, employee engagement, and parent satisfaction. And since anything that is measured improves, they're really thrilled about the progress they see. They like the Leadership Development Institutes and the techniques they're learning. In short, they're in the honeymoon phase (discussed in Chapter 4) and everything is great.

We're talking about middle and high performers, of course. The low/subpar performers are pretty much staying negative and thinking (actually hoping), "This won't last." However, change keeps happening and then all of a sudden, POW! We hit a wall.

Why? Well, high performers are getting tired. They have realized they are still carrying people they thought would be dealt with by now. So they start losing their enthusiasm and back off a bit. This doesn't mean they aren't still really, really good, but they've lost their edge. They doubt the organization's commitment to its values. They've throttled down.

Think about what happens when you're driving on the highway in a line of traffic and the lead car slows down. Let's say you're right behind it. What can you do but slow down? There isn't another choice. When these high performers back off the throttle, so do the middle/solid performers.

In the past, it wasn't unusual for us to get a call during year two from organizations we coached. The CEO would say, "We need another motivational talk. We need some more passion. Can you come do your Fire Starter thing for us again?"

Well, that made sense to us, so we threw some more motivational talks their way. But those didn't really go over so well because high and middle/solid performers didn't need them. They were thinking, "We heard this message the first time and we're there. We're not the ones who need to be talked to. It's someone over there sleeping, or maybe someone who didn't show up today, who needs the talking-to."

Thus we identified the performance wall.

This wasn't some big Studer Group discovery. The wall has been around since early civilizations created the Olympics. If you're an aspiring marathon runner who has just gotten started, you may not know if and when you will hit the wall. When you first hit it, you will stop. On the other hand, if you've been running for a while, you'll have adjusted to it. You'll know there's a wall, and it's only temporary, and you'll power through it.

The Performance Wall

Organizations face great challenges to get over that wall. When they start shaking like a plane approaching the sound barrier, they slow down and back off. It's a normal tendency. If you are driving a car and it starts shaking, you're going to slow down unless someone tells you that you actually need to speed up. Most people think this way. That's why when we saw the organizations we coached hitting that wall, we realized we had to create a way to help them through it.

The wall is why fields such as education and healthcare have been flooded with buzzwords, hot new methods, and trendy procedures over the years. Organizations have normally implemented a method for two or three years and then moved on to the next trend in management. We've realized, "The method is always the same. What we need is to come up with a better way to execute the method we have."

If we don't address performance issues—which means recruiting and retaining high performers, retaining and developing middle/solid performers, and moving low/subpar performers up or out—the organization moves backward. And we think, "Well, this no longer works. It's outlived its purpose. It's time to move on to the next idea."

At Studer Group, we've been in business long enough to work with the same organizations for years. Because they have the flywheel, the pillars, EBL, and the Nine Principles®, they find they don't have to do a new initiative. They just have to figure out which change in behavior or which new tool or technique fits into the original framework.

Let's say the tool is employee engagement, and the tactic they want to implement is leader rounding. Well, they have always been committed to employee engagement under the People Pillar. So what we do now is integrate the measure into a transparent scorecard and a leader evaluation tool. We change how we're holding people accountable for things like giving employees the opportunity to provide input, making sure they have the resources to do the job, and recognizing good work. Leader rounding influences all these results.

We make sure the leader has the skill set to apply leader rounding and that the tools and systems are in place to support it. We retain, reward, and recognize the people who have moved first on it. We try to develop everyone, and for people who just can't do it, we create a corrective action plan so they either move up in performance or move out of the position or the organization. We've implemented a new process and aligned it.

We don't need a new initiative or a new buzzword. That just turns people off and creates cynicism. Instead, put the new goal under one of the pillars and implement the needed tool or tactic. The flywheel is already turning. Change is implemented in a way that people don't see as change; instead, they see it as doing something they've always done but doing it more efficiently and effectively. We've always talked with employees. Now, we're just going to do it with focus and more efficiently and effectively, with a planned outcome and a frequency guideline.

We don't need a new initiative or a new buzzword. That just turns people off and creates cynicism. Instead, put the new goal under one of the pillars and implement the needed tool or tactic.

Let's talk about where we are now. Remember the graph (Figure 12.6) that showed organizational performance declining? The good news is that if we address performance issues quickly enough, we might not have that backward slide at all. Plus, the sooner we address them, the less painful they are to the organization because our high and middle/ solid performers are less exhausted. We're keeping the gap from getting so uncomfortable that it's unlivable, and we're applying a process that moves high and middle/solid performers over the wall (Figure 12.7).

We'll admit that performance management, particularly with sub-par performers, is really difficult. That's why we normally do it only when the pain of not doing it is worse than the pain of doing it. That's unfortunate, but it's just human nature.

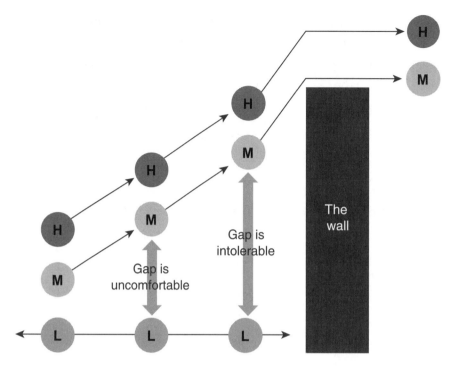

FIGURE 12.7 | GETTING OVER THE WALL

Why is performance management so difficult for organizations? Well, first of all, we have an amazing ability to rationalize why we don't need to do it (e.g., "Well, Toby might not be who we really want in that position, but we might not be able to find anyone better").

We don't realize how much money we're wasting on our "Tobys." When we ask leaders to write down how many employees they have and estimate the percentage of time they spend with each one, they're often amazed to find that they spend the majority of their time on the minority of employees who are the performance issues. In other words, they're focusing on the most difficult people to the detriment of the high and middle/solid performers, who cause no problems whatsoever.

We also find leaders who are working under a false premise. One of our favorite parts of the book *Results That Last* is the first page of Chapter 1. It essentially says we are tired of reading leadership books in which the first point is that job number one is to get everyone on board. We've been in healthcare and education for over 30 years and have met some "unboardable" people. They make a profession out of being un-happy. No matter what we do, it won't be good enough for them.

We find that leaders who believe they can get everyone on board *will* bring those who don't want to be on board home each night. Worse, they bring that emotion home. And it wears them out. Their family knows it, too. We tell people, "I know who your performance issues are. Just give me the phone number of your best friend or your closest fam-ily member and let me call them. In a matter of minutes, they'll tell me who your performance issues are, because you talk about them. A lot."

Another reason performance management is so tough is that in edu-cation, we are taught to focus on helping people. After all, we are here for all students and their families. Everything in our bodies tells us to never give up on a student, and we never want to give up on employees, either.

We've had people tell us things like, "I know she's difficult on the job, but she's got a lot of responsibility out of school that puts a strain on her finances and health. What's going to happen if I let her go?" If this is a teacher, how fair are we being to students if we continue to allow their teacher to perform at a subpar level? We're not exceptions to this problem. We're as empathetic and caring and mission-oriented and passion-oriented as everyone else—maybe even a little on the side of enabling—but we've learned that there comes a point when it is okay to say enough is enough. In fact, the sooner that point is reached, the better, because postponing it damages and exhausts the organization.

It's All About Values

We at Studer Group came up with an exercise that I think helps us get to where we're going. It's not a performance conversation—well, it is, but more than that, it's a *value* conversation. We ask organizations, "On a scale of 1 to 10, how value-driven are you as an organization?"

We generally ask people to vote on the answer to this question. If it's a group with executives present, I ask the executives not to raise their hands, because people tend to watch them or feel they're being watched *by* them. The idea is to make sure people are comfortable enough to be honest.

Before the vote, we explain that a 10 means you fulfill your mission statement and live your values. For example, at Studer Group, a 10 would mean that you're a good team player, treat people with respect, have high integrity, are generous, like to learn, like to teach, and understand measurable achievement. Those are the Studer Group values.

In our experience, organizations rarely rank themselves below a 7.5. In fact, that's happened only once in the hundreds of times we've conducted this exercise. The average is about an 8. Executive teams tend to vote a little bit higher, like a 9 or a 10, because, after all, that's what they live for. (It's almost like asking parents how dedicated they are to being parents. Of course they're dedicated!) So in general, most organizations seem enthusiastic and feel pretty good about how value-driven they are.

The next question is, "On a scale of 1 to 10, how well do you deal with performance issues?"

Again, before the vote we talk about what a 10 might look like. We all know there's no perfect world, no perfect employer. We all have challenges. A 10 means that, when someone is not meeting performance expectations, the reason for it is documented. It's clear what needs to happen to fix the problem: corrective action is taken or they're given a skill development plan. Ultimately, if they continue to not meet expectations, they're removed from either the position or the organization.

On the other hand, a 1 means not only are there performance issues, but possibly dysfunctional friends and relatives have been hired as well. In fact, three generations of performance issues might be working right now in one department.

So people usually laugh and shake their heads, and then they vote. We don't get any 10s on how well an organization deals with performance problems. We don't get any 9s. We get very few 8s. The response we usually get averages between 4.5 and 5. In other words, the response is usually 3 to 3.5 points below the response to the values question.

Then comes the bad news. We say, "Now, you have to change the answer to your first question. You have to reduce it to match the answer to your second question." Why? Because if we're not dealing effectively with performance issues, we're not living our values. Because it's not fair to students to be taught by someone who is not meeting expectations. And because it's not fair for team members to have to work with or be affected by someone else's poor performance. One mountain climber in a chain can bring down all the others.

A Lesson on Poor Performance

A parent was scheduled to meet with the principal about her child. The administrative assistant had failed to record the meeting on the principal's calendar, and the principal was not on site when the parent arrived. Not only was the principal not there, but the assistant was gone for the day as well. Now the principal had to take the call by phone and deal with not only the original issue of the meeting but also an irate parent on the phone.

So the principal's performance had been influenced directly by someone else's poor performance. One may think, "These things happen." They do. But the truth is that this was not the first time this type of incident had occurred, and the assistant's previous poor performance had been ignored. Ignoring poor performance affects the whole organization.

Poor performance that's not addressed puts the entire organization at risk. It causes safety issues, jeopardizes student achievement, and negatively influences the work environment for others. What's more, it's unfair to the people who work alongside subpar performers.

When we ask leaders if they're fair, they almost always say yes. And when we ask them to define fairness, they'll pinpoint things like scheduling, compensation, and benefits. Sometimes they'll mention performance expectations. But when we talk to the employees and ask them if their leader is fair, they don't mention scheduling, compensation, or benefits. They *always* talk about expectations. And if coworkers aren't meeting them, that's not fair to the 92 percent of the people who are.

When we position it like this, we find that the leader is willing to do those tough things.

Quint's Story: A Willing Leader

I once got a phone call from a healthcare leader who said, "Quint, I had to have a tough conversation with a person who's had performance issues for a long time. It was not something I wanted to do. In fact, I've avoided it for all too long, but I prepared like you said. And I actually was sort of hoping that the meeting would go much differently than it did."

In the back of our minds, we're always hoping the person says, "Yeah, you're right. I realize that I'm the problem. I'll change." Normally, though, it doesn't happen this way. People generally don't just have issues with a single organization or a single department; they have issues elsewhere, too. This situation was no exception. The leader told me her conversation didn't go well—in fact, it went about as badly as it could have gone.

At this point, I was sort of cringing. I'm like most of us: I don't want to cause pain, either. I figured that now she was probably mad at me because she had to do this, and it was painful. But she surprised me.

She said, "I just want to thank you. Even though this was a difficult conversation that didn't go well, I want you to know it was a big weight lifted off my back. I feel better walking out of this hospital today than I have for a long, long time."

Dealing with low/subpar performers can be painful. But ultimately, it's far less painful than doing nothing.

So we've got to deal with the elephant in the room. And we also have to tell leaders it's okay to admit that they've fallen short. When we've worked with organizations on this issue, we've found that people are afraid to come forward and tell us that they have no documentation of the subpar performer's problems. We've had to create amnesty, which means being straight about it. We all make mistakes, but the biggest mistake would be to not start now.

High, Middle/Solid, and Low/Subpar Performer Conversations

Remember how we discussed the importance of positioning things not as "new" but as "better"? That's a good way to handle the implementation of high, middle/solid, and low/subpar performer conversations. We just say, "It's only fair that we give people consistent feedback. This is an area that we want to get more consistent and reliable in, so now we're going to be meeting with everybody one-on-one, just to give them feedback on performance."

Here's how to hold each type of conversation.

The High Performer Conversation

It's best to meet with the high performers first. They're the people who, in the past, have been neglected. And they're the ones we most need on our side. If we're going to move the system and we know that they move it first, we've got to move *them* first.

The New Teachers Center published a study in 2012 called *The Irreplaceables: Understanding the Real Crisis in America's Urban Schools*. The original purpose of the study was to determine whether or not leaders were using new rules that loosened the requirements for removing low-performing teachers from the classroom. They found that the new rules did not precipitate that change and that many high-performing teachers were leaving urban classrooms. Here's why correcting this issue with high performers is critical. In an average school, when a high-performing teacher leaves, the school has a 1 in 6 chance of replacing that teacher with another high performer. In a low-performing school, the chances drop to 1 in 11. When exploring what high-performing teachers want, here's what they found. First, ask me to stay. Second, provide feedback and professional development opportunities. Third, give me more responsibility and opportunities for advancement. Fourth, recognize my accomplishments. Fifth, ensure that I have the resources to do my job.

In an average school, when a high-performing teacher leaves, the school has a 1 in 6 chance of replacing that teacher with another high performer. In a low-performing school, the chances drop to 1 in 11.

Having professional conversations with high performers is one of the most important jobs for leaders to do. Equally important, leaders have to solve the problem of addressing low-performance issues.

We suggest that leaders follow the process outlined in Figure 12.8 when talking with high performers. First, thank them for their efforts and work. Be sure that as you thank them and show appreciation, you tell them that you want to retain them.

In very specific terms, tell them how important they are to the school system. Be aware that when you thank them, they will want to know why. High performers don't like generalities. They gag when they're in a room with a thousand people and they hear that everybody is doing a good job. They know it's a nice thing to say, but it's probably not accurate.

Explain where the school system is going and what is being done to meet goals. This will excite them. High performers like being on winning teams. They like being the best. So we tell them about the system's commitment to being the best and include some of the things being done to meet goals, including these performance conversations.

Next, we ask them for input. We say, essentially, "We want to retain you, so is there anything that we should be doing better? What do we need to do for you?" We have never, ever had a high performer say, "Well, I want more money or benefits." Typically, if they ask for anything, they're going to ask for more responsibility, more opportunity, more development.

Janet's Story: Challenging High Performers

A teacher leader told me he didn't think his supervisor valued him because she never asked him to lead teams or to be part of committees that make a difference in the school. The teacher leader wanted an opportunity to show his leadership skills and didn't understand why people weren't giving him a chance, even if he made some mistakes along the way.

When I mentioned this to his leader, the leader could not have been more surprised. She had actually been worried that she and others were already overwhelming this

> teacher. She said, "Here I was thinking I was doing him a favor by not asking him to do more, and he actually volunteered to do more!"
>
> That's the value of high performers.

Sometimes high performers get so overwhelmed during these conversations that they become emotional. We've seen plenty of employees cry. We've also seen leaders cry because the employee says, "If I feel good, you've got to feel good. You do a good job, too." Their compliments are usually along the lines of "You'd never ask me to do anything you won't do" or "You're very approachable."

We leaders often get used to hanging out in the wrong neighborhood—the low/subpar performer neighborhood. We normally hear what's wrong: "Nobody likes you" or "Nobody wants to work here." We're constantly swallowing all that negativity instead of spending time with high performers. So these conversations can feel pretty good.

Here's the status thus far: You've had conversations with all your high performers. If there are 30 employees, and 30 to 40 percent of them are high performers, you've now had 10 to 13 really good meetings. You're starting to realize, "Hey, maybe I'm a better leader than I've been thinking, because I've been listening to the wrong people!"

FIGURE 12.8 | HIGH PERFORMER CONVERSATION

GOAL: REWARD, RECOGNIZE, AND RETAIN INDIVIDUAL

Thanks and Appreciation	Thank them for their effort and work.
Importance	Outline specifically why they are so important to the organization.
Organizational Direction/Plan	Explain where the organization is going and what is being done to meet those goals.
Input	Ask them for input. • "We want to retain you. Is there anything that we should be doing better? • "What do I need to do for you?"

Now it's time to take that newfound leadership confidence into conversations with middle/solid performers.

The Middle/Solid Performer Conversation

Generally, we start by explaining to the middle/solid performer that we're meeting with everybody one-on-one. Then we get right to the point and say, "We want you to stay. We want to keep you." Whatever words are used, the clear message demonstrates that this is a positive conversation. We might even bluntly say, "When you leave here, I want you to feel better than when you came in." The idea is to alleviate any anxiety that the middle/solid performer may have.

After we say we want them to stay, we tell them why (Figure 12.9 outlines the support-coach-support strategy). We spell out exactly what benefits they bring to the department. They're not as worried about where the organization is going as high performers are—they're more concerned about where they're going right now because they want to do well and they know they have areas that need developing.

Next we talk about their developmental needs. We know from our work/life balance study that it's vital for people to feel that we've invested in them. So we say, "We want to develop and invest in you and your career." If there's one thing we want that person to do better, we go over it. If there are multiple things, we still keep it to one. Remember, we don't want to overwhelm them; we want them to walk out feeling positive.

If there's one thing we want that person to do better, we go over it. If there are multiple things, we still keep it to one.

Maybe there's an extra certification they need or some extra training or some more experience. We might even share some specific tips on how to do their job better. (In conferences, we sometimes show a video of a leader holding a performance conversation with a person who works in food services. The leader talks about how to make sure everything in the refrigerator is the right temperature and is labeled with the right date, and then he shares a couple of systems that other food service workers have in place.)

Finally, we close with what's right. We talk about what they do well, and they leave feeling better than when they came in. They know we want them to stay. They know what they do well. They know we're committed to their development. And now the middle/solid performer might even be more excited than the high performer.

FIGURE 12.9	MIDDLE/SOLID PERFORMER CONVERSATION— SUPPORT, COACH, SUPPORT	
GOAL: REASSURE AND RETAIN INDIVIDUAL		
S	Support	Describe good qualities—calm down their anxiety.
C	Coach	Discuss development opportunities.
S	Support	Reaffirm good qualities.

The Low/Subpar Performer Conversation

Finally, it's time to tackle the task we dread the most. The good news is that having a proven template to follow makes the low/subpar performer conversation much less difficult than just "winging it" would be.

People don't meet performance goals for various reasons, but for this example, let's assume it's an employee with an attitude problem that's gone on for a while. The good news is that we've got the standards of performance signed, so not only can we cite what the low/subpar performer has done wrong, but we can show them that they agreed up front not to do it.

Now, before bringing in the low/subpar performer, we need to do a lot of preparation. First, be completely straightforward with your own supervisor. Share it all—the good, the bad, the ugly: "Here are the things I've documented, as I was supposed to do. Here are the things I haven't done. Here's where I am." That conversation will bring a sense of freedom. Remember, it isn't about going backward—it's about moving forward. You're going to leave the room a different leader from the old leader who didn't document.

Next we take a trip down to Human Resources. We let HR know that we're here for straight talk—we're not here to protect people. We're here to give people a chance to develop, but they have to do the work. The leader can't carry them. We're going to hold people to strict guidelines, and either they meet expectations or they're going to have to leave either the job or the school system.

We share with HR everything we've got and create a game plan. We ask, "Do I have to start with a verbal warning? Can I go straight to the written warning? Can I go to the final written warning, or do we have enough documentation to make the person leave the organization if things don't go well?"

We're still not done. This low/subpar performer has had these types of conversations before. They're not afraid of them. So we'll need to decide whether we want somebody from Human Resources with us. Do we want a supervisor with us, or another manager with us, or are we going to do it alone? This is a decision to make with your supervisor. Sometimes it's okay to do it alone, but sometimes it's not.

The person might interrupt or even go on the offensive, so it's important to be prepared. Role-playing can help. Ask a colleague to take the role of this person so that you're prepared for resistance. Remember, the only way to get good at something is frequency, and you'll never have a lot of frequency in low/subpar conversations. They're an exception, not the norm, and that means a lot of preparation is needed.

Now we're prepared. We bring the low/subpar performer into the room. Let's say, for this example, it's just the two of us. We tell the low/subpar performer that this is a serious conversation. We might say we've been meeting with everybody one-on-one, and then we follow a strategy we call DESK (Figure 12.10).

FIGURE 12.10	DESK, THE LOW/SUBPAR PERFORMER CONVERSATION STRATEGY	
D	Describe	Describe what has been observed.
E	Evaluate	Evaluate how you feel.
S	Show	Show what needs to be done.
K	Know	Know consequences of continued same performance.
	FOLLOW-UP	

The issue we discuss might be attendance, a problem with a coworker, or a lack of preventive maintenance. While we've got them there in the room, we have to *describe* the issue. That's "D."

Next, we're going to *evaluate*—this is "E"—exactly where the person is not meeting expectations and how that makes us feel. Perhaps they're being difficult about scheduling, or when someone asks for help the low/subpar performer is always "too busy." This is the chance to connect their behavior to a larger issue—say, commitment to coworkers.

At this point we may say, "As you'll recall, you signed the standards of performance, including the 'commitment to coworkers' part. Your attendance is affecting the team."

The person will either claim they didn't sign the standards, or they'll say they did but didn't understand it. Around this time, we'll likely be interrupted, so we will have to ask the person to please be quiet and let us finish, and when we're done they can talk.

Chances are the low/subpar performer will try to point fingers or shift the attention to someone else. We have to keep reminding them we are here to talk about them and no one else. In other words, we show them leadership that they have not seen from us before (otherwise, we wouldn't be in the situation we are in now).

Now we move to "S," which means to *show* the low/subpar performer what needs to be done. We say, in essence, "Here's what I'm looking for, here's 'what right looks like,' here are the expectations."

Now for "K," which stands for "*know* the consequences," we spell out the current consequences of the low/subpar performer's behavior and also the consequences they will face if it continues.

The low/subpar performer may think that once they're out the door, life will return to normal. So it's vital that we talk about follow-up: how often we're going to meet with them, what the meetings will look like, what we expect them to do between now and then. The point is to make sure the low/subpar performer knows this thing is not going away.

We find that a third of these low-performing employees will self-select out. Once they know they can no longer do what they've been doing, they'll leave. Another third will adjust their behavior. The remaining third we will probably have to ask to leave. Remember, if we have 30 employees, we're talking about only two or three people.

We find that a third of these low-performing employees will self-select out. Once they know they can no longer do what they've been doing, they'll leave. Another third will adjust their behavior. The remaining third we will probably have to ask to leave.

We've just discussed the technique for moving performance when we hit that wall. It's a crucial part of creating a culture of high performance. When we talk about creating consistency and reliability, human capital is our biggest investment, our biggest responsibility, and our biggest opportunity.

Summary

We learned about the three levels of employee performance. In most organizations, only 8 percent of employees are low/subpar performers, 58 percent are middle/solid performers, and 34 percent are high performers. We also learned how each of these categories of people responds to change.

Low/subpar performers are the rotten apples in the barrel. If we don't deal with them, they will spoil the organization's culture. They may infect middle/solid performers with their bad attitudes and we/they behavior, and high performers may disengage or even leave.

One thing's for sure: when we don't address low/subpar performers, our organization's improvement will hit the wall. Only good performance management will get us over the wall.

Here are the three types of conversations that organizations need to implement:

- High performer conversations: The goal here is to re-recruit these employees. We thank them for their contributions and let them know we want to retain them, we share the organization's goals, and we ask for input on what we can do to help them.

- Middle/solid performer conversations: Here the goal is to move middle performers up. We describe their good qualities, go over development opportunities, and reaffirm good qualities (support, coach, support).

- Low/subpar performer conversations: These conversations have one purpose—to move low/subpar performers up or out of the organization. We use the DESK technique to frame this discussion: **D**escribe what has been observed, **E**valuate how you feel, **S**how what needs to be done, and **K**now the consequences of maintaining the same performance. (Follow-up meetings will determine the fate of the low/subpar performer.)

CHAPTER THIRTEEN:

PROCESS IMPROVEMENT: STANDARDIZATION AND ACCELERATION

FIGURE 13.1 | EVIDENCE-BASED LEADERSHIP^{SM} EDUCATIONAL FRAMEWORK

We've come to the last part of the EBL framework, which focuses on the processes we apply to build efficiencies into our systems, the programs we select to support high student achievement, and the technology systems we choose to accelerate our work flow. This chapter focuses on two aspects of process improvement. One is the validation component of the Execution Flywheel[SM], which requires setting up processes to validate Always Behaviors[SM] and follow-through. The second aspect is process-improvement methodologies, which help leaders engage the workforce to analyze information so they can solve problems associated with everyday actions.

The purpose of this book is not to detail process-improvement methodologies such as Lean, Six Sigma, Total Quality Management, and so on. Rather, we focus on validation processes embedded in the EBL framework and on improvement science spearheaded by healthcare and translated to education by the Carnegie Foundation for the Advancement of Learning.

Studer Group has always been committed to process improvement. Our efforts to improve the processes by which our own firm performs led to our receiving the Malcolm Baldrige National Quality Award in 2010. We've been able to share many of the lessons we learned from this experience with the organizations we coach.

In our work with school districts, we've discovered that many systems fall short of creating and applying good processes. K–12 leaders have had difficulty coming up with the right process and implementing it properly, as many of us have. School systems seem to have trouble holding onto a process over time and applying it with fidelity and consistency.

Consider the many ways we use process improvement in our daily lives. Whether we are figuring out the best sequence to clean and cook, the best route to take when driving, or the most efficient way to prepare and pack for a family vacation, we naturally want to take the fewest steps to achieve the greatest impact. It is amazing to watch teachers juggle all their activities and commitments with students. Great teachers have their sequence and processes down to a science.

It is amazing to watch teachers juggle all their activities and commitments with students. Great teachers have their sequence and processes down to a science.

The EBL framework guides leaders to align goals, actions, and processes to improve educational systems. Processes do not exist in a vacuum. They align to and rely on key performance measures that drive individual accountability and strategic actions to help people achieve the goals. Good processes should help leaders achieve the organizational and departmental goals they are accountable for.

Good processes should help leaders achieve the organizational and departmental goals they are accountable for.

Priorities and Process

Charleston County School District in Charleston, South Carolina, places a high priority on improving its overall district services survey score. The school leaders complete a district services survey by responding to items that reflect the level of service schools receive from the district offices. The goal is for all departments to score a 4.50 on a 5.00 scale. Some units achieved the goal, but about 80 percent did not.

Deputy Superintendent Audrey Lane and Performance Management Officer Erica Callaway designed and facilitated process-improvement sessions with district department leaders. Audrey and Erica reviewed the results with district leaders. They also highlighted the processes of leaders who scored high marks on the survey. After this session, Audrey and Erica had department leaders work with their individual units to create a process to solve one or two core problems identified by principals on the survey. Then the department leaders engaged employees in their units to come up with possible improvements to try out.

The district support services survey is administered about every 45 days so the units can see their progress over short cycles. Most units have shown an increase in their survey scores. Consequently, the overall district services survey has improved every year and is getting closer to the 4.50 mark.

The EBL framework naturally focuses leaders' attention on system-wide improvement. As part of this framework, the goals and actions cascade from the executive team level to every leader of departments and schools. So do the processes. As leaders, we think about how to apply process-improvement strategies and tools to improve the systems as well as the unique problems in a given unit.

Every day, we apply many processes and go through the same steps each time. For example, we have processes for answering the phone, recording data into a system, meeting with others, and so on. In almost any process we've observed in a K–12 system, however, we run across inconsistencies. Consequently, we hear from unhappy employees, students, and parents.

A process may be a set of steps we take to offer a service, create a product, achieve a goal, implement a program, or provide value to others (e.g., recognizing people for their good work). When processes work well, they improve the effectiveness and efficiency of our educational systems. When they don't, they create stress, frustration, anger, and impaired goal achievement—even student achievement.

As a simple approach to creating effective processes, we recommend that teams work together to map the process by using a flowchart or similar tool and then teach the process to colleagues. The goal is for everyone to hardwire a process consistently. Here's what's important: sometimes we change a process or a program when the problem was not the program itself but its poor execution. One of the most important aspects of EBL is creating a way to validate the expected strategic actions and the accompanying processes as well as any workflow processes that help us do our jobs in the most efficient way.

Validation Processes

We've diagnosed where we need to set our goals, determined the aligned strategic actions, and provided the development and coaching needed to support leaders to perform. To get results, people need to apply the standardized behaviors consistently and well. The goal is to shift validation from compliance only to a quarterly review of the individual execution of the action.

As part of the K–12 EBL framework and the Execution Flywheel, validation is a formal process for supervisors to determine how well Always Behaviors are being carried out. Are they being executed with high quality and producing the expected results? The collection of documented evidence is the validation of the expected action.

We'll review the validation process associated with leader rounding as an example.

An Example of Validation

Dr. Steve Sperry is director of administrative and human resources in the School District of Janesville, Janesville, Wisconsin. In that role, Dr. Sperry supervises and evaluates school leaders. Each semester, he presents a leader rounding schedule to school leaders that defines expectations for the number of times school leaders will round with staff. Dr. Sperry validates in two ways: at a monthly meeting and by accompanying school principals on their rounds. School leaders are expected to keep a rounding log for each rounding session and to post and update a Stoplight Report, which includes the status of processes that can be improved and the resources needed.

At the meeting, Dr. Sperry verifies the number of teachers and staff on the rounding log and then asks the leader, "What are the main things you have learned from this past 45 days after rounding with teachers and staff?" "What are the wins?" "What areas are of greatest concern?" In this way, he engages the school leader in a process-improvement conversation by capitalizing on the wins and noting the issues. The school leaders leave the meeting with an action plan for engaging teachers and staff to create improvements.

Here's what we've learned: solid and high-performing leaders want validation processes in place because they realize it makes them better and more accountable. It is human nature to let things slide if someone is not validating our actions. Also, we've learned that at first, superintendents and senior leadership teams tend not to see the need for validating. They believe they should be able to trust people to always apply the action. When results slip, one quickly realizes that the missing piece of the puzzle is a clear validation process for those actions and processes, in which doing them *always* is the only option.

When results slip, one quickly realizes that the missing piece of the puzzle is a clear validation process for those actions and processes, in which doing them *always* is the only option.

Improvement Research

As we apply the EBL framework in school districts, we've begun to rely on the concept of improvement research, which aligns to the extensive work in healthcare on improvement science. The primary goal in healthcare is to determine which improvement strategies work to increase patient safety and quality of care.

The Carnegie Foundation for the Advancement of Teaching and Learning has developed and is promoting a research and development infrastructure called improvement research, which synthesizes the evidence from best practices, rapidly develops and tests prospective improvements, and deploys the improvements to continuously improve the performance of systems. Improvement science in and of itself is often compared to other sciences, such as evidence-based practice and strategy utilization. The conceptual frame of reference allows a broad scope of study about improvement strategies that work best in complex systems.

The systems approach builds process improvement from the bottom up. It relies on a series of tools for quality management that help workers identify and solve problems on their own. Every solution needs to push the organizational system closer to the overall measurable goals and evidence-based improvement strategies.

For example, sometimes we hear leaders complaining about survey results that look bad in a particular area. Their concern is that respondents fail to give them the information they need in order to improve. We've heard leaders say things like, "If someone gives us the lowest score, the survey tool should force the person to say why he or she gave a score of 1 or 2 (the lowest two ratings)." Here we reinforce two things. First, a survey shows how people feel and is not intended to define or solve problems. Second, the process-improvement system helps engage teams to identify problems, explore potential solutions, and experiment in the workplace to determine if the applications need to be adopted, adapted, or abandoned. Good processes arise from the workforce being highly engaged to identify and solve problems in order to achieve excellence. The process-improvement part of EBL reinforces and accelerates a culture of performance excellence.

> The process-improvement part of EBL reinforces and accelerates a culture of performance excellence.

We have embraced Carnegie's six core principles of improvement, and we've seen that they have great relevance for improvement research (Figure 13.2; see also http://www.carnegiefoundation.org/). Because they are central to the work we do, we introduce the six core principles to our partners so leaders can study ways to improve processes. For instance, as we study programs by doing a mini program evaluation, we apply improvement research.

FIGURE 13.2 | IMPROVEMENT RESEARCH CORE PRINCIPLES

	SIX CORE PRINCIPLES OF IMPROVEMENT RESEARCH	CARNEGIE DESCRIPTION
1	Make the work problem-specific and user-centered	It starts with a single question: "What specifically is the problem we are trying to solve?" It enlivens a co-development orientation: engage key participants early and often.
2	Variation in performance is the core problem to address.	The critical issue is not what works, but rather, what works, for whom, and under what set of conditions. Aim to advance efficacy reliably at scale.
3	See the system that produces the current outcomes.	It is hard to improve what you do not fully understand. Go and see how local conditions shape work processes. Make your hypotheses for change public and clear.
4	We cannot improve at scale what we cannot measure.	Embed measures of key outcomes and processes to track whether change is an improvement. We intervene in complex organizations. Anticipate unintended consequences and measure these, too.
5	Anchor practice improvement in disciplined inquiry.	Engage rapid cycles of Plan, Do, Study, Act (PDSA) to learn fast, fail fast, and improve quickly. That failures may occur is not the problem; that we fail to learn from them is.
6	Accelerate improvements through networked communities.	Embrace the wisdom of crowds. We can accomplish more together than even the best of us can accomplish alone.

Plan, Do, Study, Act

The Plan, Do, Study, Act (PDSA) cycle is one of the most popular process-improvement approaches applied in educational systems that have won a state-affiliated or national Baldrige award. Because it is noted as one of the core principles of improvement research, we provide a brief overview of how PDSA is included in the EBL framework.

So far with the EBL framework, we have described a systems scorecard with key performance measures by pillar, with aligned progress-monitoring measures and key strategic actions. All are cascaded to unit levels in an educational system.

In the Plan phase, our goal is to enlist process-improvement teams in the workforce to review the progress-monitoring results and other useful information in order to determine performance gaps or accelerators, possible causes of a problem, and potential ways to improve. Leaders then work with teams to gather evidence and gain input for identifying gaps and coming up with potential solutions to problems. To complete the Plan phase, a plan of action is put in place to test the possible solution on a small scale.

During the Do phase, the test site implements the plan, data are collected, and problems are documented. The Study phase pulls the results together to be analyzed so that during the Action phase, one of three decisions is made: adopt, adapt, or abandon.

Technology as an Accelerator

Technology is one of the greatest drivers in process improvement today. Done poorly, technology can be one of our greatest frustrations and expenses. Done well, new technology can accelerate a system's progress. Speed is important because the goal is always to improve quality while reducing cost. Some cost reduction might come in the form of pure cost savings to the budget. Other savings might be realized when we improve productivity, which allows people to do more things in the same amount of time. Technology that facilitates either type of cost reduction can be a worthwhile investment. The technology we use includes well-thought-out ways of applying the tools and systems as well as user training. Leaders should be able to explain why the district has selected a technology system. Purchasing technology has to be a strategic decision that aligns to one of the key pillar measures.

Technology is one of the greatest drivers in process improvement today. Done poorly, technology can be one of our greatest frustrations and expenses.

Technology Talking

At our last visit to Stoughton Area School District, Stoughton, Wisconsin, we were discussing bad decisions that cost systems a lot of money with no increased student achievement outcomes. Stoughton's technology director spoke of a potential bad decision that technology directors are facing. He said, "We are under constant pressure to provide all students with iPads. I'm not against iPads, and I think it would be nice for all students to have access to one. However, we need to gather evidence on the advantages and obstacles the district would face in making this decision, like the potential need to increase staffing in the Technology Department to provide support and the training needed for teachers and students."

We then talked about applying improvement research by selecting a small pilot group. This would guide the district to define a hypothesis, test it in the field, and provide the results in the form of good evidence to leaders and the school board.

Process-Improvement Tools

This section does not provide an exhaustive set of tools for leaders to use; it does present some tools we tend to rely on. We highlight some of these tools with brief descriptions.

In our work with school districts, two tools are fundamental to helping us know our partners. A tool we use as part of our strategy meetings is a SWOT analysis (Strengths, Weaknesses, Opportunities, and Threats). We can apply this tool to the school system and then to each department and school as part of the strategic planning process. To review efficiencies, we also use a common tool—a flowchart—to map out the steps for essential strategic actions and the accompanying workflow processes.

As described throughout the book, Studer Education focuses on training and coaching leaders to create best-place-to-work environments. Here we present some tools that leaders can use to gather input from employees to solve problems or build on areas of strength and opportunities. As we've mentioned, one of the lowest-scored items on the Studer Education employee engagement survey aligns to employees perceiving that they have opportunities for providing input into decisions that affect their work. The sample tools summarized here help leaders do that.

Brainstorming

Brainstorming includes both individual and group brainstorming to address a problem or opportunity. Once ideas are recorded, the participants complete a ranking process, using number rankings and/or dots, to determine which solution the group thinks is most viable. We encourage leaders to apply brainstorming when rolling out survey results or any other results that indicate areas where improvements can be made.

Brainwriting

At times it's important to allow people to capture their own thoughts as well as others' creative thinking. One way to do this is to ask people to write down, say, three ideas on a sticky note for solving the problem and then pass the note to the next person. Each person looks at the others' ideas and adds their thoughts. This continues through several iterations. The final information is posted and then analyzed.

The Five Whys

To analyze the failure of a process, a group of people answer this question five times: Why did the process fail? The purpose of asking the same question five times is to get to the root cause of the problem. The technique is simple, effective, and engaging.

A facilitator leads the session and makes sure that the responses are connected to the process, not to people. The goal is to keep people from applying we/they during this exercise. Making a mistake in any one answer can lead to misleading results. A facilitator's responsibility is to guide the team to get to the root cause of a problem that needs to be solved.

Affinity Diagram

Narrative comments on surveys can be analyzed using the affinity process. The information is analyzed and placed into themes and labeled under broad categories. To create the Affinity Diagram, we place the problem at the top and then list categories underneath with the ideas for each category.

Fishbone Diagram

Some problems are serious enough that we need to explore everything that could be causing them. Addressing one part of a problem while ignoring other factors may cause the problem to recur. A Fishbone Diagram is a cause-and-effect approach to solving a problem. It requires teams to identify the problem, identify the factors that might contribute to the problem, identify possible causes, and investigate and test which of these causes is most likely to contribute to the problem. As teams go through these steps, the members diagram the factors and the root cause as a way to create a visual for the problem at hand.

Stoplight Report

We use a Stoplight Report to communicate the information leaders receive from rounding. This report shows how the ideas and concerns that have come up are dealt with. Posting Stoplight Reports in a communication bulletin, on boards, or through other existing communication protocols is an excellent way to disseminate information. Green items are things that have been addressed and are complete. Yellow items are things in progress. Red items are things that cannot be done and are followed by an explanation of why they can't be done. We also use the green-yellow-red breakdown to track status on short-cycle initiatives. Leaders can use this approach in multiple ways. Here's an example: We coach superintendents to round with their senior leadership teams. One question they ask is, "What processes can be improved to make your work more efficient?" Superintendents gather the responses and determine how to follow through. The Stoplight Report is the communication tool they use with their senior teams. Figure 13.3 shows one superintendent's Stoplight Report after a 45-day cycle, or one set of rounds.

FIGURE 13.3 | SAMPLE STOPLIGHT REPORT

STOPLIGHT REPORT SENIOR LEADERSHIP TEAM

GREEN	YELLOW	RED
• Hold weekly meetings on time. • Provide agendas at least 24 hours in advance. • Give everyone a chance to provide input (create a process for speaking and apply the Rules for Engagement).	• Create a better process for cascading information to the school district within 24 to 48 hours of meetings (team creating and defining the process due in 20 days).	• Move meetings from weekly to every two weeks. (Before changing the schedule, we are going to work to improve meeting processes.)

These are just a few of many tools that help us build better processes and, most importantly, engage our workforce in the decision-making process to help us improve. The Aligned Processes part of the EBL framework focuses on finding ways to standardize what everyone needs in order to maximize performance. These tools can help accelerate results.

It's All About Critical Thinking

We want to see leaders striving to hit the sweet spot for aligning goals, behaviors, and processes. As we close this chapter, we would be remiss if we failed to discuss where critical thinking fits into good leadership. Linda Elder and Richard Paul wrote a book titled *The Thinker's Guide to Intellectual Standards*. In the introduction, they write,

> Humans live in a world of thoughts. We accept some thoughts as true. We reject others as false. But the thoughts we perceive as true are sometimes false, unsound, or misleading. And the thoughts we perceive as false and trivial are sometimes true and significant. The mind doesn't naturally grasp the truth. We don't naturally see things as they are. We don't automatically sense what is reasonable and what is unreasonable. Our thought is often biased by our agendas, interests, and values. We typically see things as we want to. We twist reality to fit our preconceived ideas. Distorting reality is common in human life. It is a phenomenon to which we all unfortunately fall prey. . . . Each of us views the world through multiple lenses, often shifting them to fit our changing feelings.

The EBL framework, a systems-improvement approach, focuses and depends on leadership. We propose that leaders apply the intellectual standards shown in Figure 13.4 with other leaders and with teachers and staff. These standards and the associated probing questions are the work of Elder and Paul.

As we set measurable goals, align individual leader evaluations, analyze leadership gaps, manage individual performance, and create the most efficient and effective processes, we should ask these types of questions. The best leaders are great critical thinkers.

FIGURE 13.4	INTELLECTUAL STANDARDS FROM ELDER AND PAUL, *THE THINKER'S GUIDE TO INTELLECTUAL STANDARDS*
CLARITY	· Could you elaborate further on that point? · Could you express that point in another way? · Could you give me an illustration? Could you give me an example?
ACCURACY	· Is that really true? · How could we check that? · How could we find out if that is true?
PRECISION	· Could you give more details? · Could you be more specific?
RELEVANCE	· How is that connected to the question? · How does that bear on the issue?
DEPTH	· How does your answer address the complexities in the question? · How are you taking into account the problems in the question? · Is that dealing with the most significant factors?
BREADTH	· Do we need to consider another point of view? · Is there another way to look at this question? · What would this look like from a conservative standpoint? · What would this look like from the point of view of...?
LOGIC	· Does this really make sense? · Does that follow from what you said? · How does that follow? · But before you implied this, and now you are saying that. How can both be true?
FAIRNESS	· Do I have a vested interest in this issue? · Am I sympathetically representing the viewpoints of others?

Summary

The EBL framework is a systems-improvement approach that holds superintendents and the senior leadership team accountable for driving excellence throughout the school district. For school districts to be excellent, all schools and all departments must be excellent. The framework reinforces alignment of leadership throughout the system.

This chapter focuses on the last part of the framework: standardization of processes and programs, and acceleration with technology. All parts of the framework work hand in hand to maximize leadership performance. We describe the relevance of the validation component of the Execution Flywheel as a critical part of Evidence-Based Leadership^SM. We explore some existing process-improvement methodologies, including summaries of several tools that leaders can use to better engage the workforce. Leaders engage the workforce by setting up teams that provide input on what and how improvements need to be made. We include two components that reinforce disciplined and creative thought by applying improvement research and the intellectual standards.

This chapter is not intended to provide the detail associated with process improvement. A number of good books do this. We include aligned processes in the EBL framework as one of three important systems-improvement considerations. All three—aligned goals, aligned behaviors, and aligned processes—must be in place for school systems to achieve and sustain results.

CHAPTER FOURTEEN:

Reflection: Connecting with Hearts and Minds—A Set of Qualities and Skills Every Leader Needs

We have worked in healthcare and education for a long time. Each of us has found that people who are the most successful in aligning actions to achieve the desired results in a department, division, or organization have certain characteristics in common. These characteristics, which we'll look at one by one in this chapter, come together in one overarching skill: the ability to connect with both the heart and mind of those they lead, work with, or provide services to. To create highly effective K–12 educational systems, leaders must be able to make these connections.

Why is it so important to connect with both the emotional and rational aspects of people? Well, many people working in education are both scientifically minded and deeply passionate about their work. When we connect to the mind, we're appealing to their logical, data-driven, evidence-seeking side. When we connect to the heart, we're appealing to people's passion and to the values they bring to work every day—the same values that led them to this career.

> When we connect to the mind, we're appealing to people's logical, data-driven, evidence-seeking side. When we connect to the heart, we're appealing to their passion and to the values they bring to work every day—the same values that led them to this career.

It's the same with students: we diagnose where they are, create a lesson plan, monitor their progress, give them feedback on their performance, and assess the outcome. That's the mind part. We also need to provide comfort, reassurance, and hope. That's the heart part.

So, what characteristics do high-performing leaders exhibit? They are authentic and they show empathy. They can bring conversations back to point. They have an instinct for knowing when to push an individual and when not to. Other key qualities are the ability to limit and sequence changes, to break things into understandable steps, and to connect back to a group's mission, vision, and values. Finally, they can also connect the dots for people—to pull the various elements together. Let's look at these characteristics one at a time.

Authenticity

Authenticity is basic to connecting with another human being. It creates the trust necessary to construct a culture of high performance, one person at a time. Authenticity can exist on both organizational and individual levels. And while it's important in all fields, in education it is absolutely vital.

Today, leaders are under the scrutiny of people who are professionally trained in evaluating honesty, who constantly ask, "Do I agree with what I am hearing/reading?" We have seen leaders who have, at best, average communication skills in the literal sense but who get high marks from people in the organization on their ability to communicate.

286

We have also seen people with superb verbal skills who are viewed as ineffective communicators by those they lead.

What is the difference? Authenticity, otherwise known as believability.

Becoming an authentic leader is not necessarily easy, but it is simple. We just start telling the facts even when it's difficult—*especially* when it's difficult. We stop sugarcoating. We stop practicing we/they. We learn how to have the tough conversations rather than avoid them. We start being who we are no matter whom we're talking to. When we can become more authentic, those we lead are more likely to believe us and comply with our requests. Authenticity creates followers.

When we can become more authentic, those we lead are more likely to believe us and comply with our requests. Authenticity creates followers.

Empathy

What is empathy, anyway? Basically, it's the ability to understand and share other people's feelings. When we demonstrate empathy, people connect better with us. They know they are understood. When people feel cared about, they listen better; they are more comfortable asking questions and asking for help. They also work harder and are more likely to stay in an organization long term.

Being an empathetic leader doesn't mean we get caught up in the emotions of our staff or try to "fix" them and take on their burdens. (As we discuss elsewhere in the book, that's never a good idea. People really have to take responsibility for themselves.) What it does mean is that we make an attempt to truly listen to employees and understand where they are coming from.

Empathetic leaders really focus on employees when they are talking. While we may not agree with them or give them the answer they want, we make sure they know they are heard. We don't issue commands or "talk at" people. We talk *with* them and listen to them. Leaders who know they tend to be short on empathy can, by cultivating the practice of careful listening, develop this quality.

Empathetic leaders tend to get plenty of "listening experience" by getting out of their ivory tower and connecting with staff regularly. Many of the classic Studer Group tactics (such as rounding for outcomes, 90-day meetings, and employee forums) help leaders listen to staff members. To empathize with people, we must truly know them, and that happens only when we make ourselves a part of their world.

> To empathize with people, we must truly know them, and that happens only when we make ourselves a part of their world.

Finally, empathetic leaders are vulnerable. We're open about our own shortcomings because we believe others can learn from them. We don't mind saying, "I made that mistake myself, so I know where you're coming from. Let me tell you about it." You'll see stories throughout this book that share mistakes we've made in our careers.

Empathy means approaching other human beings with the full awareness and disclosure that we, too, are human and have flaws—but it *doesn't* mean we wallow in those flaws. It doesn't mean we stop trying to get better and better.

Moving a Conversation Back to Point

Empathy is a needed quality in a leader, but at times it must be set aside and conversations moved back to the issue at hand. For example, a superintendent was talking to his chief academic officer (CAO) about some concerns he had about the department that reported to the CAO. The CAO provided a list of reasons that performance had fallen short.

Most of these reasons had merit, but a few of them were a bit of a stretch. After showing empathy with his good listening skills, the superintendent said to the CAO, "Okay, now tell me what actions will be taken to get the department on track." One of Quint's connections in healthcare, Tom Cassidy, said that defensiveness goes down when a leader moves to the right question, namely, "What is going to happen to get performance back on track?"

Of course, many occasions arise when we need to take the past into account. However, the faster someone can move into the present and future, the better the present and future will be.

Early on in our careers in leadership positions, when we met with our supervisors for regular monthly meetings, we would talk about challenges and obstacles, expecting empathy for our situation. Sometimes our supervisors empathized, but other times they did not. If the question recommended by Tom Cassidy—"What is going to happen to get back on track?"—had been posed, those meetings would have been more productive. Now when we're working with our staff or coaching other leaders, we practice what Tom recommended, and it really works to get the conversation back to how the problem can be fixed.

"What is going to happen to get back on track?"

When to Push and When to Hold Back

Knowing when to push people or the organization forward, and when not to push while still getting forward movement, is an important part of the art and science of leadership. Being a leader (which includes leading students to achieve) is about being able to manage the gap between where people are and where they need to be. Too much pushing can shut people down. Too little pushing will not create enough action to achieve the goal.

> Too much pushing can shut people down. Too little pushing will not create enough action to achieve the goal.

After observing many highly effective people at work, we've come to see that the best time to push is when things are going well. Why? Because that's when people are feeling the most confident. Jack Welch, past CEO of GE, said that people and organizations with self-confidence (not cockiness) work more quickly and smoothly (and less expensively) in all aspects of their work.

On the flip side, when an organization or person is not achieving the desired outcome, support may be the best way to lead. The key is to build self-confidence. This doesn't mean accepting poor performance. It means pulling a person or an organization out of a self-defeating mind-set. Methods vary from saying, "I have confidence in you, and we're committed to your development" to saying, "I understand what happened, and I know we will do better." Other effective tactics are making a gesture of sincere caring or simply moving on to what comes next.

Quint's Story: Moving the Team Forward

I knew a sports medicine physician who at one point worked with a team in the National Basketball Association. I happened to see one of their televised games during that time. I was excited as the game started and thrilled to spot the physician behind the bench. But as I watched, I became more and more dismayed as the man's team endured one of the most lopsided losses I had ever seen. They were normally a much better team.

The next day, I called the physician to let him know I had seen him. I told him I was curious about what the coach, Don Nelson (who is now in the NBA Hall of Fame), had said to the team. Frankly, I had imagined a really challenging locker room scenario. The answer I got surprised me at the time, but as I have gained more experience and knowledge, I now see why this coach was successful.

The physician said that when they got into the locker room, the coach gathered the team around, handed out the scouting report on their next opponent, went over the report and how confident he was that they would be ready, and then went into his office. He literally acted as though the game they just lost had not happened. That's because he understood that his job as leader is to move the team forward.

I thought if the team had won, he would have gathered them around, acknowledged the win, and pointed out areas they needed to improve on. Good leaders know when to push . . . and when to push in a much different manner that doesn't feel like pushing.

Limiting and Sequencing Changes

Most times when we are asked to assess an organization, the problem is inconsistency in results. By this, we mean they're seeing too much variability in outcomes or, after some positive gain, performance has flattened or is falling off.

While there are all sorts of possible reasons for the two issues (which can be closely related or at times one and the same), we find that one cause shows up more often than others: people are trying to do too much. Our partners have great dedication to outcomes and are prone to thinking that doing more is always better.

Because people in education are so passionate about making things better, we may try to do too much too soon and get overwhelmed. Too much too soon is passion's sneakiest side effect. As we know all too well, even good things can have not-so-good side effects.

Building an Emotional Bank Account

We've worked with principals in high-need schools, or schools that have high poverty rates and low student performance. Many of these schools receive funding from School Improvement Grants, so they may freely hire instructional coaches and purchase programs, training, and materials. As external consultants, we often find that principals and the leadership team in such schools pile too many things on teachers to apply in their classrooms. We've seen up to ten new programs or offensives implemented at one time. As you might imagine, teachers get frustrated, feel defeated, and lose confidence under this pressure.

We encourage the district leaders to apply Evidence-Based Leadership[SM] as they choose strategies for teachers to apply. First and foremost, however, we teach tactics that allow leaders to build emotional bank accounts with teachers. A positive balance in the emotional bank account results from leaders rewarding and recognizing performance by praising three times as much as they criticize. The process of recognizing teachers' efforts connects with their hearts, and then they can move on to the science of applying just two or three strategic actions.

With passion—bolstered by new skills and new knowledge—the desire to make things better often leads to short-term pain but long-term gain. We have read, and we believe it to be true, that the less change a person tries to make at one time, the better their chances of success.

No, we are not saying no change is the way to go. Our point is that people and organizations can handle only so much change at once. We recommend one or two items per leader. That way, lots of change is taking place, but it is manageable.

People and organizations can handle only so much change at once. We recommend one or two items per leader.

So why did we mention the short-term pain? In our experience, when leaders go into a unit with new or enhanced methods to improve performance, they implement a wide variety of actions. This means people end up either working harder and longer or reducing time spent on other needed actions that the new actions displace. In time, adding many new actions to current work means a drop in consistency in previous work. Then the tasks that had fallen off because of the new actions must be completed, which causes an easing off of the new actions. Or a big project comes up and delays the actions being taken on the previous change, so that change never becomes fully operational.

Our suggestion is to be patient and select one or two items to implement or enhance. Work on it frequently and stay at it long enough to see the outcomes, and only then decide if another action is needed. When we ask attendees at skill-building sessions what they will do when they get back to their work areas, we hear a list of four, five, six, seven, or even more actions. They're all good ideas, and all may need to be implemented in time; however, we encourage people to reduce the number of actions they introduce right away.

Breaking Actions into Understandable Steps

We find that organizations often fail to break down new initiatives into doable steps. This is a mistake because any process will be more successful if it is broken into doable steps during implementation. In fact, taking small steps can lead to phenomenal results. It also reduces the anxiety that people may encounter with a new challenge.

Similar to many of you, when we were high school teachers, we would teach our students how to break down the steps of a complex project or problem and not move to the next step until the current step had been mastered. This process helped our students achieve things that they believed were impossible to learn.

The same process works in all settings. For example, a highly effective communication technique we teach is AIDET® (Figure 14.1).

FIGURE 14.1	AIDET®	
A	Acknowledge the person.
I	Introduce yourself and your role (and, when appropriate, share your skills and experience and/or introduce coworkers, other departments, and/or individuals).
D	Duration: Educate the person on the time it will take to complete the project or initiative.
E	Explain the *why, what,* and *how* regarding what has occurred, is occurring, or is about to occur.
T	Thank the person for trusting you and choosing you.

AIDET is used as a communication tool when we are trying to reduce someone's anxiety about a situation. When we introduce a situation using several or all components of AIDET (depending on what the situation calls for), the person stays with us and gains a degree of comfort with our interaction. When we teach this technique, some people say, "I am not comfortable telling people how good I am." Our suggestion is to consider this introduction as a way to help the other person. It's not bragging; it's talking about the skills and experience you bring to the job so that others can have confidence in you. A parent who learns of a teacher's credentials is likely to tell others, "I lucked out with my child's teacher."

Teaching faculty deserve to use the A and I in AIDET to introduce their credentials to others. Leaders should provide opportunities for them to do so. The quality of faculty hires is one of the most important aspects of any educational system, and teachers often have impressive credentials, experience, and talents. We've found that faculty members have too few opportunities to showcase their expertise. Embedding the A and I in processes and meetings shows that we value the faculty.

Connecting to Values

There is probably no better way to capture the hearts and minds of individuals in education than by connecting what we're asking them to do back to the values of the organization. We have found that this motivates people, even in organizations that are not performing well. It shows employees that we know we're driven by values and that we're confident in our ability to achieve high performance. Connecting back to our values really captures people.

Connecting back to our values really captures people.

When we partner with school districts, we start by making it a high priority to transform theirs into "a best place to work." It becomes part of the culture. When the district sets the stage for rolling out its employee engagement survey, what better way to approach the survey than to remind them that the school district is committed to them? After all, engaging employees and making the organization a great place for everyone to work does improve human life—and everyone in the organization is an important human life who deserves to improve.

When people are responsible for applying a new tactic or changing from an existing behavior, we tie it back to values. We let people know that the reason we're introducing this new tactic is that, even though it is difficult and requires a change in practice, we all want the best outcome for the students and communities we serve.

People want to work in a place where they have purpose and do worthwhile work. Leaders show the values of an organization by connecting their actions to this desire.

> People want to work in a place where they have purpose and do worthwhile work. Leaders show the values of an organization by connecting their actions to this desire.

Connecting the Dots for People

The most effective communicators are those who can connect the dots for others in a way that creates clear understanding and leads to the desired outcome. Good leaders are effective communicators. Great leaders use good communication strategies *and* have a special touch with people. This is the science and art of communication and leadership at their best. Here's a quick tip for improving communication skills. After connecting with a group, our goal is always to accomplish three things: (1) make sure the listener understands the outcome or the result of the technique or tool, (2) explain how to implement the expected action, and then (3) tell a story that illustrates the impact.

If this is done well, those who are most influenced by the metric outcome will hear a call to action and the *how*. Those most moved by the human impact will also hear the call to action and the *how*. Most people respond to both the metric outcome *and* what it represents in human terms, but some favor one more than the other. Either way, the key is moving people to action. Let's look at an example.

Selection of talent is a make-or-break skill for a leader. When recommending new or enhanced selection processes for leaders who are mostly financially driven, the argument is clear: Better selection leads to lower turnover. Low turnover reduces orientation costs, overtime, and agency use. For the quality-driven group, the metrics show that better selection and low turnover mean better student learning outcomes and better retention rates for employees as well as for students.

For those driven primarily by heart, or feeling, we explain that better selection leads to a better cultural fit, better teamwork, a better place to work, and staff members who feel respected and trusted because they were involved in the selection process (via peer interviewing). Plus, the new hires feel more cared about because the organization took time to make sure they were the right fit, and they have already met some of the people they will be working with.

Each type of leader sees the benefit that resonates with them—and this gets them ready for the *how*. The point is that in communication, the three important elements are the outcome, the *how*, and the stories. Using these elements gains the support of those who lead with their mind, those who lead with their heart, and those who use both, which is most people.

The point is that in communication, the three important elements are the outcome, the *how*, and the stories.

Connect Back to Purpose

We've been in leadership positions most of our professional lives. Both of us are passionate about people working with purpose and feeling worthwhile so they can make a difference in education. Teachers want to make a difference in the lives of students and their families. Here's what we've learned: leaders make a difference in the lives of the people in an organization. That's what makes us passionate about our work in leadership.

The Evidence-Based Leadership framework embeds processes and practices that urge leaders to connect with the hearts and minds of those they lead. Building better educational systems is all about leadership and about every person in a system having opportunities to lead every day.

Summary

Leadership is both an art and a science. Therefore, as we seek to hardwire excellence and maximize performance, we must be able to connect to people on both the heart and mind levels.

Eight qualities make up this ability:

- Authenticity
- Empathy
- The ability to bring conversations back to point
- An instinct for knowing when to push and when not to
- The ability to limit and sequence changes
- The ability to break things into understandable steps
- The ability to connect back to values
- The ability to connect the dots for people

We do believe that certain people are "naturals" at most of these skills and thus make powerful leaders. Other leaders are strong in some skills and weaker in others. However, we also believe that the vast majority of people use both their minds and their hearts to make decisions and take action—and therefore most of us can learn the skills to connect with others on both levels.

When we can make sure all our leaders know the techniques for connecting with both aspects of the human beings who make our organizations work, we're well on our way to creating a high-performance culture that can weather any storm.

As we close this final chapter, let us connect you with our *own* hearts and minds. We are deeply appreciative of the many people we have had the privilege of meeting in our work with education—people who have shared in the journey of making our professions better.

We are grateful to you for being our role models, our teachers, and our mentors. We hope we can continue to carry the message and do everything in our power to make working environments better for those we serve, our employees, and our key stakeholders. We know we all share the same goal of making educational systems better. As we continue on our journey, we truly hope that our paths will cross as we all strive together to do work that has great purpose, that's worthwhile, and that makes a difference in every life we touch.

REFERENCES

Collins, Jim. *Good to Great: Why Some Companies Make the Leap...and Others Don't.* New York, NY: Harper Business, 2001.

Covey, Stephen R. *The 7 Habits of Highly Effective People: Powerful Lessons in Personal Change.* New York, NY: Simon & Schuster, Inc., 1989.

Glaser, Susan R., and Peter Glaser. *Be Quiet, Be Heard: The Paradox of Persuasion, 4th Edition.* Martinez, CA: Communication Solutions Publishing, 2006.

Heath, Chip, and Dan Heath. *Switch: How to Change Things When Change Is Hard.* New York, NY: Random House, Inc., 2010.

Kotter, John P. *A Sense of Urgency.* Boston, MA: Harvard Business Press, 2008.

Paul, Richard, and Linda Elder. *The Thinker's Guide to Intellectual Standards: The Words That Name Them and the Criteria That Define Them.* Tomales, CA: Foundation for Critical Thinking, 2011.

Pilcher, Janet. *Who's Engaged? Climb the Learning Ladder to See.* Pensacola, FL: Studer Education, 2012.

Pilcher, Janet, and Robin Largue. *How to Lead Teachers to Become Great: It's All About Student Learning*. Gulf Breeze, FL: Fire Starter Publishing, 2009.

Senge, Peter M. *The Fifth Discipline: The Art & Practice of the Learning Organization*. New York, NY: Random House, Inc., 1990.

Shenkar, Oded, and Scott Berinato. "Defend Your Research: Imitation in More Valuable Than Innovation," *Harvard Business Review*, April 1, 2010.

Sherman, V. Clayton. *Creating the New American Hospital: A Time for Greatness*. San Francisco, CA: Jossey-Bass Inc., Publishers, 1993.

Studer Group. *Organizational Change Processes in High-Performing Organizations: In-Depth Case Studies with Healthcare Facilities*. Gulf Breeze, FL: Alliance for Healthcare Research, 2005.

Studer, Quint. *Hardwiring Excellence: Purpose, Worthwhile Work, Making a Difference*. Gulf Breeze, FL: Fire Starter Publishing, 2003.

Studer, Quint. *Results That Last: Hardwiring Behaviors That Will Take Your Company to the Top*. Hoboken, NJ: John Wiley & Sons, Inc., 2008.

The New Teachers Project. *The Irreplaceables: Understanding the Real Retention Crisis in America's Urban Schools*, 2012. Accessed online October 10, 2014, at http://tntp.org/assets/documents/TNTP_Irreplaceables_2012.pdf.

The Right Stuff. Dir. Philip Kaufman. Warner Brothers, 1983.

ABOUT THE AUTHORS

Quint Studer
Founder
Studer Group

Quint Studer is the founder of Studer Group®. A recipient of the 2010 Malcolm Baldrige National Quality Award, Studer Group is an outcomes firm that implements Evidence-Based Leadership^{SM} systems and practices to help organizations achieve, sustain, and accelerate performance in service, quality, finance, people, and growth.

Quint has been in the healthcare field for over 29 years and spends much of his time creating and sharing best practices with hundreds of healthcare professionals each month. Quint spent ten years working in education, earning his master's of science in education, before entering the healthcare industry. A frequent keynoter at national and organizational events, he regularly meets with healthcare leaders around the country at client engagements and Studer Group-sponsored institutes. He is also a frequently interviewed healthcare leader in national media.

Inc. magazine named Quint its Master of Business, making him the only healthcare leader to have ever won this award. *Modern Healthcare* has twice chosen him as one of the 100 Most Powerful People in Healthcare. In March 2014, he was also named one of the 40 smartest people in healthcare today by *Becker's Hospital Review*. In September 2014, Quint became the first recipient of *Modern Healthcare's* Healthcare Marketing Visionary Award. He is currently part of the 21st Healthcare Leadership Curriculum Task Force at Harvard Business School. Quint has served as a Board Member for the Association of University Programs in Health Administration (AUPHA) and the Healthcare Financial Management Association (HFMA). Quint has also served as a Think Tank Panelist in Washington, D.C., and is Faculty in Residence at George Washington University and a Guest Professor at Cornell University. He currently serves on the board of a major healthcare system.

Quint has written and contributed to a number of books, including his newest *A Culture of High Performance*, which was released in October 2013. His first book, *BusinessWeek* bestseller *Hardwiring Excellence*, is one of the most widely read leadership books ever written for healthcare, with more than 700,000 copies in circulation. His book *Results That Last* hit the *Wall Street Journal's* best-seller list of business books. *Straight A Leadership* provides a methodology for organizations to assess their alignment, action, and accountability. One of his most popular books, *The Great Employee Handbook*, provides actions that employees can take to better enjoy both their work and life.

Janet Pilcher
Senior Leader
Studer Education

Janet Pilcher earned a PhD in measurement and evaluation from Florida State University. She also earned a master's degree in educational leadership and a bachelor's degree in business. She has published a number of research articles and several books, and has trademarked online tools that help leaders and teachers improve their performance. She has led research and development projects that have resulted in more than $17 million in grants and contracts, and has created Web and mobile learning systems. Dr. Pilcher has published a book for teachers, *Who's Engaged? Climb the Learning Ladder to See*, and coauthored a book for school leaders, *How to Lead Teachers to Become Great*.

Dr. Pilcher is the Senior Leader at Studer Group and creator of the education division, called Studer Education. She leads a team of professionals who work with senior executives, board members, and institutional leaders of educational organizations to apply a system-wide continuous-improvement process developed by Studer Group called Evidence-Based Leadership. Dr. Pilcher spends most of her time working with outstanding leaders in educational institutions throughout the United States.

Dr. Pilcher began her education career as a high school math teacher and tennis coach. She joined the faculty at the University of West Florida (UWF) in Pensacola, Florida, where she served as professor, associate dean, and then dean of the College of Professional Studies during her 19-year tenure. She was the first dean at the university to lead faculty to develop online programs, which today are some of the largest programs on campus. She also led UWF to begin its first doctoral program. In 2005, she launched an entrepreneurial center affiliated with UWF, where she led the development of TeacherReady®, a premier virtual program that today prepares second-career teachers all over the world. TeacherReady continues to flourish in partnership with Studer

Education and UWF; currently the program certifies teachers in over 25 states and over 18 countries.

Dr. Pilcher and her team partner with school districts to apply the principles described in *Maximize Performance: Creating a Culture for Educational Excellence*. The Studer Education team is designing online leadership instruction focused on supporting educational leaders to create best-place-to-work environments and analyze performance data to coach teachers and staff to achieve at their highest potential.

ADDITIONAL RESOURCES

About Studer Education, a division of Studer Group

Studer Education is a division of Studer Group®, which is a leading service provider focused on improving education and healthcare outcomes in organizations throughout the world. Studer Group coaches have partnered with more than 1,000 organizations to help them achieve exceptional results while sustaining and accelerating success over time. Our work centers around a framework called Evidence-Based Leadership℠ (EBL). At Studer Group, we use this framework to help leaders align organizational goals, behaviors, and processes to build skills, get results, and change culture.

In particular, Studer Education coaches work with partner school districts and schools to:

- offer training through institutes, speaking, books, and online learning,

- provide onsite and virtual coaching to maximize organizational and leader performance, and

- transform school district culture by hardwiring evidence-based practices.

Books

Straight A Leadership: Alignment, Action, Accountability—A guide that will help you identify gaps in Alignment, Action, and Accountability; create a plan to fill them; and become a more resourceful, agile, high-performing organization. Written by Quint Studer. www.firestarterpublishing. com

The Great Employee Handbook: Making Work and Life Better—This book is a valuable resource for employees at all levels who want to learn how to handle tough workplace situations—skills that normally come only from a lifetime of experience. *Wall Street Journal* best-selling author Quint Studer has pulled together the best insights gained from working with thousands of employees during his career. www.firestarterpublishing.com

Hardwiring Excellence—A *BusinessWeek* best seller, this book is a road map to creating and sustaining a "Culture of Service and Operational Excellence" that drives bottom-line results. Written by Quint Studer. www.firestarterpublishing.com

Results That Last—A *Wall Street Journal* best seller by Quint Studer that teaches leaders in every industry how to apply his tactics and strategies to their own organizations to build a corporate culture that consistently reaches and exceeds its goals. www.firestarterpublishing.com

How to Lead Teachers to Become Great—An education book by Studer Education leaders Janet Pilcher and Robin Largue that presents tactics for school leaders to apply to engage teachers and staff in the workplace, students in learning, and parents in their child's education. www.studereducation.com

Who's Engaged: Climb the Learning Ladder to See—A book for leaders and their teachers that reinforces the essentials for engaging students in learning. Written by Janet Pilcher. www.studereducation.com

Institutes

Studer Institutes for Educational Leaders

Throughout the year, Studer Education offers leadership institutes focused on the content of the book *Maximize Performance*. The topics and dates for the institutes are provided at www.studereducation.com/events/

What's Right in Education®

What's Right in Education is a peer-to-peer learning conference offered at the same time as Studer Group's What's Right in Healthcare® event. This event brings school districts together to share ideas that have been proven to improve education. Hundreds of leaders attend this institute every year to network with their peers, hear top industry experts speak, and learn tactical best practices that allow them to accelerate and sustain performance.